DAVID E. SMITH is a member of the Department of Economics and Political Science at the University of Saskatchewan and author of *Prairie Liberalism: The Liberal Party in Saskatchewan 1905–71*.

During the past twenty years, the Liberal party has shown a marked failure to hold a place in the hearts and minds of the voters of Manitoba, Saskatchewan, and Alberta. Professor Smith here argues convincingly that the party is largely the author of its own downfall through insensitivity to regional concerns and ignorance of the implications of its centralizing tendencies.

Smith views the reforms which helped restore the Liberals to federal power after defeat in 1957 as a primary cause of the party's continuing poor electoral performance in the region. He chronicles the shift from a political structure dominated by strong provincial spokesmen like Gardner and Garson to the reorganized federal Liberal party, which emphasizes control from national headquarters and favours a more scientific approach, relying on opinion polls, ad agencies, and campaign colleges for candidates.

The result has been a decline in voter support and a lack of regional participation in party councils – and the adoption by the party of policies unacceptable to the West. The West thus has come to perceive the Liberal party as dominated by eastern Canada and preoccupied with the problems of Quebec separatism. The consequences have become increasingly evident at election times.

CANADIAN GOVERNMENT SERIES

General Editors

R. MACG. DAWSON, 1946–58 / J.A. CORRY, 1958–61
C.B. MACPHERSON, 1961–75 /S.J.R. NOEL 1975–

DAVID E. SMITH

The Regional Decline
of a National Party:
Liberals on the Prairies

UNIVERSITY OF TORONTO PRESS
Toronto Buffalo London

© University of Toronto Press 1981
Toronto Buffalo London
Printed in Canada

ISBN 0-8020-2421-1 (cloth)
    0-8020-6430-2 (paper)

Canadian Cataloguing in Publication Data

Smith, David E., 1936–
    The regional decline of a national party
    (Canadian government series; 21)
    Includes index.
    ISBN 0-8020-2421-1 (bound). – ISBN 0-8020-6430-2 (pbk)
    1. Liberal Party (Canada) – History. 2. Prairie
    provinces – Politics and government – 1945–   *
    3. Canada – Politics and government – 1963–   *
    I. Title. II. Series.
    JL197.L5S64   324.27106   C81-094251-8

FOR GENE ANNE

Great prairies swept beyond our aching sight
Into the measureless West; uncharted realm,
Voiceless and calm, save when tempestuous wind
Rolled the rank herbage into billows vast,
And rushing tides which never found a shore.

Charles Mair, *Tecumseh*, 1886

Contents

Acknowledgements

I am indebted to many people and institutions for assistance given me while writing this book. Among these is the University of Saskatchewan, which provided both time to write the manuscript as well as money to carry out the initial research, and the Social Sciences and Humanities Research Council of Canada, whose grant of a leave fellowship in 1978 allowed me to complete the work. The archives and archivists of the following institutions have been of great help: Public Archives of Canada, Archives of Manitoba, Glenbow-Alberta Institute, University of Saskatchewan Archives, Archives of Saskatchewan, and Public Record Office, London. Because most of the manuscript was written while on leave in Great Britain, I am especially grateful to the staff of the Library of the Royal Commonwealth Society for their help. Finally, I could not have written the book without access, freely given, by the national director to the papers of the Liberal Party of Canada and by Senator Richard Stanbury to his personal papers for the period he was president of the National Liberal Federation. One of the conditions for use of both sets of papers is that all living persons must give their permission before being quoted. I wish to thank these Liberals, many of whom I met only through correspondence, as well as those I interviewed for their co-operation.

I especially would like to acknowledge the help and encouragement of my colleagues Norman Ward and Duff Spafford, who generously agreed to read earlier drafts of these chapters. The final copy has benefited from their criticisms and suggestions. I alone am responsible for any errors or omissions.

This book has been published with the help of a grant from the Social Science Federation of Canada, using funds provided by the Social Sciences and Humanities Research Council of Canada.

DES

Note on Abbreviations and Citations

AM Archives of Manitoba
AS Archives of Saskatchewan
IBR Immigration Branch Records
NLF National Liberal Federation
PAC Public Archives of Canada
USA University of Saskatchewan Archives
WP *Western Producer*

All material unless otherwise noted is held by the Public Archives of Canada. This includes the papers of the National Liberal Federation and of Senator Stanbury, none of which have been catalogued but remain in the sequence in which they arrived at the Archives. In a number of instances, especially with respect to the Federation's papers, the date and subject order of material do not correspond with the notations on the folders within the boxes. Where confusion might occur, I have given the folder notation as well as the volume number of the records.

Introduction

The genesis of this book is the observed decline of the Liberal party on the prairies in the last two decades. The rate of deterioration may have varied depending on local conditions, but there has been no deviation in its direction. In Alberta, in the wake of a Progressive Conservative upsurge, collapse from an already feeble state. In Saskatchewan, a series of cumulative reverses from historic strength, most recently before an improbable Progressive Conservative rival. And in Manitoba, retrenchment within the boundaries of greater Winnipeg before the combined forces of the Progressive Conservative and New Democratic parties.

Except in Saskatchewan, the condition of provincial Liberals as a partisan force on the prairies has been desperate for so long that their most recent plight does not require comment. It is the state of the federal Liberals in the region that marks the significant change. Their failure to revive following the party's rejuvenation in central Canada in the sixties established a discontinuity of support across the country which was confirmed repeatedly under Pierre Trudeau's leadership. As a result, a realignment in the party system has occurred, equal in this century only to the plight of the Progressive Conservatives in Quebec, with the Liberals the major casualty. The party system now fails to encompass the distribution of governmental power in Canada and thus to moderate its politics.

Yet to attribute this decline to Progressive Conservative appeal or even, as more frequently happens, to the popularity of John Diefenbaker, is to beg the question. Why the Liberals were displaced and continue to be deprived of support is more than a question of personalities no matter how luminous or grey the individuals in question. In this case, party organization and policy, subjects which are often depreciated by party politicians in their evaluations of electoral success or defeat, deserve particular attention.

To these reasons for studying prairie Liberals may be added others. The national unity debate has waxed while the prairie Liberals have waned. It may be an overstatement to say that the relationship between the two is direct, but that it exists is clear nonetheless. National unity has never been tried so severely as it has recently, except perhaps in 1917, and then the West overwhelmingly came to the aid of the federal government regardless of party. In response to the strains placed on Confederation by Quebec's transformation in the last twenty years, the federal government has sought to disengage itself from responsibilities previously undertaken on behalf of the provinces, thereby giving all of them greater autonomy. The coincidence of this new freedom with the economic windfall due to the rapid rise in energy prices has placed Alberta and Saskatchewan in a position unprecedented in their histories: they may assert their provincial objectives restrained only by the knowledge of the burden their demands place on the federal system.

That natural resources should have returned to prominence in national debate and that two of the prairie provinces and Ottawa should again be lined up so clearly on different sides of this issue contributes to the continuity of Canadian history if to nothing else. No issue identifies more acutely the region's sense of discrimination or resurrects historic antagonisms towards the centre more clearly than this ancient feud. Among the West's bundle of grievances, resources and their exploitation touch provincialism to the quick. 'Provincial' and 'regional' are not necessarily synonymous, but as far as the prairie provinces are concerned the fight for natural resources, which ended with their transfer in 1930, was a regional question par excellence. This refurbished issue as much as the hoary subjects of the tariff and freight rates, which in the West are 'local' issues, is thus easily fashioned into a repository for all former wrongs. Economic dependence, real or remembered, explains a great deal about the region's traditions of political independence.

The focus of this study is the three prairie provinces. There was a time when the assumption that these three constituted a region would have gone unquestioned, although that is no longer true because the term 'prairie provinces' has gone out of fashion, replaced by the more inclusive designation 'western Canada,' to which British Columbia is seen to belong. Recent analysis suggests, however, that such categories, embracing more than one province, should be suspect: 'Why rank ten entries in a table when you can get away with five? ... The probability that combining data for the Prairie Provinces may be about as meaningful as combining data for Ontario and Quebec and calling it Central Canada simply hasn't occurred to everyone as yet.'[1]

That may be. The data on occupational composition of the prairie provinces suggest that it was never so homogeneous an area as was assumed. But the wheat economy and the immigrant population in the years before 1914 as well as the repeated references in the East to 'going out West,' by which the speaker did not mean British Columbia or he would have said so (or at least have talked about 'the coast') created an accepted regional category that continued in use even as the provinces diverged in terms of urbanization, population growth, and resource development. Politically, they had demonstrated separate patterns of development early and yet the federal Liberals continued to think of them as one unit. After 1958 when federal Liberals did as badly in Saskatchewan and Manitoba as they had done for two decades in Alberta, past practice seemed further confirmed. While a change in usage appears to have taken place recently, for most of the period considered here it is useful to consider the prairie provinces as a region. It is also an accurate reflection of the view the Liberals themselves held.

Like the historic region it discusses, this book is divided into three parts. Part I examines the distinctiveness of the prairie West, taking as its themes the heterogeneous population, the evolution of its economy, and the divergence of its political traditions. The people and the one-crop economy they worked forced associational and demographic patterns which still are salient even when the economy is less homogeneous and the people increasingly urban. The need to discuss these characteristics is clear enough every time the West is depicted as anti-French in its views on the language question or anti-Canadian in its position on natural resources. If not misconceptions, these are oversimplified interpretations of the region's attitudes. Those attitudes were amply demonstrated when the federal Liberals, returned to office in 1963, sought to deal with what they saw as crucial national issues. The search for a new accommodation of the original partners of Confederation aggravated tensions with the western provinces.

Part II discusses the Liberal party's organization and policies in the period between 1957 and 1977. In the search for a route back to power after their trouncing by John Diefenbaker, Liberal leaders became enamoured of new organizational theories and techniques which had a detrimental effect on the traditional influence exercised by prairie Grits. The reorganization that went on throughout the sixties was a two-stage affair, first under Senator Keith Davey and then under Senator Richard Stanbury, but neither reform appealed to westerners. The second reorganization introduced the party to participatory democracy, but with the paradoxical result that prairie Liberals were less active than before. If the effects of reorganization were contrary to its intention and helped separate rather than bind Liberals, federal Liberal policy during the Pearson and Trudeau years widened the gulf further. Farmers, farm organizations, provincial governments, and westerners generally became alarmed and then angry at federal policies intended to reform the wheat industry, to direct the development of natural resources, and to promote bilingualism. Their criticism was directed as much at the formulation of these policies, which in their opinion ignored regional sentiments, as at the policies themselves, which frequently were viewed as contrary to the interests of the West. Together, party reorganization and policy reform contributed to the decline of the party while it accentuated regional feelings.

Part III examines the West's relationship to the nation. The theme which has characterized that tie is the 'hold of the centre.' In virtually every field but most surely in the minds of westerners, the centre is seen to direct their destiny. Whatever the objective conditions for greater independence, this continuation of past attitudes is most striking. But conditions have changed and not only in the West. The rapid disengagement of federal-provincial relations that began under Lester Pearson continued apace in the late seventies and opened the door to a fundamentally different relationship between periphery and centre. The ramifications of this change for party politics in the federation and especially for the Liberal party is examined in Part III. Party ties, which once bound the units of the federation, seem almost severed today. In the world of executive federalism such popular links appear both old-fashioned as well as unmanageable. The concluding chapter of the book analyses the West's relationship to the nation and the ties of the Liberal party to both.

Research for this book began shortly after the 1974 general election, when there was some evidence that the Liberal party's decline in the West might have been reversed and the slow process of rebuilding on pockets of strength begun. That interpretation proved deceptive, as the 1979 and 1980 elections confirmed. The book was completed with the Liberals out of power nationally and bereft once more of members of Parliament from Saskatchewan as well as Alberta. (It was submitted to the publishers on the day Pierre Trudeau's second ministry was sworn into office.) Politics is a subject of perennial and universal interest on the prairies, so much so that during the academic procession that attended the interment on the grounds of the University of Saskatchewan of John Diefenbaker, the university chancellor, some faculty members predicted that with Diefenbaker gone, the Liberals would return. It was perhaps irreverent but not unexpected to discuss politics on such an occasion. Not for Liberals alone is the West still considered next-year country.

PART I: THE REGION

1

'Nothing Less than a "New Nation"'

It was here [in Manitoba] that Canada ... learned ... that her historical territories ... though themselves more extensive than half a dozen European kingdoms, were but the vestibules and ante-chambers to that still undreamed of Dominion. (Speech of the Marquis of Dufferin and Ava, at Pembina in 1879. Quoted in E.B. Osborn, *Greater Canada: The Past, Present and Future of the Canadian North-West* [London 1900])

The quotation that forms the title of this chapter is from a letter, written in 1910, by the Bishop of Qu'Appelle to the Archbishop of Canterbury in which the Bishop described the spectacular growth then evident on the prairies. The sentiment expressed was neither unique to him nor limited to the region. In the same period, imperialists in central Canada as well as on the periphery held firmly to the belief that the prosperity of the Dominion and the Empire lay in promoting even more immigration, most desirably from the British Isles. But because economic and social factors joined to promote the most rapid development in their history, and to effect what another Anglican clergyman described as a 'Greek feeling of civicism' among the new settlers, the prairie provinces offered the best locale in the country for realizing imperial ambitions.[1]

Although British immigration and the interests promoting it were important influences, they did not determine the settlement pattern which in the last analysis was crucial to the region's development. The moulding influence here, as in few other instances in Canadian history, was clearly attributable to one man – Clifford Sifton – whose career as minister of the Interior from 1896 to 1905 it is essential to review.

Sifton himself was not unaware of the personal nature of his rule, recognizing, he once remarked, that while 'there are a great many people whose opinions are perhaps just as valuable as mine who do not agree with me ... my opinion whether it be right or wrong is very strongly entertained.'[2] On this point he spoke with some authority, for he had set conditions when accepting the Interior portfolio, thereby hoping to implement 'the integrated system of policies' he favoured for the West in respect of the tariff and transportation as well as immigration. As it turned out he was to be disappointed with the Laurier Government's policies in the former areas and especially its reluctance to promote a Canadian merchant marine to carry prairie grain seaward.[3] But on land settlement, over which he demanded and received a free hand, there was no similar regret.

Nor should there have been. At the outset of his federal career Sifton restructured the Department of the Interior by amalgamating into a separate branch the disparate offices previously responsible for immigration. He took care, too, in his choice of principal advisers so that they should be as devoted as he was to the West's interests. Westerners were chosen wherever possible and Manitobans, whom he had known since his time as Attorney General in that province's Greenway Government, preferred.[4] His singleness of purpose in promoting western development, which to him and to most westerners of the period was identical with that of the nation, commanded the respect if not always the assent of Liberals and opponents alike. As a result Sifton became the first popularly recognized spokesman for the region in Cabinet. It was a role a series of distinguished politicians from the West were to perform in this century, though none more capably than its creator who, unlike his successors, never had to face stiff competition from prairie premiers in federal-provincial relations.

But Sifton's policy was not simply to people the prairies; immigration and settlement were levers 'by which both investment and employment were to be increased and the East made prosperous as well as the West.'[5] This view of national economic development was more popular in the West at the time he espoused it than in later years when the import of its conditions was realized. Particularly repugnant later on was federal retention of natural resources, a requirement Sifton regarded as so indispensable that he even argued against federal payments to Saskatchewan and Alberta being treated as compensation for the resources. But because the fiscal arrangements of autonomy were widely regarded in 1905 as generous, isolated disagreement at the terms was short-lived. Certainly there was no hint of any fundamental wrong done or of the fierce debate to come.

The minister also held strong opinions as to which immigrants could be placed on the land with profit. In order of preference, these were: American farmers, European peasants, and northern English, Scots, and Irish agriculturalists. This priority ran counter to the imperialists' thesis which, while not vigorously propounded in the West early in this century and probably at no time the predominant view, nonetheless grew in popularity before and after the First World War in the presence of large numbers of non-English immigrants. Here, too, was potential not only for sharp conflict but also for lingering resentment.

The departmental regime was thus marked by the minister's strong personal views expressed in plain speech and by an impatience with bureaucrats and politicians whose beliefs or actions interfered with the transmission of these views into policy. In short, Sifton was a benevolent autocrat with principles. It was personal disagreement over the educational clauses in the original provisions of the autonomy bills which caused his resignation from the government in 1905.

On no subject was he more adamant in his opposition than to assisted immigration. The idea of paying an immigrant's passage, in whole or in part, both preceded and survived Sifton's years as minister. Its durability arose from the proposition that there were too few good immigrants to be shared by the competing 'new world' countries in North and South America and in Australasia, so that inducements must be offered to attract them. Sifton believed Canada could compete successfully without subsidizing its immigrants. She still possessed fertile but unoccupied land and her proximity to Europe, not to mention the United States, were advantages enough to attract the right immigrants. Indeed, Australia's recognition of Canada's attractiveness had led her to initiate assisted passages in the first place. A subsidiary argument in favour of assistance was the imperialists' claim that to keep the Empire British transportation must be made available to migrants at cheap rates. Sifton rejected this proposal on the same grounds as he rejected all schemes for assisted passages: Canada could compete in the free market for immigrants. But behind his laissez-faire response was the belief that offers of assistance would only attract unqualified settlers, especially the unemployables that a legion of charitable organizations in Great Britain seemed always ready to send to Canada.

The fact that some countries did give assistance meant the market was not entirely free, however, and, as a result, as early as 1890 the Canadian government had instituted a system of bonuses to be paid to booking agents in the United Kingdom and Europe. Over the years the amounts varied between $1.75 and $5.00 for each adult depending on his location, and was paid to agents to secure their co-operation in directing desired settlers to Canada. Sifton accepted the practice and even its utility, for it allowed the government to select the prospective immigrants on which the bonus would be paid and thus to help regulate the flow and direction of the movement. He even tried to improve on it by helping to create a syndicate of continental booking agents – the North Atlantic Trading Company. Except for Holland, the European countries generally did not favour their peasants being attracted overseas, and in Germany and Austria-Hungary Canadian agents were prohibited from circulating promotional literature. Some found themselves threatened with imprisonment, and even Lord Strathcona, the High Commissioner in the United Kingdom, was once the subject of a complaint from Berlin after he had journeyed at Sifton's request along the Rhine with a view to gauging the supply of prospective immigrants. In return for promising to spend fixed sums promoting settlement opportunities in Canada, the NATC agents were to receive a bonus for every immigrant settling in the West. The syndicate, whose members were kept secret to protect them from harassment in Europe, became the subject of parliamentary criticism and speculation in Ottawa and, soon after Sifton left the cabinet, the agreement was cancelled by the Canadian government.[6]

These bonuses, it should be stressed, were paid to agents and not to the settlers. In the nineties a scheme to pay homesteaders had been instituted by the Conservative government in the hope of encouraging settlement but the results were disappointing, in part because of the economic depression in the last quarter of the century.[7] Sifton was not disposed to revert to the practice and once the boom began inducements were unnecessary in any case. In his mind the telling argument against them was the belief that state aid of this kind, as opposed to emergency or educational help to farmers, killed individual initiative: 'Once a man is taken hold of by the Government and treated as a ward he seems to acquire the sentiments of a pauper and ever after will not stand on his own feet.'[8]

It was Liberal conviction that the agriculturalists who were needed would pay their own way. This certainty overrode other considerations, including the immigrant's nationality and religion, which proved so important to Sifton's critics then and later. To fellow westerners of Anglo-Canadian background, who expected a society composed of familiar institutions to evolve on the prairies, Sifton appeared perverse in his lack of concern for the suitability of immigrants. He also struck some as unfaithful to his early promise when as Attorney General of Manitoba he had overseen the abolition of that province's separate schools. The mistake was to read racial motivations into his support for national schools. He was neither anti-French nor pro-British and throughout his long public career (he was knighted in 1914 for his part in organizing wartime munitions) national questions, not sectarian or parochial interests, occupied his attention.[9]

Next to the resolution of the Manitoba School Question itself, Laurier's invitation to Sifton to join the Cabinet probably had greater significance for the West than any other single action of his government. Whatever the prime minister's feelings about the establishment of separate schools on the prairies (and they were far from unequivocal if one compares his course in Manitoba with the original provisions of section 17 of the later Alberta and Saskatchewan acts), the selection of Sifton as architect of western development not only made cultural dualism an unlikely first principle to guide future decisions but also prejudiced the prairies' evolution as a British bastion as well.

Critics of his immigration policy focused on the central Europeans, the man in the sheepskin coat, who after the beginning of this century appeared in large, and to them, alarming numbers, and on the American farmer from the mid-west, an area renowned for its antipathy to Great Britain.[10] The figures on the influx of immigrants into the prairie provinces between 1901 and 1911 are indisputable enough: American-born 189,000, British-born 190,666, Continental-born 160,338, and Canadian-born 182,769. Their interpretation is less straightforward, although as the Dominion Statistician once warned, 'the factual detail' is all the more essential as 'the corrective of loose thinking.' Seeing the tide of settlers moving north, Goldwin Smith prophesied in 1903 that the 'North-West will be American.' That the prediction proved wrong, despite the obvious impact of American settlers in some parts of the prairies, is less interesting than the reason why: the remarkable dispersal of American-born immigrants across Canada in conformity to the ethnic and occupational composition of the existing Canadian population. For the prairie provinces the significant effect of American immigration was that it reinforced the continental European population coming from abroad. Only in Saskatchewan and Alberta were there large majorities of foreign American-born stock and in rural Saskatchewan 'other origins' of American-born 'actually exceeded' the British and French.[11]

Nor could British settlers confidently be looked upon to right the balance. As compared with the American or continental European, the British immigrant more frequently possessed an urban background and a skilled trade and was less attracted to farming or less fitted to succeed at it. A comparison of the peaks and troughs of homestead entries as a percentage of immigrant entries from Great Britain, the Continent, and the United States between 1900 and 1908 makes the point: British 9.33 and 7.33 (that is 8,097 British homestead entries for 86,796 British immigrants in 1905–6 and 4,091 homestead entries for 55,791 immigrants in 1906–7), Continental 19.57 (1902–3) and 8.62 (1906–7), and American 22.17 (1902–3) and 11.26 (1901–2).[12] The British homestead entries were especially low when it is remembered that in the same eight-year period British immigration exceeded American on five occasions and Continental on six.

In the years before the First World War these demographic trends were visible to those who lived on the prairies and accounted for the unease many felt. But the extent of the change from the recent past, when Edmund H. Oliver could describe Saskatchewan as 'somewhat homogeneous in population,' had yet to be appreciated;[13] by the time of the 1921 census the West, with a combined population smaller than that of Ontario, had fewer British-born immigrants but three times as many foreign-born residents. Again, while over 90 per cent of the population of the four eastern provinces was Canadian-born, and for Ontario the figure was 78, in the West it stood at 58 per cent. It was on the basis of data like these that W. Burton Hurd concluded: 'Such a marked difference between the east and west in the proportion of foreign-born in the population cannot but result in radical differences in their attitude toward the problems of government, education and business.'[14]

If the effect of immigration was to separate east from west, it created a second dichotomy on the prairies by heightening the contrast, and sometimes conflict, between city and country. The differences and especially the adjustments necessary for those who moved from one to the other have seldom been depicted in prairie writing. Yet rural and urban solitudes existed in the West with few bridges between them until after the Second World War. The exceptions would be successful political organizations like the Liberal party in Saskatchewan and to some extent the farmers' movements, which depended on the support of rural electors; then as now no group could expect to triumph if its appeal was restricted to the cities. The checkerboard pattern of land settlement 'devised,' said Sir Richard Cartwright, 'apparently at the instigation of the devil,' whose servant he identified as Sir John A. Macdonald, accentuated the rural apartheid through individual isolation.[15] Community co-operation to overcome the psychological and economic costs flourished up to 1930 but was enfeebled by the ravages of drought and depression afterwards. Thus the unifying effects of mechanized agriculture, rural electrification, and improved communications came late to the prairies.

A distinctive feature of the rural landscape (literally if one is interested in domestic architecture), which contributed to the contrast between country and city, was the founding of ethnic settlements either by directing settlers of the same origin to one place or by deliberate government policy of helping locate groups of immigrants whose language and religious customs set formidable barriers to individual migration. Although recognizing it as 'misguided,' Sifton later defended his reserve policy on the grounds that 'in the early days of the immigration movement ... we were forced to do anything and everything to get people.'[16] There was another reason for creating the reserves which Sifton did not mention in his correspondence but which was bruited in government circles: the reserves were a means of attracting and keeping immigrants who too often slipped across into the United States. By allowing and even promoting use of the immigrant's native tongue the reserve proved a powerful drawing card in the contest for settlers with the United States where, according to Marcus Lee Hansen, 'social minorities of European nationalities were almost as unwelcome as if they were political minorities.'[17]

By 1903 disadvantages had come to outweigh one-time advantages. In addition to the factionalism which was spawned within some of the ethnic settlements themselves, there was mounting criticism from outside that the reserve system discouraged the integration of the larger rural community. Complaints were supported by the publicity given to British immigrants who left their homesteads because of the appalling loneliness of prairie life, where such neighbours as one had frequently did not speak English. Finally, there was the unhappy experience of the Barr Colony at Lloydminster, where Sifton had 'given way,' as he said, 'to the demand for this reserve solely because the people were British.'[18] The result of this unique experience with a reserve that was British was enough to make even a man of Sifton's convictions change his principles. The problems originated with the unsuitability of some of its members, who almost needed someone to 'hold the plough' for them, and in its Anglican leaders, the undependable Isaac Barr and the mercurial George Exton Lloyd, whose energy and perseverance were to goad Canadian governments for nearly three decades but whose influence was always less than the pressure applied.

The political importance of ethnic enclaves continues to the present day, as any glance at election returns, party campaigns, or government policy will show. But at the opening of this century their very existence was the subject of public debate. Those who decried the adverse economic and social effects often appeared to disapprove of the foreigners themselves. Sifton treated the complaints he received in this manner: 'The cry against the Doukhobors and Galicians is the most absolutely ignorant and absurd thing that I have ever known in political life.'[19] For each party there was an element of advantage to be had from misconstruing the other's position: the Conservatives might curry favour with the British immigrant by claiming the government gave preference to the Europeans, while the Liberals, invoking British principles of fair play, would keep the continental immigrants apprised of Tory 'prejudice.'

Behind the verbal ripostes lay a matter of signal importance for the future of the West. Sifton was confident that through his policies of natural resource development the West would prosper. But the social implications of the accompanying massive influx of settlers from the Continent seem not to have concerned him, if he ever considered them. And except for intermittent reverses in the period before the First World War, there was little to criticize on the score of prairie prosperity even after Sifton left the government. His undoubted devotion to the West's interests had buoyed Laurier and the Liberals and legitimized them as the region's most dependable advocates of expansion. But there was a social side to the ledger whether Liberals recognized it or not. It was uncertainty about the future of the new society being created on the prairies – not small-minded bigotry alone, as Sifton would have it – that explained the rising dissent.

The immigrants, whether from Europe, Great Britain, or other parts of North America, saw themselves as filling up a new land. This perspective was at odds with the presence of an Indian and métis population, but for most of this century that fact was ignored. Most important, it was never seen as a restriction on the options open to the new settlers. The word options is both apposite as well as misleading. In one sense the settlers were free to choose the society they wanted. Notwithstanding the imperialists' opinion that 'the cultural pattern already fully imprinted upon western Canada would limit the extent to which immigrants could alter Canadian values and standards,' the unity this belief fostered was illusory.[20] Although there was undoubtedly a similarity in institutions between west and east, as there was to a significant degree between Ottawa and Westminster, their operation depended on the ends to which they would be used and that was to be determined in the region. But the description was misleading, if each immigrant stream was interpreted as carrying a model of development and ready to do battle on the prairies to implement it.

There never was a war of the fragments in the West. It was true, as Robert England said, that 'every emigrant settler in Canada carried a memory of past culture [just as] an amputee sometimes feels the phantom pain of a missing limb.'[21] But the discomfort was not the same for all. Some central Europeans found in Canada the freedom and material advantages to express their culture more fully than in their homeland. This opportunity did not extend to changing employment, however. It could not be said of Canada, as it has been said of the neighbouring republic, that 'only a very small proportion of the peasants who flocked to the United States in the several decades before 1914 became farmers.'[22] The difference was crucial to the development of the two countries: in the United States the impact of the immigrant was to accelerate 'the social mobility also of the natives,' while in Canada, where he passed through its settled regions and out on to the plains, his influence was indirect and reduced.

Religion more than any other characteristic identified the continental immigrants, for while the education system might accommodate up to a point the language differences of the prairie settler, ultimately it pressed towards uniformity in its medium of instruction. The very wealth of ethnic memory in the West discouraged the formation of structures comparable to those created by smaller groups elsewhere, such as the Acadians of New Brunswick. In their stead the intellectual institutions of the prairies, dominated by the three great provincial universities, recognized and respected the cultural differences of their region's population; so much so that they pre-empted plans by the Roman Catholic church to found its own prairie colleges or university.[23] The rough society of the prairies before the First World War embraced almost as many traditions as it did settlers. Canadian traditions, in particular those founded on the experiences leading to Confederation, had no more authority than any other. It was to provide the order necessary to construct the mosaic that the settlers, British and non-British alike, invoked British ideals of individual freedom, justice, and fair play.

In a region recently settled by so many nationalities it would be surprising if data could not be found to link political variables to a score of ethnic sources. But the relationships established, are less than satisfactory explanations of regional political development, as the case of the Americans shows. The movement which undertook (but failed) to introduce into the constitutions of the prairie provinces the apparatus of direct democracy – the initiative, referendum, and recall – so popular in the adjoining states of the Union, is insufficient evidence on which to build a theory of settler contagion. The same is true of individuals like the American-born Henry Wise Wood and his theory of group government (again of no enduring success). Wood's mesmeric qualities came from his evangelic style and not from his Missouri childhood. What either says about American influence in the West is less than clear. What is remarkable is the diffuse impact of so many articulate immigrants on Canadian society and politics. Laurier's quip that the Americans cared more for money than politics was intended to mollify 'the alarmists' who pictured Canada swarming with Yankees after the achievement of reciprocity.[24] But there was scant evidence around to refute it.

One can only surmise the reasons for such political passivity among a people often depicted as quite the reverse in character. Canadian institutions were not congenial to the traditional methods of American political persuasion, as the Non-Partisan League discovered when it tried to invade the prairies during the war years. Again, the designation 'American' embraces a diversity of origins which in this instance (although the figures have been described by Harold Troper as a 'nightmare') are known to include prodigal Canadians and adventurous Europeans.[25] In any case the vast majority who were from the border states were familiar with Canada and not disposed to change the system. In Saskatchewan at any rate they were given little chance. The government took precautions to check the emergence of group sentiment among American settlers by recruiting their prominent leaders into Liberal ranks. As a mass of voters, American immigrants influenced party fortunes just as other ethnic groups did but the political initiative always rested elsewhere; they never sought it.

Of approximately equal numbers but in very different circumstances were the Europeans. Grouped in reserves in the country or isolated in districts of the larger cities, their sense of identity reinforced by language and religion, they were easy and willing targets for Liberal organizers. Until the nineteen-thirties, at the very earliest, their political participation was limited to rewarding with their votes the party in power at the time of their arrival in Canada. Notable and aspiring leaders might be co-opted into party candidacies or recruited into the bureaucracy but the ethnic voter otherwise remained quiescent, taking no active role in party politics except to be mobilized at election times. The dislocations of drought, depression, and war, beginning in 1939, the succession of generations with different memories and less acute feelings of obligation account in part for the disappearance of the old political dependence of immigrants on the Liberal party. But ethnic politics by no means disappeared; in fact it has assumed new significance as a result of emphasis in the last decade on multiculturalism.

The option the West might have chosen was the one closest to hand – the cultural dualism of central Canada. The embryonic federalism that was the counter-principle but hallmark of the United Canadas from 1840 to 1867 had testified that Canada would have dualism or not exist. After 1867 it was the organizing principle necessary to the new polity's survival, recognized by the leaders of both parties if not welcomed by all of their supporters. Politics in the old North-West originally pitted old settler against new, the new being the advance guard of the Canadians who appeared after mid-century. Only gradually did religion and language emerge as issues in Manitoba to align provincial politics along the same axis as federal. This distribution of support in turn was destroyed during the battle over the Manitoba School Question and the institutional structure to maintain dualism did not survive the opening of the new century.

In Alberta and Saskatchewan, where separate schools were entrenched by section 17 of the autonomy legislation, which repeated the guarantees of section 93 of the British North America Act, religion (and inevitably language) was given another chance to become a central political issue in the West. And in Saskatchewan it did remain contentious until 1930. Significantly, in Alberta after 1905 the school question ceased to be a partisan issue and as a consequence so did its potential for convulsing the political system.[26] This helps to explain the different history of educational policy in the two provinces, but it may also explain another difference which has puzzled observers for some time – the contrasting party development of the prairie provinces. The original political parties of Confederation, constructed to bridge the cultural cleavage of central Canada, succeeded on the prairies only so long as that cleavage was maintained in provincial politics. By this analysis the eclipse of the old parties on the prairies would come first in Manitoba, but with the decline retarded until 1916 by the Laurier-Greenway compromise; next in Alberta where the old parties never had any relevance for this issue; and last in Saskatchewan where religion, language, and education remained lively issues until the early thirties.[27]

In the West, dualism became a principle shorn of meaning or, more accurately, an article of faith which waned for lack of believers, of whom the most crucial were the French. As the French-Canadian proportion of the population dwindled before the surge of immigrants from abroad, the federal government was pressed to check the decline and thereby assure the French Canadians a place in the West commensurate with their role in Canadian history: 'Les deux éléments réunis contribueraient éfficacement à contrebalancer l'influence étrangère et développeraient et fortifieraient le patriotisme vraiment canadien.'[28] The Department of the Interior sent clerical agents to the United States to promote immigration to the prairie provinces. These particular enterprises were part of a wider move to repatriate the French-Canadian diaspora in New England, which had seen the

Department go so far as to violate its own prohibition on assisted immigration (in the name of 'charity') and pay the costs of transporting French Canadians from the United States to the Lake St John country.[29] The West gained few French-speaking settlers from this effort, in which it had to compete with Quebec's own attractions for those about to move as well as clear the hurdle of a federal bureaucracy not at ease with the French language. Delays in translating regulations into French were not uncommon, nor were miscalculations in the distribution of bilingual material unfortunately rare. As one Canadian agent wistfully commented in a letter to Ottawa: 'There does not seem to be a great call for French [atlases] in Montana.'[30]

Nor did the Department do much better with Quebeckers, whose objective condition might have been expected to prompt thoughts of migration. The appeal of the Canadian West was to men who found tradition restrictive, wanted to make a new start, and thought they could better their lot on the prairies. But for the French Canadian in Quebec the very promise of the West posed a threat to his way of life, one which could not be easily transplanted intact if the individual French settler followed the lead of most of the other immigrants. The economic argument therefore did not carry the day even though the European immigrants passing through French Canada were held up as people 'pauvres aujourd'hui, demain ils seront riches' while the French Canadian would remain 'comme si nous étions tous des rentiers.' But the example of the European immigrant could be used as well to discourage migration because of the threat he represented: 'Jean-Paul craint trop ... l'absorption des nôtres par les éléments étrangers.'[31]

The wave of foreign immigrants created a striking illustration of cross-pressure, particularly for the Roman Catholic church in the West, which found itself torn between duty to the immigrant and solicitude for its French patrimony. As one observer noted in 1911, the job of saving the souls of the Ruthenians and others was 'sufficient to fire the zeal of an apostle. What do we find our Archbishop doing? His whole energy is taken up in trying to bolster up a lost cause, so far as the west is concerned. The great western provinces are now, and will always be, English. Every foreigner coming there will become English in speech if not in sentiment.'[32]

The other obvious sources of French immigrants were France itself, and Belgium, where Canadian representatives were established early in the century and continued to operate until the onset of the war. Efforts in France were concentrated in Brittany, where the Canadian agents tried to work through the clergy as they had for some years in Great Britain. But official reluctance to see French citizens come to Canada 'which is really a foreign nation to them' as well as personal disinclination to move helped to explain the discouraging results: between 1899 and 1910, '2,585 inscriptions de homesteads au nom de Français ...

[et] pour la seule année de 1910 ... 41,568 droits d'entrée pour des homesteads.' A number of suggestions were made in Ottawa as to how the immigration propaganda might be improved. Among these was the interesting observation, which seems never to have been acted upon in any identifiable way in the sphere of immigration, that 'it is in the interests of European powers that Canada should remain independent of the United States and ... that we should be a rival to the American Republic rather than that there should be any political union between the two.'[33]

The diminished numbers of French would therefore have made the achievement of dualism improbable had there been agreement even to try. But its failure was a question of neither lack of will nor intolerance. The rejection stemmed rather from the belief that it had nothing to do with Westerners. They were not parties to the bargain of 1867 and the society of immigrants that grew up on the prairies was seen to have no counterpart in the older sections of Canada. How this sense of difference affected the prairies' perspective of the rest of the country requires explanation before the region's economy and politics are discussed in Chapters 2 and 3.

The West's view of itself as distinctive has historical roots which scholars like W.L. Morton and Lewis H. Thomas have traced to the Red River settlement, whose ties were as much with Britain as with Canada and who looked more frequently north through Hudson Bay to Europe or south up the Red River to the United States than it did east. Early contact with Canada after 1867 – the turbulent events leading to rebellion, the creation of the province of Manitoba, and the federal government's insensitive domination – established a relationship a legion of critics has labelled imperial both for its historical dependence and for its origin which George W. Brown aptly summarized: 'Canada gained an empire because she was herself part of an empire.'[34]

But if unity based on a sense of equality was absent right from the start, the belief in unity nonetheless prevailed until the First World War. The imposition of national political parties, the rounding out of the federal system, and the creation of a wheat economy – these were achieved while 'a vast British peace brood[ing] over it all' instilled a false confidence in the beneficence of institutions.[35] Fragile nationhood must be tended in its early years and the literature of the period is replete with references to 'the protecting walls of British institutions' and to 'the machinery which promotes that *ism* [positive Canadianism] by almost mechanically transforming newcomers to Canadian purposes.'[36] But the place of culture in a society composed of immigrant nationalities and the part played by institutions in transmitting that culture were more subtle and intricate than the institutionalist imagined. The subject was further complicated by the imperial dimension: Canada's expansion on the prairies before the war coincided with the palmiest days of Empire but to those in the West who sought some unifying principle to make whole that region of parts, the Empire and indeed the United Kingdom afforded no certain guide, for each embraced a diversity of peoples and traditions that defied modern concepts of nationhood.

With a high disregard for the pervasive influence of Canadian regional geography and history, immigration was assumed to be a kind of reductionist process whereby those entering the new land would be 'emancipated' from their old ways and beliefs and would accept new ones.[37] But it assumed what had never been proved, that there was a set of agreed-upon values and that the immigrant would conform to them. Not the least to be questioned was the substance of those values, lost too frequently in the fog of rhetoric that enveloped appeals to race and Empire or Canadianism, which were synonymous for the passionate advocates, like J.T.M. Anderson and George Exton Lloyd, who used them.

As is the fate of majorities elsewhere, the Anglo-Canadians have received less scholarly attention than their numbers deserve. Studies of the course and impact of British immigration have been few and there is nothing so comprehensive as Marcus Lee Hansen's *The Mingling of the Canadian and American Peoples* or the volume by R.H. Coats and M.C. McLean on *The American-Born in Canada: A Statistical Interpretation.* As a result, much (perhaps too much) has been inferred about British influence from the existence in Canada of institutions modelled after those found in the British Isles. But where once the attribution British was given to traditions and practices essentially Canadian in substance and evolution regardless of appearance or terminology, now concern for national unity has led governments to reject not only the designation but on occasion the objects to which it is applied. It would be a great help to Canadian unity to unravel what is and is not British in Canada's heritage.

In this century British immigrants were attracted to the West for the same reason other immigrants were: free land. Few were mobilized and fewer still succeeded out of patriotism. The history of the Empire Settlement Act of 1923, which was designed to strengthen the Empire by directing migration to the Dominions through publicly and privately sponsored settlement schemes, is instructive on this point.[38] The correspondence between government departments in London and Ottawa and between administrators in both capitals and in the field discloses that British settlers were seen principally as leaven to the mass of foreigners and that the schemes of settlement were judged by how well they accomplished this objective. It is also clear that there was a gap between intent and result: two-thirds of those who settled on farms specially prepared to receive them left and virtually all other British immigrants in the twenties who declared their intention to settle in the West failed to appear. Gross figures can disguise notable individual exceptions and a large number of British immigrants after 1920 did make a success of prairie farming. But aside (and it was a crucial difference) from the factor of language, the British enjoyed few privileges over European immigrants. Nor did they exert a dominating influence; rather they were one people among many: 'Northwards they trek, far over the Saskatchewan River and south close to the boundary, the builders of the Empire all right ... men of all nationalities and ages.'[39]

Like those from Ontario, the British found their origin 'too heavy to carry around with them indefinitely.'[40] The region's demands cut across all ties and appeals, including the evocative 'Canadian values' the immigrant was supposed to adopt. Instead of divesting themselves of their cultures as they moved from the docks of Quebec City or St John, the immigrants quickly passed through the heartland but remained untouched by it. W.M. Martin, a premier of Saskatchewan, once prophetically commented on the implications this direct passage had for the country. The settlers from abroad had 'never known eastern Canada, and ... stubbornly hold to the view that the west is Canada.'[41] He might have added that the American and European immigrants were no better acquainted with British institutions and practices.

Immigration instilled local patriotism, which was in turn strengthened by the shared experience of pioneer life, whose cardinal qualities were determined by distance. The immense size of the region affected every westerner but most directly the farmer and his family. The Immigration Branch of the Department of the Interior might dispute the accuracy of the following description of the region given intending immigrants in London and argue that 'it would be nearer the truth if revised' but it conveyed, if starkly, what was surely the newcomer's most vivid impression: 'The whole of this country consists of a vast plain covered with prairie grass extending several hundreds of miles and broken only here and there by a small town, a farm house or a shanty.'[42] More to the point, it was distance and the costs associated with overcoming it that provided the stimulus to co-operation which moulded prairie institutions: local protestant amalgamations long before the creation of the United Church of Canada in 1925 (with larger congregations to be addressed from pulpits on matters social as well as spiritual), public utility monopolies and, best known of all, the co-operative elevator companies and the wheat pools. The effect was, as one commentator said, to make them 'all Progressives in the West.'[43]

But localism, the feeling of separateness that became the basis for regionalism, entrenched itself for other reasons, most obviously as a reaction to central dictation. Canada is distinguished when compared to the United States, which for better or worse is the comparison Canadians usually make, by its linear development. What Northrop Frye calls the 'longitudinal mentality' has had a profound impact on the prairies, as the work of Harold Innis, Donald Creighton, Vernon Fowke, and George Britnell has revealed.[44] Economically and politically the frontier could never be tolerated,[45] although it was the experience of party coalition in the Union government and collapse of wheat prices after the First World War which brought that message home. The retention of natural resources, made acceptable in 1905 because of Sifton's vision of an integrated system of policies to develop the West in Canada, ceased to be tolerable in the twenties when the West saw itself being developed for Canada. The transfer was only a matter of time once 'the purposes of the Dominion' seemed fulfilled.

The press of events – drought, another war, and post-war prosperity – disguised once again the provinces' position with regard to their resources. More recent events have belied the importance once associated with ownership as far as beneficial use of resources is concerned. Transfer has increased the scope for friction, and in the 1970s the western periphery became locked in a new dispute with the centre which led this time to demands for access to the fields of direct taxation and even international relations.

Frustration fed by economic grievances and, as W.L. Morton demonstrated in his study of the Progressive party, sectional impotence, explained the political localism that came to identify the West. The search for influence followed a seesaw path from support for the dominant party of the time to third-party experiments to opposition party loyalty, but with each shift in allegiance the region's insularity in national politics and issues grew more evident. Continuity through change is the paradoxical character of the West. In its pantheon of grievances, the issues remain the same as they were thirty, even fifty, years ago: the tariff, freight rates, the price of wheat (since the creation of the Canadian Wheat Board in 1935, a preoccupation of the federal government as well). Even the questions of language and culture, which have dogged the French, the Europeans, and the Anglo-Canadians of the region for most of this century, endure, this time revived by the federal government and its policies of bilingualism, biculturalism, and multiculturalism.

The new policies may be more effective at establishing unity than the old institutions, which were once assumed to be adequate for the job. It is too early to say, although not unrealistic to doubt. The history of the West indicates that a heterogeneous people does not readily transform itself into a multicultural society. If that were the case, it would have happened long ago. 'Fiction' may, as Robert Kroetsch has written, make a people 'real'; so, too, presumably do art and music.[46] But it is a moot point how faithfully these arts have asserted the pluralism of the West. Moreover, any regional identification of this kind must compete against the pull of federal ties which, in Canada, are strongest among those who must adopt the regional perspective if it is to succeed. The interplay of region and nation has been mediated in the past by a number of institutions, foremost of which have been the political parties among whom the Liberal party has succeeded in establishing the broadest spectrum of support. Its failure in the West over the last quarter century demands explanation if the consequences for region and nation are to be understood.

2

Economic Opportunities

There are, perhaps, some justifications for the prairie farmer's point of view. They are firstly economics, secondly economics, and thirdly economics. ('Secession in Canada,' the *Canadian Forum*, June 1924)

No region of the country has been as influenced by a single industry as the prairies have by grain. The settlement pattern, the transportation network, the society itself reflect it. The massive organization required to collect and transport the product over hundreds of miles to ocean-going ships helped integrate the region in a way that later economic development has failed to do. Natural gas, oil, and potash are found generally within single provinces, subject to unique technologies and governed by individual jurisdictions, when not in conflict with federal legislation. The effect of their exploitation has been to undermine the cohesion of the wheat-growing provinces by creating alternative and even competitive industries. The horizontal movement of grain within Canada as well as to markets abroad has thus been challenged by a series of vertical structures within each of the provinces which are, in turn, connected to the North American economy.

Diversification emphasized what was often overlooked: wheat was grown in only a part and at that the smaller part of the vast territory embraced by the three prairie provinces. The plains and parkland which comprise this arable area form a wedge whose rough boundaries are the Shield and Rocky Mountains to the east and west and the invisible forty-ninth parallel of latitude to the south. Natural and political boundaries isolate the region equally well. If the former pose formidable obstacles to communication with the other parts of Canada, the latter is no less effective a barrier to the United States, whose populace in its northern tier is sparse and scattered. By contrast, in southern Manitoba, Saskatchewan, and Alberta the population is both more evenly distributed in the rural districts and more concentrated in larger metropolitan centres than in the adjacent American mid- and far west. Winnipeg, Calgary, and even Regina with 150,000 people are larger than any city to their south for over six hundred miles. Nowhere else in Canada is the United States as accessible and contact so limited as on the prairies.[1]

Defined by their geography and economy, the prairies constitute a sub-region within the three provinces. But in the 1970s the boundaries of that larger area were themselves subject to alteration, principally for the strategic purposes of federal-provincial negotiations, as the old distinction between the regions east and west of the mountains was ignored in favour of a newer entity designated 'western Canada.'

Several reasons explain the change in usage. The prosperity and growth of Alberta and British Columbia after the Second World War created problems and interests common to them but foreign to Saskatchewan and Manitoba, whose economies languished.[2] As well, federal initiative contradicted the old dichotomy: the new formulas to amend the British North America Act, as provided in the Victoria Charter of 1971, and to redistribute seats in the House of Commons, as agreed to by Parliament in 1974, treated the eastern and western pairs of provinces in the enlarged region differently.[3] Important, too, was the federally-inspired Western Economic Opportunities Conference of 1973, which provided a forum where the premiers from all four provinces might criticize federal policies for their adverse effect on western agriculture, industry, transportation, and financial institutions. At about the same time, international events stimulated national debate over the region's energy resources and subsequent jurisdictional disputes kept it from subsiding. Finally, a series of provincial elections beginning in 1969 changed all four governments, so that instead of the prairie premiers being content to co-operate for limited purposes, while W.A.C. Bennett held himself aloof from interprovincial co-operation, four premiers (three of whom in the first half of the new decade were from the New Democratic Party) saw profit in making common cause over a range of issues which affected their relations with the federal government.[4]

If potential for co-operation among the four was great, joint activity beyond pressing Ottawa to redress provincial grievances remained minimal, with the result that in 1978 practice still endorsed tradition in viewing the prairies and coast as separate regions. At the same time the prairies' distinctiveness continued to rest as before on the thorough, if no longer absolute, hold of grain on the region's economy and outlook. A prolonged and acrimonious debate about the industry's future testified to its enduring strength even when in relative decline,[5] while the continued willing submission of thousands of farmers to monopoly control by the Canadian Wheat Board underlined its unique position among Canadian industries. But beyond the practical consequences of change and proposals for change, which will be considered later in this chapter, there is another reason for giving special attention to the grain industry. The perceptions westerners have of themselves and the rest of Canada are intimately bound up with the wheat economy that has dominated their lives for more than three-quarters of a century. It is no exaggeration to say that it is the principal source of those attitudes that have come to be identified with the region.

The wheat economy, symbolized by an elevator on every horizon, marks the minds of all prairie dwellers: 'The elevators are in our prairie landscapes what the church spires are in the Quebec villages, along the shores of the St Lawrence. ... They interpret an ideal.'[6] Grain has preoccupied debate since the earliest days of settlement and if the immediate issues have varied – branch lines, pools, quotas – there has been only one subject – wheat. The contribution of memory should not be dismissed; no resident of farm or city today can fail to be reminded of the depression or drought or of their imminent return when the price of wheat falls or the spring rains do not. Such unabating interest in a favourite topic may impress others as obsessive but the listener is reminded that the prairie tale chronicles ancient wrongs as well as current complaints.

The source of western attitudes, however, is less one of dissonance than one of puzzlement over the region's place in confederation. In his studies of the West and national policy, Vernon Fowke demonstrated that except for the golden years of this century before 1914, when 'all parts of the Dominion with the exception of the maritime provinces expanded their industrial and other economic activity in direct response to the opening of the prairies,' the interests of the centre and the prairie periphery have never coincided.[7] If it is true that at any one time units of a federal system enjoy a variety of relationships with the centre – that federalism in fact is no system of uniform ties but a spectrum of relations and that some embody or articulate more faithfully than others the purposes of the federation in a specific period – then in the years before the First World War the prairie provinces more than any other region might be seen to represent the ambitions of the nation.[8] It was in this period that prairie expectations were formed; but because of the war and then post-war industrial development elsewhere they were never realized. One could go further and say that the expectations were unrealistic and could never have been fulfilled for, as Fowke argued and others have confirmed, western agriculture was intended from the outset to serve as 'an instrument of empire.' In any case, it is possible to interpret all economic and political development in the West after the imperial implications of federal policy became known to the region's inhabitants either as initiatives to redress this course of events or attempts to mitigate its adverse effects.

Not only did industrial growth outstrip agriculture in the twenties, but in the following decade there was an accelerated shift of population from farms to cities. The census of 1931 recorded a rural peak, with the rate of decline thereafter in

Saskatchewan, for example, occurring 'at about the same rate as settlement took place up to 1930.'[9] It was another forty years before the balance in that province finally tipped towards an urban concentration but depression, a second world war, and post-war changes had long made the inevitable obvious, even if it occasioned little comment.[10] Few western farmers were ready to institute internal passports or break machinery to reverse the trend, but they did resent the country's equanimity before such epochal change, especially when it was assumed that the farmers should bear the costs of adjustment. To westerners, this complacency indicated that the rest of Canada did not grant agriculture the primacy ceded it on the prairies.

In 1953 the *Western Producer* appositely summarized regional sentiment when it lauded papal criticism of the modern industrial age 'for the absolutely abnormal way in which agriculture has become a mere appendage of the industrial world.'[11] Injunctions to the contrary stressed the farmer's worth to a hungry world where millions in developing lands needed food, to a vulnerable world where capitalist agriculture might be used to fight Communism, and to a commercial world in which Canada must compete for her livelihood. Western farm leaders never tired of reminding other Canadians that 'agriculture is vital to our nation both as a supplier of basic food needs and as an earner of foreign exchange.'[12]

If agriculture was so important, then any suggestion which would have the effect of curtailing production deserved to be stoutly resisted. The first defence was to label the proposal as 'defeatist.' Thus did a Liberal (John W. Dafoe) mock a Conservative plan (by R.B. Bennett) to cut wheat exports when the prime minister and his principal grain adviser, John McFarland, were groping their way out of the wheat morass in the early thirties towards participation in the first International Wheat Agreement. So, too, did a Conservative (John Diefenbaker) disparage a Liberal (Otto Lang) for his program to Lower Inventories for Tomorrow (LIFT) and rid the industry of mountainous surpluses in 1969 and 1970.[13] The heart of the criticism, as Dafoe had made explicit, was that such plans served notice that 'the West was through as the leading producer of wheat for export.'

To be palatable, proposals for reform had to be tied to affirmations of confidence in the region's future, as they were in the Report of the Hall Commission, published in 1977. The Commission dealt with subjects that touched prairie nerves like rail line abandonment, but even where it 'sensed frustration and disappointment ... in Western Canadian developments,' the fact that 'the optimism of the pioneers, persists undiminished' was cause, in the Commission's view, to assert 'great faith in the future of Western Canada.'[14] Only the Report's favourable reception need be noted now, along with the comment that because it did not recommend taking men off the land or the land out of production, both of which suggestions have always been treated as unnatural propositions by western farmers, it had a better chance of being welcomed than preceding reports no matter what else it said. On the other hand, R.B. Bennett, Otto Lang, and W. Ross Thatcher (the premier of Saskatchewan between 1964 and 1971) were identified with one or both proposals and excoriated for them.[15]

One who never fell into this category was J.G. Gardiner, whose tenacity in promoting western interests raised criticism only from some Liberals who were not westerners. His proclivity for expensive schemes to help depressed farmers, which Mackenzie King attributed, curiously in light of Gardiner's life-long antipathy against the CCF, to 'a kind of socialistic instinct,' was nonetheless tolerated, because as his leader said: 'He is not only Minister of Agriculture [1935–57] but a former Premier in a Western province, and I think knows the West as well as anyone. I feel, in such a situation, there is nothing left to do but to accept his advice and let him proceed.'[16] Gardiner's ability to deliver beneficial programs in part explained his political longevity and popularity among those who were not electoral enemies, but there was another reason for his success which lay in the nature of the programs themselves. Typified by the Prairie Farm Rehabilitation Act (a final act of the Bennett Government in 1935 but always identified with Gardiner because of his personal devotion to making it serve prairie needs), they aimed to improve the farmer's lot by improving the land he farmed. Critics have described this approach as 'rural fundamentalism,' meaning by that that it placed individual betterment ahead of industrial efficiency.[17]

Gardiner's objective, in his own words, was 'to set up as many homes as can possibly be maintained on farms in the prairie section of western Canada.' For this aim he cited reasons that echoed Clifford Sifton's theory of economic development: 'We believe that to do so will assist in solving our labour problems, our railway problems and every other national problem ... our whole rehabilitation program is directed to this end that more families may be maintained in the area that has been known as the drought area in recent years.'[18]

After the Liberal government's defeat in 1957, the job of conserving the prairie homestead and the values identified with it passed to the agricultural spokesmen of the Progressive Conservative party and in particular to Alvin Hamilton who, as minister of Agriculture, followed his predecessor in promoting another major piece of self-help legislation, the Agricultural Rehabilitation and Development Act (ARDA). The value worth preserving most, according to agrarian advocates, was the farmer's independence, which in a grain industry as controlled as the Canadian had a peculiarly limited meaning. Essentially, it meant freedom from bureaucracy, whose growth alarmed many observers, but in the context of this discussion its focus was on the 'expert.' Hamilton's suspicion of 'mandarins' was greater than Gardiner's because for most of his time in Ottawa he had seen administration from the opposition benches and because no matter where one sat it was equally clear that the number of advisers to government increased yearly. But his concern had a singular origin in the planning and research groups that came to surround the minister responsible for the Wheat Board, Otto Lang, after he assumed that job in 1968. Under Mr Lang, the wheat industry saw the greatest number of far-reaching policy innovations in its history and notwithstanding prior consultation with those affected or the credentials of the specialists in question, these changes prompted some westerners to see advisers as 'back-room boys' or 'magician[s] in the east' insensitive to local feelings and therefore dangerous to regional interests.[19]

The programs of Gardiner and those philosophically attuned to him stressed protection and production. The farmer was expected to grow wheat and for the last forty or more years the Canadian Wheat Board has been expected to sell it. The time between planting and sale can be very long, a year and more sometimes, and separated by innumerable decisions of the railway and elevator companies, among others, over which the farmer has no control. It is perhaps not surprising then that the Hall Commission discovered among farmers 'a considerable lack of understanding of the marketing process.'[20] That the producer had no monopoly on misunderstanding was demonstrated in 1969 when the prime minister, pressed to reveal his government's plans to move mounting surpluses, waspishly replied: 'Why should I sell the Canadian farmers' wheat?'[21] Mutual ignorance made a poor base on which to run a partnership, but it helped explain bitter references to 'callous neglect' and 'Bourbon' arrogance, which the farmers periodically directed towards the federal government.[22]

The contrast between the theory of independent production and the reality of dependence upon controlled deliveries, pooled product, and shared returns creates a situation where expectations outrun results and where blame for disappointment may easily be shifted. Conditions then are ripe for the rhetoric of oppression. Populist demonology in which the 'interests,' banks and railways, for example, are villains is as old as prairie settlement itself and has been modernized only by adding new devils in the form of regulatory agencies, like the Canadian Transport Commission, whose errors the Hall Commission attributed 'to being Ottawa based ... [and therefore] unaware of ... and not responsive to Western problems and needs.'[23] Diatribes against the Canadian Pacific Railway are probably as common as before but they tend to reflect modern constitutional and political realities rather than the more archaic criticism of the railway's having been 'grubstake[d]' by the Macdonald Government.[24] The importance of including regulatory agencies (or the Bank of Canada or Air Canada) in the indictment of 'interests' is that complaints immediately become political and, more particularly, grist for the federal-provincial mill. They become partisan, too, because the appointments are within the gift of the ruling party. It brings government, usually the federal government, into disrepute since regulatory agencies are more susceptible though not necessarily more sensitive to this type of criticism than private organizations. Public institutions are expected to respond. One constant in the history of the CTC and its predecessors back to the Board of Railway Commissioners has been the attempt by westerners to compromise its political neutrality either by influencing appointments or the subjects coming before it.[25]

Nowhere in her book, *Survival: A Thematic Guide to Canadian Literature*, does Margaret Atwood refer to parliamentary debates, committee discussions, or farmers' conventions for evidence to support her thesis. Nor should she; for whatever description may be given them, literary scarcely applies. But nonetheless they are populated by many of the same images – victimization, betrayal, and sacrifice – which she divines in Canadian prose and poetry.[26] At times, the emotive language joined to moral judgments approaches the fervour of the Anti-Corn Law League, with the crucial difference that where that group of Victorians sought removal of protection to improve conditions the Canadian wheat farmer generally favours its continuance (but minus the tariff) for the same reason. Wheat farmers in Canada are not usually thought of as enjoying much in the way of protection. Indeed, it has been one of their stock complaints that when compared to the American farmer, they are devoid of government support. Perhaps for that reason the indisputable strengths they have, the Crow's Nest Rates and the Canadian Wheat Board, are championed importunately as equivalent to a 'Farmers' Magna Carta.' It would be a more enlightening description of the Board and its position in the grain industry to compare it to Rousseau's legislator. But choice of language and its zealous exercise are sufficient to suggest that on these matters one is at the *sanctum sanctorum* of the wheat economy. Criticism of either is rare, although less so than in the past, and together they help sustain one of those 'garrisons,' where 'moral and social values are unquestionable,' which Northrop Frye has espied as characteristic of Canadian society.[27]

The fact that the Rates and the Board were determined by political debate and bargaining casts doubt on the region's vaunted – vaunted by itself more than by others – impotence in politics. Moreover, each may be credited to a different source of strength: the first (without depreciating the Liberals' contribution) to third-party activity and the second (again with deference to the Bennett Government for the Board's genesis) to the labours of individual cabinet ministers, of whom Gardiner and C.D. Howe were among the most important.

The Crow Rates are the easier of the two to explain because their chief characteristic is immutability. They arose from an agreement between the federal government and the CPR, concluded in 1897, under which the railway agreed to reduce in perpetuity rates on grain and flour moving east to the Lakehead. As well, rates were reduced on some products useful to the settler moving west. In return for these concessions, the railway received a government subsidy not to exceed $3.7 million for the construction of a line through the Crow's Nest Pass from Lethbridge, Alberta, to Nelson, British Columbia. The Rates were suspended under the War Measures Act towards the end of the war but were restored (by statute in 1925) when the Liberals, their unity on the question frayed but intact, voted with the Progressives in realizing what W.L. Morton has described as 'the most notable legislative achievement' of that transitory group.[28] Within five years, the restored rates had been applied to grain and flour moving east to Fort William on all railroads, and not just the CPR, west to Pacific ports and in 1931, north to the Port of Churchill.

The railways did not want the Rates restored after the war and fifty-five years later were even less pleased with the old agreement for the simple reason that it was uneconomic: 'The U.S. rate for identical distance was between 4 and 6 times the rate charged under the Crowsnest agreement.'[29] From these exceptionally low charges flow a sea of problems not just for the railroads but for the wheat producers and the region as well. In the first place, because it is not profitable to haul grain, the railroads avoid expenditure to improve the system and even seek ways to contract it. The government must offer subsidies to help keep branch lines open but while millions ($290 million between 1967 and 1975) have been paid, they have not helped improve the necessary track and have been used instead to underwrite the railroads' general losses. Second, these low rates when joined to the higher costs of shipping finished products have had a depressing effect on the region's economy, for they encourage the movement of unprocessed raw materials to the detriment of local industrial development. The Hall Commission showed how the statutory grain rate when applied to the shipment of rapeseed, for example, as opposed to the higher rate charged for meal or oil, created a disparity between processed and raw products of 19.7 cents per cwt on a journey from Lethbridge to Montreal.[30] Finally, unrealistically low rates whose explanation is historic rather than economic shield the producer from bearing the costs of his industry or even being fully aware of them and thus further contribute to the farmer's misunderstanding of the system.

The defence of the Rates is that they help Canada compete with other grain-producing countries and by aiding sales benefit all Canadians. Canada's wheat region is nearly a thousand miles from her principal ports, only one of which is open the year round. Compared to Australia, whose crops are grown much closer to her several warm-water harbours or the United States, where year-round shipping is accessible in three directions, Canada is at a great disadvantage. Never are the limitations of the country's linear development more apparent than when compared to the circumferential development of her major grain competitors. From a regional perspective, therefore, the Rates are seen as essential if the West is to do what it does best. Criticism or proposals that they be substituted with comparable support administered in a different fashion elicit strong adverse response. To Mr Lang's suggestion that 'the right to receive the benefit can be enshrined every bit as formally and finally as the existing Crow rate,' the retort from one Saskatchewan Wheat Pool delegate that 'it would be like rewriting the Ten Commandments' was distinctive only for its reference to Mosaic Law. For many westerners, like the general manager of the Pool, it was 'shocking ... a startling announcement, especially coming from a Saskatchewan minister of the government.'[31]

Compared to the evolution and operation of the Canadian Wheat Board, the history of the Rates is relatively straightforward, which is part of its potency for those farmers who adamantly refuse to countenance change. An account of the Board's history is more complicated, although considerably easier to relate since the publication in 1978 of Charles Wilson's mammoth study, *A Century of Canadian Grain*.[32]

Briefly, until the 1930s government involvement in the grain industry was limited to setting the ground rules for its regulation early in the century and to using its emergency powers between 1914 and 1919 to counter disruptions to the trade caused by war. The latter activity culminated in 1919 with the creation of a Wheat Board whose distinctive characteristics – advance payments and pooled returns – presaged the later board of the thirties and whose brief life coincided with exceptionally high prices for wheat. Rapid decline in those prices coincided with the Board's demise and encouraged farmers to press for its return. But in the post-war period the federal Liberal government was neither constitutionally able nor philosophically disposed to interfere in the market. Nor was it alone in its reluctance. In 1922 the prairie provinces failed to act to bring federal enabling legislation for a new Board into effect. Among Progressives and Liberals alike, there was a lack of will to see compulsion imposed. The Saskatchewan Liberals, the most progressive of Grits, opposed government dictation and the Progressives themselves were divided, with the Manitoba group from whom the party's first parliamentary leader, T.A. Crerar, was chosen, adamantly against it.[33] By mid-decade, pooling had replaced 'return of the board' as a single answer to the farmer's problems and it was the collapse of the pools at the beginning of the depression which dragged the federal government inexorably into wheat marketing.

The Conservatives under R.B. Bennett grudgingly accepted responsibility only after the free market had proved itself incapable of meeting the emergency and when they were convinced there was no other alternative.[34] The Liberals, on the other hand, had the benefit of being in opposition, from where they could give vent to their prejudice against government interference. The Board created in 1935 and which the Liberals inherited the same year was voluntary (for the Grain

Exchange continued to operate) and as such, it reflected the compromise necessary to meet Conservative exasperation with current conditions and Liberal devotion to laissez-faire. But it was no less permanent for that. Once made, the change proved irreversible, despite Liberal distaste at what W.D. Euler, minister of Trade and Commerce from 1935 until 1940, called, in a letter to Mackenzie King, 'class legislation of the worst kind.'[35] The Board's strength lay in its popularity. 'Orderly marketing,' as the system became known, meant removal of domestic competition and realization of the farmer's dream of first-line protection in the international market. The peaks and troughs of the futures market were replaced by the assurance of an initial advance payment based on projected sales and a final payment calculated on the pooling of returns from actual sales. The Board thus became a steward of producers' interest and the fervour with which the vast majority of farmers defended it revealed how great was the need it satisfied.

In the last four decades the Board's operations have changed very little with the exception that in 1943, when the press of war demands on limited supplies threatened the government's price control system, it was given monopoly control of grain. Another wartime innovation, which became a permanent and distinctive feature of the Canadian industry, was the introduction in 1940 of delivery quotas. Through the adjustment of the quota, it was possible to regulate the flow of wheat entering the system at the local elevator. The full impact of this new device was demonstrated the following year when delivery quotas, announced before seeding, were combined with acreage payments to encourage wheat farmers to grow some other grain crops or to summerfallow the land. In this way, it became a means of controlling production without limiting acreage as occurred in the United States.[36]

But if the mechanics of the Board's operation remain virtually the same, the atmosphere surrounding them has changed out of all recognition. While the Board was conceived in a time of depression with poor harvests and declining incomes, the intractable problem it has faced in the post-war period has been recurring surpluses which have plagued the grain handling system and the federal government whose responsibility it has now become. For the Liberals, the party in power for all but six of the Board's more than two-score years, this responsibility proved particularly costly. The electoral fortunes of the parties on the prairies will be examined in more detail in the next chapter, but here it will be useful to sketch the contrasts and note their effect on the broader question of regional attitudes.

It is no exaggeration to say that wheat caused the Liberals' defeat in 1957. At that time, a record volume of 670 million bushels of unsold wheat was piled up on the prairies, although the average annual marketing of all grain between 1945 and 1950 had been only 458 million bushels. The huge carry-over, according to the *Western Producer*, was a principal cause of the St Laurent Government's unpopu-

larity: 'We do not say that the manner of financing pipelines is not important …
But we do state that at the time when the future of agriculture may be at stake it is
sheer madness – a modern version of fiddling while Rome burns – to devote the
time of the government and Parliament to what in comparison are minor
matters.'[37] But it was less the government's inability than its apparent disinclination to move wheat which angered farmers. Economic orthodoxy once again
proved the stumbling block. This time the lightning rod for discontent was C.D.
Howe, minister of Trade and Commerce after 1948, whose formidable talents and
energy in different portfolios had piloted Canada's expansion for two decades
(coincidentally up to the pipeline legislation itself), but whose knowledge of the
grain trade as builder of most of the country's terminal elevators was even older.
Anxious to increase sales, western farmers and farm organizations pressed the
government to grant easy credit and accept cheap money. Howe would do neither,
arguing instead that sales on credit or for foreign currency would discriminate
against and lose old customers.

A related issue which harmed Liberals most was the debate over advance
payments. Since farmers got paid only for wheat delivered to elevators and since
this was regulated by quotas which, because of the glut, were low or non-existent,
they argued for some payment in advance of delivery. The suggestion was not
new. It had been made at the beginning of the war before there were any quotas on
deliveries and where congestion had occurred. After investigating the initial
proposal, the Liberals had decided the scheme could not be administered
efficiently or fairly since it did not get to the root of the problem of income
disparity between rich and poor farmers. It would also impose on the Wheat
Board, the only feasible administrative agent, a relief function which would
conflict with its primary job of selling wheat. Thus, in the mid-fifties, the Liberals
rejected the resurrected proposal with a finality which implied that they knew
better and, perhaps more inflammatory to westerners, that the problem was not as
serious as claimed. Both Howe and St Laurent reminded prairie audiences that
they should be thankful for not critical of 'Providence's bounty.'[38] Eventually, the
government did respond with a scheme for low-interest bank loans, but farmers
everywhere rejected this alternative, claiming that it meant they had to 'pay' for
their own money.

For the Progressive Conservatives, the story was very different. Their grip on
the West grew after they came to power. They won only 17 per cent of the region's
seats in 1957 (compared to 87 per cent in the following year's election), while in
Ontario, the respective figures were 72 and 79 per cent. But beginning with the
Prairie Grain Advance Payments Act, which was assented to less than a month
after Parliament opened in October 1957, the Diefenbaker Government identified

itself with the interests of the western grain farmer and particularly with the thorny problem of the surplus.

Again, where the Liberals failed to act upon the rankling problem of unavailable box cars, the Tories lost no time in appointing John Bracken, former Liberal-Progressive premier of Manitoba and later Progressive Conservative national leader, as a one-man royal commission to inquire into their distribution. Like the Crow Rates, box cars are one of those incandescent subjects which kindle western wrath with regularity for the good reason that they are the farmer's entrée into the system. Without them, he cannot compete.

In the battle with the CPR and the elevator companies early in this century, the farmers fought all the way to the Supreme Court, and won, the Sintaluta case, which upheld the individual producer's right to equality of treatment by the railroads in the distribution of cars needed to transport grain to lakehead terminals. The first-come, first-served principle in allocating box cars was a vital part of the farmer's much-vaunted freedom of choice. But fifty years later when the cooperatives owned the majority of elevators, a large percentage of which were plugged with wheat, that freedom seemed illusory. Equality of box car distribution did not help clear a system whose member companies were unequal, nor did it guarantee individual producers the right to patronize their own companies. Complaints which accompanied congestion increased in the wake of the Liberals' ineffectual response.[39]

The Diefenbaker Government's disagreement with western demands, the latter of which after 1958 and in response to the ever-bulging granaries took the form of petitions and delegations in support of deficiency payments, was never viewed in the same light. Deficiency payments were subject to wide interpretation but their irreducible minimum was a commodity support price which gave some surety of income. The familiar argument against the proposal, which the government employed, was that it favoured the large and prosperous over the small and marginal farmer. Although the Tories' alternative, acreage payments of up to $200 per farm, did not meet demands for income security, it was welcomed as an income supplement scheme but most of all, as an indication of government responsiveness.

The claim of the Progressive Conservatives on the loyalties of the West was nurtured by the change in government attitudes, but it took root and flourished because of two events which occurred early in the sixties. One was the sale of massive quantities of wheat to Communist China. The sale meant a dramatic rise in income for prairie farmers and the onset of the greatest wave of prosperity in memory. Equally important was the buoyancy of spirit that followed. For the first time in ten years, delivery quotas were removed and farmers were told to grow all the wheat they could. While the Diefenbaker Government had not been responsible for the Chinese crop disasters that led to the demand, it did claim credit for Canada's being chosen supplier of the needed wheat. The purchase had been promoted through the introduction of new credit arrangements that later became acceptable practice but at the time, because they were seen as unorthodox, earned the Tories lasting gratitude in the West.[40]

The other event was really not a single happening but a series of government moves which together indicated confidence in the region's traditional institutions and way of life. Among these was ARDA, which has already been mentioned above, and the decision to go ahead with the South Saskatchewan River Dam, a project which had been promoted for a quarter century by Saskatchewan politicians of all stripes, including M.J. Coldwell and T.C. Douglas, John Diefenbaker and J.G. Gardiner, the last of whom, however, had to acquiesce in a royal commission recommendation and a government decision in 1956 not to proceed with construction. Although the plan's irrigation scheme made diversification of agriculture a possibility, the project was seen, by supporters and detractors alike, as basically a rehabilitation undertaking which would increase grain productivity. Thus, for those who wanted to see wheat farmers more secure in their livelihood, the dam was a vote of confidence in prairie life.

A vote of confidence is what the West wanted from its federal government and what it came to believe it could not get from a Liberal government. In power after 1963, the job of the Liberals and more particularly of those few members from the three prairie provinces (14 per cent of the 231 members elected in Manitoba, Saskatchewan, and Alberta at general elections between 1963 and 1974) was to persuade the region that it benefited from the government's policies. With the significant exception of language policy, the debate centred on economic questions, with most attention being paid to the state of the grain industry. As the government uniquely responsible for the operation of that industry and at the same time responsible to all the people of Canada, its commitment to prairie interests was held suspect as long as the Liberals were in power.[41] In particular, Liberal attempts to increase the industry's efficiency were viewed as a threat to the induced stability which fixed rates and monopoly control provide and which many westerners jealously guard.

The components of the grain handling system include the minister responsible for the Wheat Board, the Board itself, the farmers, the railway and elevator companies, and the farm organizations. Of course there are others, like handlers and shippers, as is made plain when either group strikes, but those listed have traditionally influenced policy more than any others. For three and a half decades after 1935 these participants remained comparatively stable, but since the beginning of the seventies they have changed in two important respects. First, the long decline in the number of elevator companies and in the elevators they own accelerated so that by the mid-seventies farmer-owned companies controlled nearly 80 per cent of the market. Offsetting this trend was the appearance in 1974, in what had hitherto been a distinctively Canadian enterprise, of a United States company, Cargill Grain, who had purchased National Grain and who for its efforts was viewed by some as a candidate for the West's list of devils.[42] Second, the prairie farm organizations which for so many years had been synonymous with the provincial pools and the United Grain Growers' Company were augmented by new bodies critical of existing practices and attitudes.

Most visible among the newcomers were the National Farmers' Union and the Palliser Wheat Growers' Association. Founded in 1969 and 1970 respectively in response to the drastic decline in the wheat market (which saw the government introduce the LIFT program), each started from a different premise as to the nature of the industry's complaint and proposed very different remedies. The Palliser group questioned the values of 'orderly marketing' and 'freedom of choice' when in the form of delivery quotas or fixed freight rates they operate so as to penalize incentive, discourage efficiency, and compound costs.[43] The NFU defended the same values not as shibboleths but for the very real protection the small, individual producer enjoyed when the institutions of the grain trade adhered to them. The NFU describes itself as an organization of farmers, not a farm organization, and stresses the family farm, the rural community, and the detrimental effects of change upon both.[44]

The influence of each organization has been to increase the temper of debate by making farmers generally and the older farm organizations in particular more alive to the effects of change and potential change. They also immensely complicated the job of the federal government, which traditionally looked to the inclusive pools for guidance and leadership but must now treat with a spectrum of farm spokesmen.[45]

There is and always has been more to the prairie economy than grain. The cattle industry, for example, has a venerable history in southern Alberta and southwestern Saskatchewan. And its interests are not those of grain (cattlemen, for one thing, need cheap feed). Nor do hog and sheep raisers share the cattlemen's concerns. But whether the interests are the same, related, or different – as they most certainly are when one turns from agriculture to resources – regional sensitivity, first identified with the wheat economy, has come to inject attitudes towards the centre on all economic questions. Disagreements in the last quarter century that have accompanied the rise of the oil, gas, uranium, and potash industries can be traced even more directly to federal decisions and policies than those of grain, whose federal provenance followed by some years its initial development.

Thus as a result of its economic predominance and precedence, grain stands alone. For this reason it has been treated separately while the other resource industries and their contribution to centre-periphery relations will be examined later. In conclusion and in anticipation, it might be noted that natural resource development has been sought as an alternative to dependency upon a single staple – wheat. To the extent that federal actions limit or thwart realization of this objective, they reinforce the sense of isolation that has characterized the region and its inhabitants from the beginning.

3

Non-Conformist Politics

The Easterner [is] prone in turns to regard the West as a phenomenon, an enigma, a romance, the key to prosperity [and] a disaster to Canadianism. (Arthur L. Phelps, foreword, Frederick Philip Grove, *The Turn of the Year*, 1923)

The prairies have been distinguished as much by want of conformity in politics as by their immigrant population or once dominant staple economy. For six decades they have provided fertile soil for opposition politics to flourish either in the form of protest parties or through support for the major opposition party. In fact, with the large concentration of immigrants in central Canada after the Second World War and the comparative decline of agriculture relative to the growth of other resource industries, partisan impermanence is the region's longest lasting characteristic. That it is not a sufficient condition to define the region is evident from a glance at the party complexion of other provincial governments, the nearest one being British Columbia. But together with a distinctive demography and economy it has set the prairies apart, no more so than in 1950 (the opening date for Part II of this book) when the administrations of Social Credit in Alberta and the Co-operative Commonwealth Federation in Saskatchewan had yet to run half their uninterrupted courses and the chameleon-like Liberal Progressives of Manitoba, already nearly a generation old, still had eight more years in power.

Explaining prairie political protest – its early appearance, continual strength, and variability – has kept a legion of social scientists busy. In turn, the fruits of their labour have stimulated succeeding students if only because the answers to the questions asked have appeared so varied and irreconcilable. The best known and most ambitious undertaking was the multidisciplinary, ten-volume series on Social Credit in Alberta, which appeared between 1950 and 1959, and in which the attraction of the movement (or of its leader, for they were one and the same) is described, its rise charted, and subsequent political and constitutional conflict with the federal government analysed. Some of the volumes look beyond Alberta and even the West for their subject matter, but the further afield their focus the more the relationship to Social Credit must be inferred. Oddly enough, Social Credit in power is not studied nor are Alberta's governmental institutions or processes.[1] Of the ten books, the one most productive of comment has been *Democracy in Alberta*. In this, C.B. Macpherson posits a theory of the 'quasi-party' system based on a class structure which he describes as petit bourgeois. Class politics, along with Alberta's imputed quasi-colonial relationship to central Canada, prompt his conclusion that the original parties of confederation were 'extraneous' to the province.[2]

Appearing three years earlier in 1950, and of equal durability, was S.M. Lipset's study of the CCF in Saskatchewan, *Agrarian Socialism*. The CCF was depicted as a variant of the agrarian radicalism that spread across the North American heartland after the beginning of this century but which in Saskatchewan took its unique characteristics from the exceptional breadth of community and co-operative organizations in the province. Brimming over with challenging hypotheses about farmers, socialists, civil servants, and the moderating influence of power, the book was accepted as the definitive statement about the CCF in office. Eighteen years later, in a revised edition, Lipset qualified the emphasis he had originally placed on sociological factors and gave more attention to the electoral and constitutional differences that he perceived between Canada and the United States.[3] The more informative question to ask, he now suggested, was why there was such a range of third parties in Canada. The focus then moved from province to nation. En route, Macpherson's class analysis was criticized for its limited perspective and in its place Lipset hypothesized that Social Credit had emerged out of the tension inherent between the centripetal demands of cabinet government and the centrifugal requirements of a federal society.[4]

In the intervening years, institutional explanations received a fillip from the work of Maurice Pinard and Denis Smith.[5] Pinard argued that third parties arise in situations of prolonged one-party dominance where the major opposition party so atrophies that the electorate must seek change elsewhere when it finally becomes dissatisfied with the governing party. The theory originated in Pinard's work on Social Credit in Quebec in the early 1960s, but it applied as well to what happened in Alberta in 1921 and Saskatchewan in 1944. In both provinces, the Liberals held sway after 1905, with the Conservatives becoming a spent force by the time of the crucial elections. Disaffected government supporters thus turned from old parties to new.[6]

Denis Smith's corrective to Macpherson's class analysis stressed the relevance of political leadership and, equally important, the forum in which it is exercised. According to parliamentary theory of the last century, the classic location was the floor of the popularly elected chamber, although the experience of the prairie provinces raised questions as to the accuracy of this judgment. The influence of this central institution on the evolution of prairie leadership unfortunately continues to be veiled because of the paucity of legislative research; an omission which may indicate the weakness of provincial legislatures but again may not since studies of powerful provincial executives are equally rare. Smith suggests, however, that the strength of third parties in the West may have something to do with the removal of political debate from the legislature to other locales where different values and judgments prevail. In the past, these locations were the platforms of organizations like the Grain Growers' associations; in more recent times, they are before the television camera and in first ministers' conferences.

This résumé by no means exhausts the literature on third-party formation but it indicates the scope of the research. It also underlines the structural importance of federalism with its two levels of government, which create both a standing opportunity for institutionalizing protest as well as a motive: to defend the interests of the province against encroachment by the central government. Why third parties should have been so successful electorally in Canada as opposed to other Anglo-American democracies or why they should have taken the several forms they did are questions that go to the heart of prairie protest. The nature of the original two-party system and, in particular, the response of the dominant Liberal party to the West's grievances are central to any explanation. But the different experiences of the three provinces were the result of the timing and sequence of local events, especially the fateful decision by the organized farmers to enter politics as an electoral force. In Alberta and Manitoba, the answer was 'yes' but in Saskatchewan agreement was first hesitant, then qualified, and finally reversed.

Notwithstanding the volume and tenor of the literature, prairie political protest has not been tied solely to the vehicle of third parties. If that were the case, the Liberal party would not have been dominant in western politics for much of this century nor would the Progressive Conservative party embrace the interests or enjoy the support of westerners today. It is therefore essential in any examination of prairie politics to give adequate weight to the old parties as well as the new. In order to take both dimensions into account, the remainder of this chapter will be divided into two parts: the first devoted to the evolution of third-party protest on the prairies and the second to prairie protest and the major parties. Figure I introduces the party complexion of provincial and federal governments since 1900.

THE EVOLUTION OF THIRD-PARTY PROTEST ON THE PRAIRIES

The first thing to say about third-party protest in the West as reflected in national politics is that it is framed by the success of the old parties. Up to 1921 there were

Figure 1
Governing party in prairie provinces and Canada 1900-80
(Adapted from Howard A. Scarrow, *Canada Votes: A Handbook of Federal and Provincial Election Data* [New Orleans 1962] pg. 236)

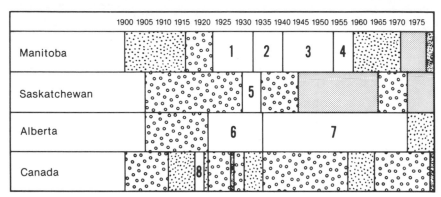

	Conservative	1 United Farmers of Manitoba	5 Co-operative Government
	Liberal	2 Liberal-Progressive	6 United Farmers of Alberta
		3 Coalition	7 Social Credit
	CCF/NDP	4 Liberal-Progressive	8 Union Government

no third parties in national politics and since 1958 (through 1974) the Progressive Conservatives have taken all but 60 of the 327 seats contested in general elections in the region; the Liberals won 25 and the remainder went to third parties. Unfortunately, the beauty of this symmetry is flawed by two facts. First, in provincial politics in Saskatchewan and Manitoba, the NDP is anything but exhausted as a political force, although only in the former has it accomplished the feat of winning, losing, and winning power again. The condition of Social Credit in Alberta is less salutary since its defeat by the Progressive Conservatives in 1971 was followed by collapse in the provincial elections of 1975 and 1979. Recent provincial election results are recorded in Table 1.

Second, there was no classic progression of third parties to power. Instead, the Progressives burst upon the scene in 1921, winning the largest number of seats (38) ever won in the West by any number of third parties in a single election. By similar blitzkrieg did the United Farmers of Alberta and the United Farmers of Manitoba sweep their respective fields and capture power in Edmonton and Winnipeg. To understand the later history of prairie protest, it is necessary to review the autochthonous origins of the farmers' movements.

Table 1

Provincial election results: legislative seats won 1966–79

Party	Manitoba				Alberta				Saskatchewan			
	1966	1969	1973	1977	1967	1971	1975	1979	1967	1971	1975	1978
Liberal	14	5	5	1	3	0	0	0	35	15	15	0
PC	31	22	21	23	6	49	69	74	0	0	7	17
NDP	11	28	31	33	0	1	1	1	24	45	39	44
SC	1	1	0	0	55	25	4	4	0	0	0	0
Other	0	1	0	0	1	0	1	0	0	0	0	0

Regional dissent did not receive expression first with the Progressives. Rather, as witnessed in the farmers' platforms of 1910 and 1916, it was made known through pressure exerted ultimately on one or other of the two original national parties. Western farmers had established their provincial organizations (the UFA, the UFM, and the Saskatchewan Grain Growers' Association) early in the history of their respective provinces and it was these bodies which quickly assumed a powerful position in provincial politics as well as an articulate and united voice in the federated Canadian Council of Agriculture.

From the distance of more than half a century, it is difficult to appreciate the authority once possessed by the organized farmers. Certainly there are no comparable entities on the prairies today, the pools notwithstanding, who wield their former influence. As educational associations committed to protecting as well as reforming the institutions of prairie society and to promoting their major industry, they performed an important integrative function. This was achieved through the social and political (but not partisan) activities of their locals in hundreds of communities and by a stream of publications, the most important of which was the *Grain Growers' Guide*, into thousands of farm homes.[7] In addition, they trained and tested leaders like Charles Dunning and Violet Macnaughton in Saskatchewan, Henry Wise Wood and Irene Parlby in Alberta, and T.A. Crerar in Manitoba, whose later contribution to regional and national politics proved exceptional. Arguably, such commanding personalities exercised as much influence over the organization as it did on them, but there is no reason to doubt Norman Lambert's evaluation of the role SGGA played in Dunning's life: '[It] took him off an obscure little farm and gave him his chance to do bigger things.'[8] Thus proven, the farm leaders were then co-opted into politics either at Ottawa or the provincial capital. Some, like Dunning, eventually did both; Wood remains the exception but so outstanding a one as to prove the rule.

Politically, the grain growers in each province formed a powerful group whose numbers and overlapping membership with the ruling political parties guaranteed a sympathetic hearing from provincial governments. Until they chose the route of direct political action in the early 1920s, they were content to press for, and get, legislation that gave them such benefits as low interest loans and greater control over the handling of their crop through co-operative elevator companies in Alberta and Saskatchewan and government-owned elevators in Manitoba.

Interest group activity in this period succeeded because governments at both the federal and provincial levels responded to the demands of the developing West. In the conflict of interests which is the hallmark of politics and the raison d'être of federalism, the West and its farmers lost only one major battle – reciprocity in 1911. The old party structure helped simplify the job of the pressure groups. As long as there were Liberals or Conservatives in power in Ottawa and in the provinces, grievances could be transmitted directly through the partisan pipeline. From local constituency officials through to the federal cabinet minister, who was the acknowledged spokesman for the province in the national capital, provincial and federal parties (this distinction is itself misleading since it was not made at the time) sought to serve one another and the organized farmer.

Nor was the benefit necessarily all one-way. The farmers' association could prove an ideal sounding board for government's good deeds, with the commendations of its members reinforcing partisan appeals to non-members. Moreover, the association could protect the government, and the old parties, by fighting off criticism that did not coincide with the interests of the organized farmers. An outstanding example of mutual self-interest occurred in Saskatchewan, where the Grain Growers' defence of established institutions and practices was crucial to the defeat of the Non-Partisan League when it infiltrated that province on its way from North Dakota to Alberta.

Integration of the old parties at both levels of government was irremediably damaged in 1917 with the creation of the Union government led by Sir Robert Borden. Except at its birth, that government, which included the minister responsible for the successful Liberal party organization in Saskatchewan (J.A. Calder), the Liberal premier of Alberta (Arthur Sifton), and the president of the Grain Growers' Grain Company (T.A. Crerar), was viewed in the West as essentially Tory in complexion and, therefore, hostile in design. The political significance of this judgment may be better appreciated in company with the returns of the four federal elections between 1900 and 1911: in the area between Ontario and British Columbia the Liberals won fifty-four of the eighty-six seats at stake. But coalition also indicted partisanship generally because its calculated disregard of past politics strengthened those critics of the system whose fortunes had fluctuated since the turn of the century. Liberals and Conservatives were never so entrenched on the prairies that they could afford to forget the original non-partisan base of territorial politics or ignore the periodic threat of groups like the Non-Partisan League, who challenged the utility, as well as ethics, of partisan politics.[9]

The temporary eclipse of prairie Grits (all but two prairie seats went Union in 1917) opened the way for disillusioned Westerners in the House of Commons to coalesce in a new Progressive party. Although the Progressives attracted much attention in 1921 when they demanded a new national policy and won all but five of the prairie provinces' forty-three seats, they were essentially reformist Liberals whose momentum was halted when the Liberals, under Mackenzie King, adopted some planks in their platform and co-opted their first two leaders, T.A. Crerar and Robert Forke.

Because both their accomplishments and failures are so ambiguous, the place of the Progressives in Canadian political history remains enigmatic.[10] Their legislative record, in terms of policies successfully carried through parliament, was meagre. Depending on the observer's partisan leanings, the Progressives were either the taskmaster or handmaiden of Liberal politicians, some of which saw the new party as a retribution for their indiscretion with Borden's Tories. The Progressives were not a protest party of the West only – over 41 per cent of the victories in 1921 were outside of the prairies, mainly in Ontario. In addition to its prairie strength as a 'sectional protest against a metropolitan economy, it was also [on the prairies as elsewhere] an agrarian protest against the growing urban domination of the Canadian economy and of national politics.'[11] For the Westerner, the Progressive movement offered an opportunity to repudiate those economic terms of Confederation that made the region a captive of the centre and which were aggravated by post-war inflation for all commodities except wheat, whose average annual price fell from $2.51 a bushel (as set by the temporary wheat board) in 1920 to $1.65 (on the open market) in 1921.[12] Eastern as well as western Progressives opposed the transformation of Canada from a rural-agricultural to an urban-industrial society.

The Progressives failed to reverse the forces against which they protested just as they failed to secure most of the legislation they promoted. Yet their short-lived revolt was significant for subsequent protest groups in Western Canada. First, it stimulated the provincial farmers' associations to consider entering politics directly as electoral organizations. The United Farmers of Alberta in 1919 and the United Farmers of Manitoba by 1922 decided to follow the federal Progressives' example, to the extent that the organized farmers in both provinces deserted the old parties. Once into electoral politics, the theory of group government set the Alberta farmers apart from their brothers elsewhere, but the effect of that initial decision was as disruptive for traditional parties there as in other provinces.[13]

The farmers of Saskatchewan, organized in the Saskatchewan Grain Growers' Association, made a hesitant entry into provincial politics in 1922 but reversed their decision two years later. This agrarian indecision was the result of the Liberal party's success since 1905 at co-opting prominent leaders and advocating popular policies with a critical eye for simple solutions. When Saskatchewan farmers wanted public ownership of elevators, as in Manitoba, the government responded with legislation to promote co-operatives, and when the Non-Partisan League's cry for cheap money was echoed by 'responsible' farmers, the province's Liberals provided long-term, low-interest loans. The Saskatchewan Co-operative Elevator Company and the Farm Loan Board were among the most popular and financially successful enterprises that Saskatchewan Liberal governments ever introduced. Thus, during the twenties, Saskatchewan's politics and parties survived the farmers' revolt, while in Alberta and Manitoba, the old party systems were destroyed. The Liberals, who had held power in Edmonton ever since the province was created, were displaced and never returned, while in Winnipeg, the success of the UFM initiated an era of non-partisan and then coalition government which was to last for thirty-five years. Rebellion against the traditional party alignment thus loosened the bonds of Confederation by increasing the opportunities for regional dissent.

The Progressives influenced the course of western protest in a second, but this time negative way. Both Social Credit and CCF enthusiasts considered the old Progressive revolt ineffectual, although each learned a different lesson from the episode. Social Credit, like the UFA before it, distrusted brokerage politics and interpreted the Progressives' fate as confirmation of the danger inherent in co-operation. The CCF, however, sought co-operation with other groups (but not the Communists) and blamed the Progressives' weaknesses on poor organization, a failing the CCF never displayed. This, however, was the extent of the connection between the Progressives and these later protest movements. Some Progressives, it is true, did join Social Credit or the CCF but many more returned to the Liberal party from whence they had come.[14]

Social Credit and the CCF represented a new form of dissent. W.L. Morton describes them (particularly Social Credit) as 'Utopian' in the sense that they sought 'to merge the nation in the section.'[15] Unlike the Progressives, who wanted to reform the existing economic and political system, the new parties each sought to replace the old order with one constructed according to new principles. At its English inception, Social Credit was an economic theory which saw politics as a means to attain a goal, but later, in Alberta, because of the Canadian constitution, this idea was abandoned. Social Credit quickly emerged as a regional protest party whose political ambitions led it to clash most resoundingly with Mackenzie King and his Liberals and with the federal government and its offspring, the Rowell-

Sirois Commission. The spectacular development of Alberta's resources after the war, which was guided by the sure hand of the Manning Government and seen to be in the interests of the province, reinforced this view, as did the party's history in power in British Columbia.[16]

Because of its socialist doctrine and diverse origins, the CCF was never a regional party like Social Credit. In Saskatchewan, the strong base provided by the United Farmers of Canada (Saskatchewan Section) and the eventual victory of the CCF over the ruling provincial Liberals gave the new party an agrarian aura. Yet its urban-industrial supporters always exerted great influence in the party's organization. The achievement of the CCF and its successor, the New Democratic Party, was the revolution it wrought in political and social thought after the Regina Manifesto – governments and individuals today accept as reasonable many of the movement's principles. But this national success deprived the party of any special claim to represent regional interests, particularly those of the West. Even in its Saskatchewan bastion, the assertion could never be supported by electoral results. In the period between 1935 and 1957 (including the elections of those years), 117 federal seats were contested in the province and the Liberals won fifty-three to the CCF's fifty-one. The Progressive Conservatives won nine and other candidates four.

By the early fifties, the protest parties of the West had become 'provincialized.' Prairie voters who wanted to vent their wrath at Liberals and who also hoped to change government policies had to look elsewhere. Eventually, they focused on the one party that has never been popular in the West, the Progressive Conservatives. In the fifty years before 1958, the party had won only 22 per cent of prairie seats at stake in general elections. (This, however, increased to 81 per cent of the region's seats in the period 1958 through 1974.) It was a dramatic swing in partisan sympathy and all the more remarkable because of its apparent permanence. Equally impressive, however, was the rejection of the Liberals in all three provinces.

PRAIRIE PROTEST AND THE MAJOR PARTIES

Identification of the West with protest has led to its identification with third parties which, as far as the old parties are concerned, is a distortion of the federal if not provincial electoral record. In this century, except for 1921, the Liberals and Conservatives have won a majority of Manitoba's seats at every federal election and a majority of Saskatchewan's in all but three (1945, 1953, and 1957). Their record in Alberta was poor, however, failing to capture a majority of that province's seats from 1921 through 1957. In terms of popular vote, though, the Liberals and Conservatives have always won a majority in Manitoba, 50 per cent or better in Saskatchewan, and failed to garner at least 50 per cent or better in Alberta only in the federal elections of 1935 and 1945.

But the fact that the distinction between federal and provincial has been made for more than half a century testifies to the havoc wrought by third-party entrenchment. Before the First World War the success of the old parties lay in the competitive attractiveness of their economic and social policies (with the Liberal party the preferred choice) and in the efficiency of their organizations nourished by the transfer of personnel between the two levels of government and the support of each for the other's policies and politicians. After the war, or more precisely, the upheaval of Union government and the farmers' revolt, this seamless web of partisanship was destroyed. For both of the old parties, a new start was needed. But for the Liberals, more ground had initially to be recovered because more had been lost: their leader, their unity, and soon two of the three prairie governments.

There are always compensations in politics, however, and especially for a party out of power during a national emergency. In addition, the Liberals had the twin advantages of being identified with prosperity before the war and racial tolerance during it. This last virtue, which the Grits were seen to possess, continued to redound to their credit in many succeeding elections. Conversely, the Tories carried the burden of the War-Time Elections Act, the War Measures Act and, for a time, Arthur Meighen, the author of both. As with the school question in Manitoba in 1896 and again in Saskatchewan and Alberta in 1905, the disfranchisement of thousands of immigrant voters had potent and long-term electoral repercussions. The federal income tax was introduced the year before the discriminatory federal franchise of 1917. There is little evidence, however, that western voters long penalized the Conservatives, if at all, for the former action, while there are still people going to the polls, some for the first time, imbued with familial resentment of the latter. Long memories may vitiate as well as sustain class politics.[17]

The Liberals' new leader, Mackenzie King, was qualified by temperament and ability to heal the schism within the party and halt the depredations of third parties from without. A sense of timing is as much prized in politics as theatre and Mackenzie King possessed a deftness in this regard, as well as a view of Canadian politics that transcended its parts, which gave him the advantage over passionate regionalists. In the often tortuous debates over the tariff, the reimposition of the Crow's Nest Rates, a new post-war Wheat Board, and the perennial Hudson Bay Railway, King was master of the Progressives and western and Quebec Liberals alike. He led Canada's first 'minority government' but demonstrated repeatedly the inappropriateness of that term.

King and his cabinets have been favourite subjects for analysis because of their longevity, the calibre of their members, and their coincidence with some of the major changes in recent Canadian politics. Much has been written about his dexterity at accommodating interests by co-opting prominent individuals as ministers. Yet the depiction of cabinet as composed of advocates of particular interests is an oversimplification if not distortion both as to the role of federal ministers and as to the mechanics whereby local interests may be represented at the centre. On the one hand, it claims too much; for in every federal system, and in Canada since 1867, the federal executive is composed so as to recognize the units. It would be the more remarkable if it did not. On the other hand, it does not claim enough; for to identify the ministers with their 'home' provinces fails to explain their strengths and weaknesses in cabinet. Which, for example, did Charles Dunning represent: Saskatchewan where he had been premier; Prince Edward Island where his last federal constituency was located; the co-operatives and organized farmers he had once led; or the financial community who so liked him as minister of Finance? It also ignores significant changes in the manner of their selection.

There was a time, perhaps in the golden age of national development, when as Stephen Leacock once wrote: 'The best politicians, the really national figures, the Lauriers, the Blakes, the Siftons, left the provinces for Ottawa. The provincial legislatures seemed turning into "sun-dogs" of the over-bright illumination from the capital.'[18] The same could not be said of politicians in the 1970s; but was it true even of the 1920s? Henry Wise Wood comes inevitably to mind. Yet more important than the fact that he never went to Ottawa (or even sought election provincially) is the fact that unlike those in Leacock's list, he was not a Liberal.

The reasons people have for agreeing to be co-opted are necessarily varied, with ambition usually a healthy element. Equally different may be the reasons for inviting them. Before the moorings of the party system were loosed by the farmers' revolt, cabinet formation was thought of in party terms first. Integration, in other words, was vertical. After 1921, and under Mackenzie King, the co-optation of opponents (or faction leaders if one saw Crerar or Forke as only wayward Liberals) made party subsidiary. Integration broadened out. It became horizontal and the accommodation of regional as distinct from party interests more possible. The cynic might say, as many did, that Liberal party considerations were now only one remove from what they had been. But the fact remained that to defuse the Progressives, Mackenzie King diffused partisanship. And the damage to some provincial Liberal parties proved irreparable. The form of accommodation remained; the reality it expressed had changed.

In the prairie provinces, where the Progressives under different guises were taking their toll on local Liberals, the situation was desperate enough without the added loss of federal men and money and the moral support of an important friend. The situation was most grim in Alberta where, once the UFA had decided to enter politics directly, the existing parties were doomed to defeat but not to disappear.

Instead, the Liberals and Conservatives were condemned to the political equivalent of a living death.

The UFA changed the electoral system, introducing proportional representation in Calgary and Edmonton and the single transferable ballot in the rural constituencies. Because of its group government theory, the UFA did not usually contest city seats, and the Liberals and Conservatives survived in Alberta politics with a base that was necessarily urban and, consequently, electorally weak. The UFA's hegemony from 1921 until 1935 resulted from the support it received in the province's rural heartland, the area with a predominantly homogeneous agricultural population.

Social Credit took more than voters from UFA in 1935. It repeated, with important differences in detail but not substance, the UFA's formula for electoral success in Alberta. It had a theory, this time monetary rather than socio-economic, a leader now more divine than didactic, and a belief in administration derived from a contempt for 'politics' and political parties at both levels of the federal government. But for all its apocalyptic showmanship, Social Credit did not signal a break in the political deviation begun in 1921 by the UFA.

If non-co-operation was the theme of Alberta politics, co-operation appeared to mould Manitoba's. A Liberal government was replaced by the United Farmers of Manitoba administration in 1922. The farmers, who had given their support to the Liberals after 1915, broke ranks because that party proved too progressive.[19] Manitoba's politics can only be understood in terms of the continuing tension between Winnipeg and the rest of the province. For most of Manitoba's history, no single party was able to bridge this gulf, but the Liberals of the First World War period were an exception. They drew support from immigrants, labour, and some businessmen in Winnipeg and from farmers outside who were disenchanted with the operation of a policy they had earlier pressed on the Conservatives: government-owned grain elevators. But post-war labour unrest and the accomplishment of social reforms close to the Protestant agrarian heart (eg, temperance legislation followed by Prohibition) loosened farmer loyalties to the Liberals. The example of federal Progressive success and the prominent part played by Manitobans in it also encouraged the severance.

But the UFM, like the UFA, disparaged traditional political parties. The farmers' entry into politics in Manitoba marked the beginning of a period first of anti-partisan and then non-partisan government which was to last for over three decades. A Liberal-Progressive fusion followed the onset of drought and depression at the end of the 1920s and a grand coalition of all parties followed the outbreak of the Second World War. The kaleidoscope of Manitoba's politics has been reflected in the progression of politicians like T.A. Crerar from Unionist minister to Progressive leader to Liberal minister, and John Bracken from provincial Progressive to Liberal-Progressive premier and finally to federal Progressive Conservative leader. In this welter of labels without meaning, where Conservative came to mean liberal and Liberal-Progressive implied conservative, provincial and federal politics evolved free from contamination through contact.

Only in Saskatchewan did the centre hold. Except for the years 1921 and 1922 when the reacting Liberals called themselves the 'Government' party and just about everyone else was a Progressive or Independent, Saskatchewan's politics remained predominantly partisan and generally Liberal. Nonetheless, temporary disavowal of partisan labels and the Liberals' reputation as a farmers' government deflected the Grain Growers from direct participation in politics at a time when their counterparts in Alberta and Manitoba were replacing the old parties. Timing was all-important, because a little later, when the organized farmers began to nominate candidates in provincial contests, the confidence inspired by post-war Progressive successes failed and the provincial movement collapsed.

As haven for Liberal partisans, Saskatchewan provided a base from which to make forays into neighbouring provinces, when it proved acceptable to the national leader. J.G. Gardiner, whose skill at organizaing equalled his commitment to Liberalism and was valued perhaps more by his national leader, disagreed with Mackenzie King's conciliatory attitude towards the Progressives. It was for this reason that his activities in Manitoba ceased at the time the Liberal-Progressive alliance was formed and before the 1926 general election.[20] The strength of the Saskatchewan organization was demonstrated by its survival at this time when the Manitoba party was disintegrating, as its Alberta counterpart had done a few years earlier.

Thus the separation of federal and provincial Liberal politics which had become evident in its sister province in the 1920s appeared some three decades later in Saskatchewan. Disagreements over party organization and to whose benefit it was to be used were heard only after the provincial party was out of power for a score of years. Complaints grew louder when the federal Liberals themselves were defeated in 1957. But policy, too, aggravated the differences. Local Liberals saw their progressive heritage, which had once saved them before the challenge of the farmers, espoused in more extreme terms, first by a provincial government with no commitment to a federal party and then by their federal namesakes. When returned to power in Regina in 1964, the Saskatchewan Liberals were in philosophic and organizational disagreement with the national party.

In spite of problems with provincial organization on the prairies, the Liberals on balance, and always remembering the Alberta exception, remained dominant in federal elections until John Diefenbaker assumed the leadership of the Progressive Conservative party. Success could be attributed to a combination of factors, the most important being the calibre of ministers identified with the region (J.G.

Gardiner of Saskatchewan and Stuart Garson of Manitoba were the outstanding examples) and the quality of their leadership. For while it has been argued that federal ministers are more than provincial spokesmen in cabinet, their responsibility for local organization in the period before 1957 and the power associated with that responsibility conferred special importance.[21] Policies, too, cannot be ignored and Gardiner's solicitude for the wheat farmers, as discussed in Chapter 2, was demonstrated in legislation intended to gird the grain industry. But federal Liberal success was based on more than specific policies or individual politicians. It originated in the widespread feeling that the goals of the national government complemented those of prairie residents. In Saskatchewan it could take the form of a hospitalization program which the federal government later made its own or, in Alberta, it could be federal development policies, generally approved of even when there was local concern to protect provincial resources, because they showed that Ottawa shared Alberta's major interest in the post-war period.

An important contribution to harmony was the translation of wheat marketing after 1935 out of partisan politics and into the hands of the federally-appointed Canadian Wheat Board. While never a placid business, wheat marketing, at the end of the 1940s and in the early 1950s, approached the halcyon days of the contract pools before 1930. Thus despite the partisan difference between the two levels of government, policies of mutual benefit helped integrate region with nation. In such an atmosphere, the Liberal election campaign in 1953 could well invoke the old 'government' appeal of territorial policies: 'You let the east elect their opposition and never mind having the west elect opposition members. ... To say you want opposition from the west is just defeating your own good interests.'[22]

If that appeal was redolent of past election strategy so, too, was the dissent that eventually broke the calm. Neither urbanization nor the development of new resources had changed the fundamental reality of the West – its dependence upon agriculture, which is to say wheat. What had altered because of migration to the city and consolidation of local services was the old community structures; the rural community had declined but not wheat farming.[23] If fewer people lived in the country, they had more invested in larger farms than ever before. They, their families, and the merchants dependent upon them were as disturbed as any pioneers by the wheat surpluses of the mid-fifties, the congested elevators, the depressed incomes, and the lack of concern of a government who no longer, in the eyes of many, took their plight seriously.

If 'every social and political movement on the prairies [has been] rooted in the land' since the days of Red River, then the kicking over of Liberal traces in 1957 and 1958 was no different.[24] With the protest parties 'provincialized,' the final act of political non-conformity on the part of prairie voters was to support a party traditionally out of favour in the region and long out of office nationally. It was also led by a westerner of non-Anglo-Saxon background who was as sensitive to his origin as he was to the origin of others.[25] The triumph of the Diefenbaker Conservatives and the rout of the Liberals for their perceived neglect of the region's basic industry was thus achieved by the combination of those elements central to prairie experience: plural society, staple economy, and non-conformist politics.

PART II: THE PARTY

4

Defeat and Reconstruction

The mountain must go to Mohammed as only Mohammed has the vote. (NLF, Volume 763, Nick Taylor, president, Alberta Liberal Association to Keith Davey, National Organizer, 18 October 1962)

To describe the prairie provinces' support for the Progressive Conservatives in 1957 and 1958 as an act of non-conformity is to take liberties with the election returns. Across the country, the results amounted to as complete a rejection of a party as any in Canadian history. In the West, the choice assumed initial significance only because of the Tories' formerly bleak record. Later when the Diefenbaker phenomenon had proved to be no more than a hiatus in Liberal dominance, and everywhere except on the prairies the pendulum swung back, then the fundamental realignment that had taken place was plain to see. To have stuck by the Liberals in 1957 and 1958 would have amounted to an act of sacrifice, although it is worth noting that the prairies were less quick to change colour than some regions. To refuse resolutely and repeatedly to return Liberals after 1963 was an act of resistance.[1]

The explanation lay not where the Liberals so often wished to see it, in some mystical union between John Diefenbaker and prairie voters, although no observer would depreciate the breadth or impact of the Tory leader's appeal, but in the response of the Liberal party's national officers to the havoc wrought by the resurgent Progressive Conservatives. To begin anew was to be expected; to rebuild so that the party should appear inimical to prairie interests was not.

It should be said at the outset that what is being discussed in this chapter are the actions of the leader and his principal advisers after 1958. In a party where the leader by virtue of his position traditionally exerts overwhelming authority, the comment need hardly be made except to note that in the matter of organizational reform at this time the party was not of one voice. Those newly placed in command favoured greater central authority exercised by the national office, while some of the rank and file wanted the provinces restored to their former prominence as the base of all organization. Everyone agreed that cabinet ministers had had too much control for too long. As a result of this difference of opinion, changes those at the top initially wanted made to the party constitution were abandoned.[2] Yet the fact remains that greater central control was achieved and that it helped transform the Liberal party into an organization viewed as unsympathetic to the West. How this happened and the effect it had on the party in the prairie provinces requires explanation.

The origin of the rift lay in the reformers' complete rejection of the past. As they set about revitalizing the party, Liberals were determined to rid themselves of a structure which had permitted ministers to play a dominant organizational role and which more to the point was held responsible for the defeat. That a number of specific grievances had accumulated against the government over its twenty-two-year history no one disputed, but it was equally accepted that government generally had grown out of touch with voters and that at the root of most complaints was a common frustration with remote, aloof and, on occasion, arrogant authority. For this, 'ministerialism' was blamed. It was accused of having promoted sectional and special interests to the detriment of the party's national good.[3] To the question, 'who had spoken for the federal party?' and by inference for the Canadian people, the reformers replied, 'no one.' The answer was taken as proof of the need to rebuild. That the question had gone unasked before 1957 was interpreted as evidence of the Liberals' demoralized condition under the old regime. In their indignation at past practice and determination to rehabilitate, the reformers displayed zeal worthy of missionaries whose object, cryptically expressed in this case, was to replace the 'old' politics with the 'new.'[4]

If it was true that the former 'barons' had adopted a limited and narrow outlook on the nature of political rule, this perspective was not wholly without redeeming virtue. As intermediaries, cabinet ministers might complicate political strategy; they might even distort national priorities – for with them politics was never tidy – but they were nonetheless keen interpreters of the local scene and, in return, committed spokesmen for party policies. Vertical integration, with a federal cabinet minister lord of the provincial organization, was never free from friction even where it worked well, as in Saskatchewan. Yet, there were reciprocal benefits at both levels, especially when Liberals were in power in each. Even when the provincial party was in opposition, it could still claim a share of federal patronage as well as a measure of influence over federal policy. However, as the years in opposition slipped into decades, provincial Liberals might be excused for wondering if allegiance had not begot an enervating dependence.

Because the new politics disdained patronage for the motives it inspired in giver and receiver, few reformers were ready to see it preserved in the new order. Instead, patronage was interpreted as an unenlightened activity which had outlived its usefulness. Mr Diefenbaker had declared that it was 'time for a change' and Liberal reformers, taking up the cry, used it against the folkways of their own organization. What they read most into the Tory victory was the need for wholesale Liberal 'modernization.' In light of the later history of both parties, there is more than a little irony in one recommendation made after the 1957 debate that 'a complete reassessment of the style of campaign to be waged should be undertaken. Our opponents have adopted the style of American political campaigns. The Liberal Party has failed to recognize the potential of ... the modern means of communications.'[5]

Those who favoured change, and just about everybody at the top did since the status quo lay in ruins, argued for a new horizontal structure that would over-arch the provincial fiefdoms and promote the party's national interest. J.G. Gardiner, identified as much as anyone with making the old system work, and on his way out in 1958, accepted the need for reform:

When the structure dependent upon the support from Provincial organizations was adopted, there were Liberal governments in most of the Provinces and strong Liberal organizations under strong leaders. The situation is greatly changed today. It is doubtful whether provincial organization can be depended upon to provide the strongest form or organization.[6]

Lester Pearson, coming in as leader in the same year, succinctly indicated what was required: 'a direct link between federal electoral districts ... and the national office of the party.'[7]

To this end, two great experiments were tried in the sixties: the first, to create 'pan-Canadian' structures free from provincial entanglements and the second to promote 'a modern mass party' that encouraged individual participation. It is these reforms, the former associated with Keith Davey, national organizer from 1961 to 1966 and the latter with Senator Richard Stanbury, party president from 1968 to 1973, and their detrimental effect upon relations between Liberals in Ottawa and the prairie provinces which are the subject of this and the following chapter.[8]

The selection of Lester Pearson was crucial to the initial course of events because it opened the door to sweeping change. He had had no great experience with organization before becoming leader nor did he indicate overriding interest in the subject afterward. But he was receptive to the idea of reform and willing to work with new structures.[9] His predecessor, Louis St Laurent, 'never had any genius for organization' either. This was not essential as long as the team was winning but after the defeat the old leader still had 'little inclination to stretch himself in this connection.'[10] Thus with Pearson, disposition combined with necessity to create opportunity. In addition, the new leader's reputation as a statesman and his detachment from the baser aspects of past partisan politics eminently qualified him to espouse the 'new politics.'

These personal advantages, when combined with the magnitude of the defeat, which all but destroyed the ministerialist structure, created a situation unusually free from the obligation and debts that traditionally hedge a leader. Seldom has less concern been shown for maintaining the established order. Policy, for example, was re-examined in light of the novel experience of forming the opposition and the consensus of opinion was to consolidate: to 'develop a very simple programme' and to 'pause in the development of our natural resources.'[11] From the regional perspective of this study, a significant recommendation was that 'the party should endeavour to deal with urban problems and lay less emphasis on rural problems.' In fact, the mood was more one of viewing both sets of problems in terms of a single set of criteria: 'We believe,' wrote Walter Gordon, that 'all Canadians, including all Canadian farmers, are entitled to some minimum standard of income and welfare.'[12] No 'rural fundamentalism' here seeking to preserve rural life as desirable in itself but rather a humanitarian sentiment that 'the poorer farmers and those on poor land' must be subsidized even at the cost of 'slow[ing] down movement to larger and more efficient farms.' The difference between rural and urban was that because of numbers and the direction of growth, urban problems were more complicated and bound to grow while rural problems, given enough time, were expected to decrease although not disappear.

Defeat freed the leaders from the past and let them impose their own solution to the problems of the time. This applied not only to experiments with party organization but to policy formulation as well. As regards the latter, the Kingston Thinkers' Conference of 1960 and the National Liberal Rally of 1961 set the party on course for greater rank and file involvement in policy matters as well as moving it slightly to the left in the substance of what was decided. The federal constituency was no longer equated with the sum of its provincial parts. For practical purposes, the old politics and the old structure had accepted, even accentuated, differences but the quest for minimum national standards started from a different premise: a nationwide community was thought to exist for which social policy goals were appropriate and desirable.[13] After 1963, the Pearson administration wrought a social revolution with its medicare, pension, and assistance plans. But the achievement of national standards was no less complicated than the creation of a national party organization. The provinces were at different stages of economic as well as political development and the response of each to 'modernization' depended on the base from which it began.

Political calculus had to adapt to the change in party organization. Canada was still a federal system and too large for any single appeal to be made without some acknowledgement of local factors. An appeal to voters from the national level became instead an appeal to the largest concentration of voters. In designing electoral campaigns, it therefore made sense to advise that 'we should give serious consideration on the strategic level to enforcing our strength in what might be described as the middle-class group of people, particularly in Ontario, where Mike's appeal seems to be most effective.'[14] The concentration of focus on Ontario and Quebec not only made sense but was attractive to the Liberals from central Canada, who had provided the impetus for organizational change in the first place.[15] To those in the prairie provinces, however, it was neither appealing nor sensible. In any electoral calculation, they, like Sir John A. Macdonald's 'rich,' would always be in a minority.

The victory of 1963 conferred the legitimacy of success on the new structure and assured its permanence until such time as another might be devised to give the Liberals the parliamentary majority they wanted or to increase the opportunities for consultation between leaders and supporters.[16] The returns then and later gave them the populous heartland and the Progressive Conservatives the prairie periphery: a partition of the electorate which mirrored the Liberal party's own internal division. That the cost proved intolerable neither for the West nor the Liberals suggests the gap that emerged between regional influence on the one hand and Liberal interests and power on the other.

Organization alone could not have created such a cleavage in national politics. But its contribution was substantial in explaining the decline of the ruling party on the prairies. In this regard, the Liberals were the authors of their own demise, although by no means did they turn away from regional questions or relax their efforts to find attractive candidates and policies. From the first, reorganization in the West had to be carried out in the uncongenial atmosphere inherited from the years before the party fell from grace. As the fifties progressed, western Liberals found it increasingly difficult to command a hearing in their party's affairs. At the start of the decade, the calibre of members returned from the region was blamed. No longer, according to parliamentary observers, were they 'a group of members of higher than average ability ... who always had the ear of Parliament and [were] influential in the councils of the Liberal party.' Instead, their opponents said, they were 'snowed under by the members from the east.'[17]

The prolonged wheat crisis illustrated in exasperating detail the nature of the problem. As surpluses mounted, incomes declined. While the government obtusely ignored the gathering storm, anger grew, and when eventually the cabinet responded with a proposal for cheap loans, feeling became inflamed even more. The farmers treated the scheme as 'an insult to their intelligence, ingenuity and industry' and laughed or booed at Liberals who tried to explain why it should be accepted.[18] Even usually prominent federal supporters like the Liberal-Progressive minister of Agriculture and Immigration of Manitoba, Donald Robertson, repudiated the plan and the financial orthodoxy of the minister of Trade and Commerce, C.D. Howe, which made it possible. Howe labelled the critics as wreckers and threatened to withdraw the loan legislation if they continued their opposition, which warning was, in turn, labelled intimidation.

This whole episode was crucial to the Liberals' loss of support on the prairies before the 1957 election and, more importantly, to the alignment of prairie voters behind the Progressive Conservatives thereafter. It demonstrated an alarming misperception of western feeling on the part of Liberal leaders. Yet those at the centre, like the Federation's General Secretary, H.E. Kidd, failed to realize how out of touch they had become: 'I suppose the wheat situation is making things a little difficult. But when all the shouting and argumentation is over, we shall probably find that Mr Howe is right. It is amazing how many times he has been right in difficult situations.'[19] Such confidence on the basis of scant information was an indictment of the ministerialist system or at least of the concentration of power in certain ministers. While J.G. Gardiner and Stuart Garson spoke for it, the plan was Howe's. The prairie ministers had no choice but to support it then, although after the election, Gardiner came out for advance payments.[20] By 1957, the political atmosphere on the prairies was charged with expectancy and even before the ballots were cast, the *Western Producer*'s prophecy for the Liberals' future was bleak:

There seems little doubt that the Prairies are now at or nearing another of those climacteric turning points which in the past have been the signal for a great leap forward. There is the same rash of meetings large and small all over the place and the same flood of discussion through available media. Oldtimers who lived through former crises will recognize the symptoms.[21]

THE REFORMS OF KEITH DAVEY AND WALTER GORDON

By the time of the 1962 election, the Liberals had rebuilt their organization so well that they were able to rob the Diefenbaker Government of its massive parliamentary majority. Accomplished in short order, this feat was not the work of a phoenix reborn but the achievement of a structure the like of which had not been seen before. The architects of victory were drawn from the ebullient young Liberals of Ontario fired by the example of their counterparts in Quebec who, without obligation to the old guard of provincial Liberals, had defeated the Union Nationale in 1960. Equally, they were enamoured of the electoral style and techniques of John F. Kennedy, which were chronicled soon after the event by

Theodore White in his *The Making of the President, 1960*. Apostles of reason and research in politics, they eschewed entangling provincial alliances if these would deflect them from their primary objective of national success.

Although success ultimately depended upon maximizing voter support, there was no question but that the initiative had come from the top and from its very pinnacle. The spark was Walter Gordon. His close friendship with Lester Pearson had admitted him to the innermost circle of advisers and because his views were compatible with those of the leader, he had been made chairman of the policy committee of the National Liberal Rally scheduled for January 1961. It was Gordon who the same year recommended the appointment of Keith Davey as national director.[22] Once the two were enthroned in Ottawa, Davey's energy and enthusiasm for change and Gordon's vision of its final form – a moderately leftish and moderately nationalist Liberal government – set the wheels of reform moving.

Their first creation was a party planning group, the Leader's Advisory Committee which, in addition to themselves and the leader, comprised the former Liberal ministers still in caucus and senior officers of the National Liberal Federation. Except for J.W. Pickersgill, it included no one with ties outside the St Lawrence Valley, and even from that region the Quebec contingent was weak. Ross Thatcher, a recent Grit convert and himself the leader of resurgent Liberals in Saskatchewan, decried this first step at reorganization where the participants were from the geographic centre and philosophic left.[23] Such orientation disqualified the committee in his eyes from knowing anything about the needs or conditions of western agriculture. More damning was its failure to recognize its limitations; it never asked for advice from him or any westerners. Whatever opinion critics might have had as to the worth of the advice rendered, the group was of organizational significance because it conferred authority on an arrangement which after all had no formal status. According to one student of this period, the Committee 'was really a device set up to ensure that Gordon would have control' regardless of the fact that he held no elected party position.[24]

As the time for the election approached, the next stage in the evolution of a new structure was to create a National Campaign Committee composed of handpicked provincial representatives and with Walter Gordon as its chairman. On paper, the Committee was to co-ordinate the campaign in all its myriad detail but in practice, the NCO met once early in its life. After that, co-ordination was the prerogative of Davey and Gordon alone as they made contact with the individual provincial chairmen. The NCO broke with a precedent which had said it was 'impractical for a political party to centralize authority in a national office.'[25] Instead, it directly involved party headquarters in the campaign and placed in charge a small group of experts rather than an unwieldy titular committee appointed to give political and geographic representation but which, in fact, deferred to the superior knowledge and command of cabinet ministers. The new structure allocated responsibilities between federal and provincial Liberals (policy primarily a federal concern, candidates mainly provincial, and finance to be shared), but the sorry state of the party nearly everywhere meant this plan was never more than a pious intent. An exception to this generalization was Ontario, where the overlap of federal and provincial party officials guaranteed that the scheme would be welcome.

The swing of the pendulum away from cabinet rule partially explained the arrogation of power by party officials. Yet it was accompanied also by a loss of respect, evident in the following comment by Gordon, for those whose influence came from having trod the traditional pathway to power: 'We appointed people whom we thought could organize and do the job. It was much more efficient than relying on the elected representatives.'[26] In Manitoba and Alberta where Liberals were weak or divided, resistance to the intrusion was ineffectual. In Saskatchewan where the atmosphere was heady with excitement as the old CCF government finally began to stumble, Thatcher proved obdurate, in effect taking command himself and in the eyes of the Ottawa hierarchy potentially jeopardizing their cause. The ease with which Davey and Gordon had assumed control of national party affairs helped confirm the rightmindedness of their cause: vestigial Liberalism of the old order should be ignored, its rampant revival resisted.[27]

An aura of professionalism pervaded the enterprise. Advertising agencies were nothing new in politics, although the one the Liberals now favoured, MacLaren's, represented a fresh start after the long service of Cockfield, Brown, whose contribution to the party had included paying the salary of its general secretary.[28] The use of public opinion polls became a characteristic feature of the new politics and received dramatic introduction in 1962 with the employment of 'President Kennedy's chief pollster,' Lou Harris.[29] An innovation unique to the party and the period were the Campaign Colleges for candidates and managers and Campaign Clinics for poll workers. Manpower to replace the discredited old system had to be found somewhere and the Colleges and Clinics were the answer the new politics provided. Seriousness of purpose was guaranteed by 'tight and total control' from the centre, achieved through a set of slides and a script used across the country without regard to 'the differing psychology of the rural areas from the urban areas.'[30] Everywhere, however, the colleges and clinics were intended to raise morale and instil confidence. To this end, it was decided early in their history that they should 'close not with a democratic question period but rather with an inspirational pitch ... giving every student the feeling that he is "in the know".' The tone of the meetings was suggested by the following exhortation: 'The Liberal Party has a firm foundation – for the Liberal Party is the political expression of reform and the feeling for progress that exists in the mind and heart of almost every Canadian.'[31]

Following the victory of 1963, Walter Gordon was appointed minister of Finance and thereafter his cabinet duties and policy interests diverted him from questions of party organization. Keith Davey's prominence correspondingly grew as he fought to keep the pre-election structure in place 'without the benefit of campaign impetus. I am convinced that it is absolutely essential that we do not allow the Parliamentary party (either in Cabinet or the Caucus) gradually to assume control of the organization. Thus we must develop a system of continuing consultation between the Cabinet and the organization across the country.'[32] The momentum of 'the newer and younger wing of the Party' had to be maintained and this could be achieved, the national organizer suggested, through the creation in each province of a Committee on Federal Organization which, out of deference to provincial sensibilities, was renamed the Federal Campaign Committee (FCC).

The new prime minister accepted the proposal and appointed in each province (in consultation with the provincial Liberal leader, provincial president, and respective cabinet minister) a federal campaign chairman and a four-man committee. The new committee had four principal functions: to act as a continuing federal electoral organization, to link federal and provincial Liberals, to be 'a valuable political sounding board,' and 'to facilitate grass roots consultation when cabinet is considering appointments.'[33] This last function meant the FCC was intended to have a key role in such patronage matters as major and minor appointments, major and minor suppliers, and legal lists.

Now government was to be joined to party by an escalator with Liberals in the constituencies making contact with the FCC, the FCC through its chairman approaching the national director, and the director (and national president) meeting regularly with a small cabinet subcommittee. Or the initiative might come from cabinet by way of a request to canvass opinion in the constituencies and then the escalator would move in the opposite direction. In the West, according to John Lamont, a prominent Manitoba Liberal, the hope for Liberals in this new structure was that it would 'overcome [their] handicap of appearing to be a party of Eastern Canada. ... Unless a close liaison can be maintained on political matters with the local organization ... it will be difficult to break down this impression'[34]

But within a year Keith Davey complained to Pearson that the system of 'grass-roots consultation' was not working because 'most ministers either are too busy or, in some cases, unwilling to co-operate.'[35] Particularly frustrating was the tenacity of old patronage habits, which obstructed the smooth operation of the federal campaign committees. Because they varied directly with 'our electoral failures,' Davey eventually accepted the possibility that 'some kind of double standard' might be required: one for Toronto and one for more traditional locales like PEI.[36] At the same time, he also wondered whether a national rather than a federated association might not be more realistic because 'the average Liberal across the country [excepting Ontario and British Columbia] has only a secondary loyalty to federal politics,' with the result that there is 'either no federal organization (Saskatchewan), inferior federal organization (Manitoba), or federal organization dependent almost entirely on the province (New Brunswick).'[37]

The new structure was not firmly established when Davey retired as national organizer early in 1966. The party was still, as he had said at the time of the 1963 victory, 'in transition.' Federal leaders speculated about further changes, even to the point of complete separation from provincial Liberals, while provincial leaders looked on the experiment with suspicion and anger. In an address on 'The Uses of Power and the Democratization of the Liberal Party,' the president of the Alberta Liberal Association spoke for many westerners, in particular, when he asserted that 'the time has passed when a group in Ottawa ... formal or informal [can] set up a power structure which weakens the provincial Liberal Association.'[38]

The party's organizational problems on the prairies as well as its disappointing electoral performance belied the promise of the 'new politics' whose eastern origin and urban focus were suspect in the West. An electoral strategy that ignored rural interests was bound to fail in a region where even 'city people are tremendously interested in agricultural affairs,' as the Liberals discovered in Alberta where 70 per cent of their support in 1963 came from the cities.[39] Liberal organizers and directors in Ottawa looked on the West as a riddle and, in a curious omission for practitioners of 'scientific' politics, never commissioned 'an extensive motivated research study – about the Liberal Party and Western Canada.' This particular failure, Davey later thought, might have been 'our single greatest mistake.'[40]

The intraparty tension that developed was not simply due to local rejection of the campaign structure promoted by officials in Ottawa after 1960. Liberal politics in the prairie provinces, as elsewhere, comprised an intricate pattern of political obligations, motives, and expectations which did not divide cleanly into support for, or opposition to, the new proposals. The root of dissension ran deep in each province and along different courses. Without the survey he wanted, Keith Davey never learned to his satisfaction whether, for campaign purposes, the three prairie provinces formed a single region or whether each was 'a separate entity.' He suspected, however, that the latter was true and that the Liberals' problem on the prairies was 'identical' to the one they encountered in the East – failure to attract the farm vote.[41]

Nonetheless, the party's bleak record (depicted in Table 2) in the five elections between 1957 and 1968 – twelve wins out of 240 prairie contests – had to be measured against its success elsewhere. And on those grounds, Davey recommended in his Final Report that the structure be retained' because this system gives us some kind of unilateral monolithic control – at least for the purposes of the

Table 2

Liberal election results on the prairies since 1950

FEDERAL

Election	Manitoba		Saskatchewan		Alberta	
	Seats	% votes	Seats	% votes	Seats	% votes
1953	8 (14)	40	5 (17)	38	4 (17)	35
1957	1	26	4	30	1	28
1958	0	22	0	20	0	14
1962	1	31	1	23	0	19
1963	2	34	0	24	1	22
1965	1	31	0	24	0	22
1968	5 (13)	41	2 (13)	27	4 (19)	35
1972	2	30	1	25	0	25
1974	2	27	3	31	0	25
1979	2 (14)	22	0 (14)	23	0 (21)	22

PROVINCIAL

Manitoba			Saskatchewan			Alberta		
Election	Seats	% votes	Election	Seats	% votes	Election	Seats	% votes
1953	35 (52)	41	1952	11 (53)	39	1952	4 (61)	22
1958	19 (56)	35	1956	14	30	1955	15	31
1959	11 (57)	30	1960	17 (55)	33	1959	1 (65)	14
1962	13	38	1964	33 (59)	40	1963	2 (63)	20
1966	14	33	1967	35	46	1967	3 (65)	11
1969	5	24	1971	15 (60)	43	1971	0 (75)	1
1973	5	19	1975	15 (61)	32	1975	0	5
1977	1	12	1978	0	14	1979	0 (79)	6

SOURCE: Hugh G. Thorburn (ed.), *Party Politics in Canada*, 3rd ed. (Toronto 1972); Canada, Report of the Chief Electoral Officer, 1972, 1974, 1979; Howard A. Scarrow, *Canada Votes: A Handbook of Federal and Provincial Election Data* (New Orleans 1962); *Winnipeg Free Press* (15 Dec. 1962) 3 and (24 June 1966) 1; Manitoba Statement of Votes, 30th General Election, issued by the Chief Electoral Officer of Manitoba; statements of election results for 1960 and 1964, issued by the Chief Electoral Officer for Saskatchewan; *Star-Phoenix*, Saskatoon (12 Oct. 1967 and 24 June 1971); and *Report of the Chief Electoral Officer, 1975 and 1978* (Regina); J.A. Long and F.Q. Quo, 'Alberta: One Party Dominance,' in Martin Robin, ed., *Canadian Provincial Politics* (Scarborough 1972) and *Canadian Parliamentary Guide* (1976).

national campaign.' As an electoral machine, the new organization might be counted only a qualified success but it had secured 'our secondary purpose': to bring together 'able, progressive' people who would work for the party in national elections. It was no mean achievement nor one the party leaders wished to see evaporate.[42]

REACTION TO THE REFORMS

Alberta
The plight of the Liberal party in Alberta in the late fifties is depicted in a description of one federal constituency's doldrums: 'We have no Liberal candidate to support. I tried to call a Liberal nominating convention and only five people came. At that meeting our president resigned as he is leaving town and there were not enough present to elect another president.'[43] On the provincial level, as the results of the election in 1959 showed, conditions were no better. In that year, the Liberals elected just one member. In a house of sixty-five, the total opposition numbered only four and since each was from a different party, the sessional allowance for the leader of the opposition was divided four ways. Even with their dismal record since 1921, it was difficult to fault *The Calgary* LIBERAL*'s* assessment of this defeat as 'the depth of the valley of humiliation.'[44] It was also a stinging rebuke after the party's brief renaissance in mid-decade when fifteen Liberals, elected in 1955, formed the province's largest opposition since the First World War. The results were bitter medicine for provincial Grits and, not surprisingly, they looked for a scapegoat who, also not surprisingly, turned out to be the federal Liberals. Thus, even as the FCC strategy was forming in Ottawa, a legacy of intraparty distrust was already established in Alberta.

The history of the Alberta Liberals is an unrelieved tale of ineffectual politics and internecine warfare stretching back to their years in government.[45] Even in the late thirties when William Aberhart's command of the Social Credit caucus was in jeopardy, the Liberals' proclivity to fight among themselves kept them from taking advantage of this rare breach in Alberta's usually impregnable government. During the war, the Grits were swallowed by an Independence movement created by themselves and the Tories, with the result that in 1945 they were once again given an opportunity to begin anew.

The post-war revival was led by J. Harper Prowse. Elected to the legislature in 1944 as a military service MLA and selected party leader in 1947, Prowse had more legislative experience than most of his predecessors and, unlike them, he and his small caucus actively set out to promote co-operation with Ottawa. To this end, they carried on federal and provincial organizational work 'simultaneously' arguing that the two were not 'severable' and that a second organization would be interpreted as an indication that 'somebody important had no confidence in the first one.'[46]

Initially, this desire for close ties was reciprocated by Ottawa Liberals, especially Alberta's cabinet member, J.A. MacKinnon, a minister in both the King and St Laurent governments between 1939 and 1950. MacKinnon consulted Prowse and John Stambaugh, the provincial president, on a number of matters, including the sensitive question of patronage, thus allowing provincial Liberals to influence the distribution of rewards for political service.[47] Relations deteriorated during the tenure of MacKinnon's successor as Alberta's spokesman in Cabinet, George Prudham, minister of Mines and Technical Surveys, 1950–7. Alberta Liberals viewed both him and the federal government as susceptible to pressure from the oil industry who, in turn, were unhappy about local Liberal attacks on the policies of the Manning Government.[48] For their part, the federal Liberals were irritated by the disposition of Alberta Grits to embarrass some of the largest investors in Canada's post-war economic development. The schism deepened when Ottawa Liberals displayed little sympathy for provincial concerns, despite repeated urging from local party officers, who finally came to view the federal party as one 'on stilts, above and beyond the provincial organization.'[49]

By the end of the decade the party was shattered. Electorally, it lost three of four federal sets in 1957 and the remaining one in 1958, while fourteen of the fifteen provincial seats won four years earlier were lost in 1959. Its leadership was crippled as well. With no members in the federal Liberal caucus, there was no tribune for the province in Ottawa or advocate of federal affairs in Alberta. In provincial politics, Prowse resigned in 1958 and was succeeded by Grant Mac-Ewan, at that time an MLA, but soon to be defeated in the Liberal rout of the next year. The Alberta Liberals were therefore a thoroughly dispirited party with 'no *effective* centralized authority within the province,' 'no organizer in the field,' no 'effective leadership,' and plagued by a continuation of the 'old jealousies.'[50]

This was the state of affairs when the FCC structure was introduced by national headquarters. The objective of the new organization was to return the Liberals to office and to do it by circumventing the cabinet warhorses, whose baneful influence, it was believed, had contributed to the smashing defeats of 1957 and 1958. In Alberta, however, there was no servile party organization subject to ministerial dictation. That had been the crux of the problem in Alberta, where for decades there had been no organizational hierarchy linking federal and provincial Liberal interests. Alberta, indeed, demonstrated a particular weakness of the new scheme that assumed the existence of a rival provincial organization. But in this province the local Grits languished without help from their federal counterparts. If, now, as a matter of policy and organization, the national headquarters refused to give assistance, except to committed federalists, then the Liberal party in provincial politics was at an end.

Alberta Liberals resented the FCC structure for several reasons, and among the most annoying was the circumscribed role it assigned them in matters of patronage. The FCC's responsibility in this area, which Keith Davey described as 'the most important ... of their activities,' brought sharp criticism of Ottawa's 'appointed darlings.'[51] Local complaints deluged advocates of the 'new politics' who were startled to see that petty patronage still mattered. In Ontario and Quebec, where the new organization flourished and the party reaped votes, the Liberals might understandably depreciate the value of patronage. But in a province like Alberta, where electoral victory was infrequent, patronage was the only reward for effort. As a former provincial Liberal leader observed: 'If these fellows who ... thought they were making a contribution to the party by taking a licking ... are now going to be penalized in the party councils for being failures, where the hell do we get our fatted calves next time?'[52]

But the FCC was criticized on other grounds as well. Its personnel were viewed as aggressively unattractive either because they came from outside the province and therefore were handicapped, through lack of knowledge and judgment, in rebuilding the party or because their élite background separated them from their fellow, though less privileged, residents. On the latter point, 'A Brief on the Federal Campaign Committee of Alberta,' presented to the annual Liberal convention in 1963 by some Edmonton area associations, noted the total lack of representation of women, workers, and non-Anglo-Saxons on the FCC.[53] As well, virtually all came from the two or three wealthiest constituencies in the province. Not only were these the characteristics of federal Liberal activists in Alberta, but they were also the characteristics of 'men of stature,' of the 'top-notch candidates,' the FCC sought. Personal, social, and business success, to the exclusion of electoral experience, became a key criterion for nomination. Indeed, electoral experience, became a key criterion for nomination. Indeed, electoral experience was translated into a liability because, in Alberta at least, it usually meant lack of success, defeat.

The emphasis on candidates originated in the national Liberals' preoccupation with 'new' and 'old guards' in the party. How applicable this dichotomy was to Alberta is debatable but it does make some sense out of the prominence given to candidates' personal attributes.[54] Also, since the Liberal party in Alberta stood for nothing in terms of policy which the other, more successful, parties did not also represent, the priority of personality over doctrinal fidelity was understandable:

Compared to Ontario and Quebec, a Prairie Liberal is a right-wing Conservative in terms of his political philosophy. This is undoubtedly more true of Alberta than it is of Saskatchewan, and of Saskatchewan than it is of Manitoba, but all three Provinces seem to be basically much further to the right than are the Central and Eastern Provinces of Canada.[55]

This philosophical difference between Liberals of central Canada and the prairies had the potential to produce considerable friction. The potential was never realized in Alberta because the FCC structure proved a failure as an electoral organization. Only one Liberal was returned from the province in three elections – 1962, 1963, and 1965 – when fifty-one seats were at stake, while 60 per cent of those who lost fell in the top quartile of Liberal losses (by margin of victory over runner-up) across the country. With no members of caucus and with a high turnover of candidates – in the above three elections, only seven Liberal candidates ran more than once and just one three times – no opportunity developed for philosophical dissent. The same could not be said of Saskatchewan, however, where a sharp dispute between contrasting interpretations of Liberalism complicated relations, already tense, over the structural innovations associated with Keith Davey.

Saskatchewan
The 'new politics' and the FCC structure were intended to replace 'ministerialism' as described by Stanbury, identified with the King and St Laurent eras, and given archetypal expression in the federal career of Saskatchewan's James G. Gardiner, minister of Agriculture between 1935 and 1957. Unlike Liberals to their east or west, the Saskatchewan Grits had for decades enjoyed the spoils of partisan battle. Except for the brief period when the Progressives originally threatened the old parties in 1921, Liberals in Saskatchewan had proudly proclaimed their name and allegiance with Liberals elsewhere. Indeed, the movement of Liberal personnel between federal and provincial office was a feature of Saskatchewan politics after 1905 for which there seemed no electoral penalty.

This heritage of intraparty co-operation encouraged the rejuvenated Saskatchewan Liberals in 1960 to believe their new and enthusiastic leader, W. Ross Thatcher, could beat the CCF. Therefore, they looked for federal help to ensure their bright prospects. When the aid proved meagre and begrudging, Saskatchewan Liberals, like the vastly unsuccessful Liberals of Alberta, became first angry and then disaffected.

Thatcher's early confidence that there was 'no difference between provincial and federal politics'[56] alarmed Ottawa officials who wanted to reform the party's organization. Saskatchewan represented exactly the type of situation they wished to avoid because there the Liberals, smelling victory for the first time in two decades, would do anything, even to the detriment of federal Grits, to gain power provincially. The situation was unusual because although Saskatchewan was the only province west of the Ottawa River where the Liberals had any hope of winning power, it was also the only province in the country where the arch enemy was the CCF/NDP. For Ottawa Liberals who saw themselves as 'small "l," reform-minded, left-wing progressive[s],' more in sympathy with the CCF/NDP than with Ross Thatcher, whose free enterprise rhetoric they labelled doctrinaire and reactionary, rivalry was distasteful.[57] It was also poor strategy for Liberal chieftains, who were trying to attract CCF-NDP voters in central Canada in an attempt to build a parliamentary majority.

In the provincial election of June 1960, seven months after Ross Thatcher was selected leader, the Liberals increased both their popular vote and legislative seats. That success, and the promise of a real victory if the provincial Progressive Conservative vote (now in one of its periodic revivals) could be tapped, fuelled Liberal passion. On behalf of the federal Liberals, Thatcher went into Alberta and Manitoba to help organize. Pleased with his progress, he was also chagrined at federal reluctance to make any financial commitment: 'This financial procrastination leaves me cold – I've had the course. I don't have to beg from anyone. ... Please count the provincial organization *out* – and *I'm not kidding*. ... I'm going farming.'[58] Contrasts in political style and objectives prevented relations between the Saskatchewan leader and the Liberals in Ottawa from being harmonious. But it was the introduction of the FCC structure which made them unproductive and bitter, a condition Lester Pearson underestimated when he described the establishment of a federal campaign committee in Saskatchewan as 'not an easy thing to do.'[59] In the sixties, few Liberals in Saskatchewan, including Thatcher, disputed the claim that 'Mr Thatcher has literally pulled the Liberal party up by the boot straps,'[60] and for this reason, equally few were willing to see another structure introduced no matter what gloss was put on its relationship to the Saskatchewan Liberal Association.

Although Thatcher agreed to the Association's president, D.G. Steuart, being named federal campaign chairman in 1961, he attached a proviso: 'If there is any detail work you want done, please continue to contact me.'[61] Active rejection followed hesitant acceptance of the new structure when Otto Lang, then Dean of Law at the University of Saskatchewan, was named late in 1962 to replace Steuart. From Thatcher's perspective, the change was unwarranted because Saskatchewan Liberals had recently helped the federal cause, unprecedented because provincial Liberals had never been excluded from a federal campaign and unwelcome, personally, because he and Lang had already crossed swords on other issues.[62]

The federal Liberals were aware of Thatcher's unhappiness but they ascribed different motives to it: fear that a successful federal Liberal organization might harm 'his right-wing coalition,' anger that someone in Ottawa was doing a 'hatchet job on him,' and self-pity that his earlier work was not 'appreciated.'[63] The costs of incurring the Saskatchewan leader's displeasure were considered bearable because with the old arrangement 'we surely could not expect to win seats,' while under the new, a federal campaign strategy could be devised to attract 'first class candidates,' train them and their workers through Campaign Colleges and Clinics, and (most heretical in Thatcher's Saskatchewan) 'campaign exclusively against the Tories in the next election.'

The results of the federal election in April 1963, in which the Liberals lost their one seat in Saskatchewan but came to power nationally, hardened attitudes to the federal campaign structure. When the Liberals in Ottawa decided to make the structure permanent, thereby depriving provincial leaders of customary patronage power, and to determine committee composition, Ross Thatcher's wrath at federal 'interference' exploded: 'Such a set up might work in Ontario – I hope you will believe me when I say it will not work in Saskatchewan.' Refusal to listen to local advice, he said, betrayed confidence in his judgment and belied wisdom in theirs, for the federal committee and its chairman were 'completely unacceptable' to him and to the Saskatchewan Liberal Executive.[64]

In an attempt to placate the Saskatchewan leader, the federal campaign committee was divided into a patronage section, whose members he was allowed to name, and an organization section, whose duty it was to work under Otto Lang's direction for the federal Liberals in the province. The experiment did not pacify Thatcher, now ebulliently anticipating victory in the approaching election. He made Otto Lang's removal a condition for further co-operation and his 'senseless and relentless' attack, 'crude by Ontario standards,' plus the election result finally forced the federal Liberals into submission.[65] A subsequent skirmish over naming Lang's successor was resolved but not amicably by the appointment of Hazen Argue, the last national leader of the CCF, now a convert to Liberalism.[66]

The results in Saskatchewan constituted a rout for the new federal party structure. As long as Thatcher was in power, it remained that way. There was no federal organization in Saskatchewan because the provincial party was strong and sensitive to interference. (In Alberta, there was none because the provincial party was weak but equally sensitive!) The federal Liberals viewed the situation philosophically, however, since they still saw the Tory party as 'the real enemy' and since Saskatchewan was still 'the Diefenbaker heartland.'[67] In light of the fact that Thatcher, the most prominent Liberal in the province, was not a Tory fighter, they could do nothing but accept their fate with equanimity.

Manitoba

The position of the Liberals in Manitoba differed markedly from that of their counterparts in either Alberta, where Liberals were impotent in provincial politics, or Saskatchewan, where Liberals were a partisan force of the first magnitude. Although there was only one Liberal government in Manitoba in this century, led by T.C. Norris between 1915 and 1922, the party played a major role in the Liberal-Progressive fusion during the depression, in the grand coalition of all parties after the outbreak of war, and in the resurrected Liberal-Progressive fusion of the 1950s.

The individual most closely identified with Manitoba's distinctive tradition of compromised partisanship was John Bracken, who became premier in 1922 as leader of the UFM government and who continued to lead the fusion and coalition governments until 1942, when he entered federal politics as the head of the newly christened Progressive Conservatives. According to Ralph Maybank, a long-time Winnipeg Liberal who from 1929 until appointed to the bench in 1951 had held a series of municipal, provincial, and federal elected offices, Bracken's move into partisan politics after a long career of championing non-partisanship created some but not much opposition in Manitoba. It also complicated but did not prevent the departure of his successor, Stuart Garson, to join the St Laurent Government.[68]

Although Bracken had made 'the first move towards coalition' in 1931 and even perfected its operating principle of 'turning the country against the city,' he did not act alone in his non-partisan sympathies.[69] Manitoba, as W.L. Morton has shown, was the seedbed of one hardy strain of Progressivism, while Alberta was another. The aggressiveness of the farmers, emboldened by J.W. Dafoe's strictures on party competition in the province, also spurred the Liberals under Mackenzie King to seek accommodation with the agrarian movement in federal politics.

The reintroduction of partisan politics in Manitoba by Duff Roblin in the fifties found the Liberals unable to compete successfully. In the eyes of the electors, at least half of whom lived in metropolitan Winnipeg, the Liberal-Progressive government led by Garson's successor, Douglas Campbell, was a rural-based organization concerned about defending its rotten-borough seats.[70] Provincial organization had languished along with partisanship, said Maybank, but federal activists were expected to help on demand. Stuart Garson, a product of this heritage, was 'actually on record decrying [party] organization,' a fact that never ceased to irritate federal Liberals in Manitoba, who resented being expected to serve Liberal-Progressive politicians without benefiting in return.[71]

The rift between the two sets of Grits had other origins as well. Conservative and not liberal or progressive ideas on matters of public expenditure and social policy dictated that the provincial government should dissociate itself from the 'socialist' St Laurent administration. It also meant that St Laurent and his supporters in 1957 would receive from the provincial premier neither public support in the campaign nor remorse in defeat: 'I never did run as a Liberal. I helped turn the Liberals out in the province.'[72]

The collapse of the Liberal party in Manitoba in the late 1950s was dramatic and swift: federally between 1953 and 1957, a drop from 8 seats to 1 and from 40 per cent of the vote to 26, while provincially, between 1953 and 1958, a drop from 35 seats to 19 and from 41 per cent of the vote to 35. Moreover, the depressed fortunes seemed permanent because the decline continued for the provincial Liberals and stopped at a cripplingly low level for the federal Liberals. This mutual fall from grace did not promote reconciliation, for the dualism of Grit politics in Manitoba remained never far from the surface.

In 1959, the left or federal wing won the party presidency with J.F. O'Sullivan, who later became Manitoba's federal campaign chairman, while in 1961 they triumphed again when Gildas Molgat won the party leadership. Ascendancy of the federal wing helped smooth the introduction and the operation of the FCC structure, allowing 'whatever personal differences there may be in the group [to be] settled in a proper backroom manner.'[73] The situation in Manitoba was not unlike that in Alberta except that the principals in Winnipeg had roots in their province's politics. The FCC structure was welcomed because it allowed committed Liberals, who for decades had sat on the sidelines, to get involved.

It was this contrast which accounted for the equanimity of the one group as it tried to explain away the fears of the other:

I am [said J.F. O'Sullivan] a strong believer in subsidiarity and I appreciate the difficulties that you have had in Alberta with respect to arranging for cooperation between the federal and provincial branches of our party ... I am disturbed at your suggestion that it is an open secret that there is an attempt being made to set up a federal organization within your province answerable only to Mr Davey and Mr Gordon.[74]

Harmony between federal and provincial Liberals in Manitoba disappeared when Molgat was named to the Senate. The old left-right schism widened after his successor described himself as 'not a left-wing Liberal ... perhaps just a little more right of centre.'[75] The triumph of the 'right' continued through the next provincial Liberal leader, I.H. Asper, selected in 1970, but faltered before yet another new leader, Charles Huband, chosen in 1974.[76] This ideological fluidity, determined as much as anything by the current provincial leader's views of federal Liberal policies, reflected the growing weakness of the provincial Grits who, between 1966 and 1973, went from 14 to 5 seats in a legislature of 57 and from 33 to 19 per cent of the popular vote.

During the period of the Davey reforms, however, the situation in Manitoba was less turbulent than in either of the other prairie provinces and, therefore, the new organizational structure had the best chance of being accepted there. Unlike Alberta, there was no traditional resentment of federal organization. Indeed, as already noted, federal Liberals from Manitoba criticized provincial Liberal-Progressives for their absolute reliance on the national organization. Again, unlike Saskatchewan, there was no vigorous and jealous provincial rival to the federal Liberals. The fact remains, however, that the FCC structure was no more successful in Manitoba than anywhere else on the prairies. The Liberals did well if they could hold their own supporters, nowhere did they show new strength.

CONCLUSION

Davey's resignation as national organizer followed the election in November 1965 in which the Liberals for a third time under the new organization failed to secure a parliamentary majority. A few months later, he was appointed to the Senate along with a phalanx of western Liberals: John Nichol, Earl Hastings, J. Harper Prowse, Harry Hays, and Hazen Argue. In Ontario, the reforms had paid dividends handsomely but on the prairies, even with federal sympathizers now in key positions in the party organization of each province, evidence of the old régime's survival was clear enough, lingering perhaps in Alberta but thriving in Saskatchewan, where Thatcher still had six more years in office. Douglas Everett, a key Liberal in Manitoba, recognized the inescapable but not surprising feature of the Liberal party: it meant 'different things in different places.' But he touched on a more revealing truth as well: 'I think it has a country atmosphere and a city atmosphere or a rural atmosphere and an urban atmosphere. ... The people who are involved in politics in the country are to a large extent the same people who have been involved for many, many years.' The newcomers were the city people and except for Winnipeg, which is an old city, the cities they came to were new and burgeoning.[77]

The city Liberals of the prairies looked a lot like the city Liberals of central Canada – middle class, comparatively highly educated, often professionals – only there were fewer of them. Thatcher's 'eggheads' were not a regional phenomenon. Old George Prudham's caution that 'campaigning in a Cadillac is a mistake in this province' was not wide of the mark, especially when the limousine was driven by a young lawyer. A former Saskatchewan Liberal leader, whose federal loyalty was never in question, echoed the sentiment in his province. Young Liberals with tenuous ties to the province or their constituency and free from experience in practical politics antagonized supporters as often as they won confidence.[78]

In the West, Davey could never satisfactorily refute the charge that the federal campaign committee structure was actually a separate organization and, therefore, a threat to local interests. Harmony might prevail in Ontario, but the westerner's reply to this inevitable observation was so predictable that it ceased to be made, although the irritation remained. Patronage, which the Alberta Liberals depended on to survive and Thatcher saw his just deserts, became the shoal on which the enterprise foundered. Federal Liberals talked about the new politics with its different attitude towards patronage, but the fact remained that the federal government possessed a reservoir of places and favours and that they had to be bestowed by someone. When the time came, the practitioners of the new politics did not flinch: 'Patronage properly used becomes an effective political tool in the hands of the organizer.'[79] The FCC in the province advised the respective minister after taking local soundings, but consultation without issue was worse than no consultation at all. Because another principle of the new politics was constant activity – to keep the organization alive – the irritation never had time to subside before being inflamed by a new clash of wills.

There was more to the new politics than organization, although at times this was easy to forget in the heat of battle over prerogatives. Earlier Otto Lang commented that 'we are becoming so mindful of organization ... that many of those who believe that policy has some importance are staying away from any meeting that sounds organizational.'[80] The importance of policy cannot be minimized in this account of the Liberals' problems on the prairies. It will be discussed in detail in Chapter 6. In the meantime, it is necessary to continue the examination of organizational change; as of 1966, only the first experiment was complete. Still, before the party lay the whole experience in participatory democracy.

5

Participatory Democracy

It's a little tougher to 'participate in democracy' from Winnipeg than it was in Ottawa. (Richard H. Kroft to Richard Stanbury, 4 February 1970)

Like the 'new politics,' participatory democracy sank under the weight of its promise. Enthusiasts who had exhorted political involvement and participation to meet 'the demands of the seventies' succumbed before their own 'time-frame.' The sense of urgency about the plight of previously ignored causes and groups faded when old concerns about the economy and national unity returned. Demands for a new political sensibility and social equity appeared ingenuous, impractical, and even cynical in light of what was accomplished. Participatory democracy thus became as easy to dismiss as it had been to advocate. But if too much had once been expected of it, now insufficient attention was paid to its legacy. However impermanent the new attitudes to politics might be, they had exerted a profound influence on the structure of the Liberal party and, in turn, on the place of the prairie provinces in that national institution. No political party ever went further or broke with its past more than the Liberals in their adventure into popular participation. For this achievement, the party owed most to its president between 1968 and 1973, Senator Richard Stanbury.

Stanbury was not a lone reformer. He could not have carried through his overhaul of the party organization without the assistance of scores of like-minded men and women, Nor could those efforts have enjoyed the authority they carried without a national party leader whose attitudes and actions after 1968 encouraged the belief that a different, more open approach to politics was possible. But Stanbury's energy and loyalty to the idea of broadened political participation within the Liberal party was fundamental to the course of the experiment. No one else had such 'evangelical fervour' – the politicians not excepted – for it was they in the election of 1972, following the greatest renovation in the party's history, who opted for the old-fashioned campaign organization.[1] When Stanbury retired as president early the next year, the momentum of change slackened but did not stop. Before the 1974 campaign Keith Davey, whose forte lay in managing elections, was back as organizer and Gildas Molgat, a former provincial leader in Manitoba and supporter of the Stanbury reforms, had become national president. The changes which Senator Stanbury had introduced in the early seventies, especially as they touched on party policy formulation, continued through the last half of the decade. What had changed were the expectations that had accompanied their introduction. Participatory democracy had chastened more than it had changed the party.

The genesis of participatory democracy was to be found in the view shared by prominent Liberals in the late 1960s that social change had outdistanced party organization.[2] Political parties could no longer perform the tasks traditionally expected of them. In particular, they had become quite inadequate transmitters of public opinion, or in the jargon of the day they had failed to provide 'feedback.' How well they had ever communicated to those in power the feelings and attitudes of the electorate was open to question, for it was widely held that the party under Mackenzie King and St Laurent had discouraged close contact with the rank and file. In those days, so the depiction went, the party's pre-eminent task was that of an electoral machine and its platforms were, in the words of an even more venerable Grit, William Fielding, like those of 'a railway coach ... made to get in on.'[3] It was not just neglect that caused the organization to die away after each campaign. The politicians wanted it that way. In the past, said Senator Stanbury, 'The idea was that an MP simply by being elected, "represented" the people of his constituency and that he could "represent" their feelings without ever checking back with them between elections.'[4] Interests, therefore, had gone unrepresented by parties and while this may have been tolerable at a time when government did less than in the modern period and when many problems could be resolved outside the formal political system, it was no longer acceptable. Those who were formerly inarticulate in society had found their voice and only at its peril could a political party fail to provide a forum for them to be heard.

In addition to the need for better communications, there were important subsidiary problems to be faced. Among these the most pressing were to extend the boundaries of party interest far beyond former traditional concerns and to recognize within these new bounds the existence of a plethora of 'publics,' in some cases already identified and organized around interests like race, income, and dwelling place; subjects which previously had not been granted prominence in Liberal politics. Nothing short of an extension of the political franchise was contemplated and it was this emancipation that set off an unprecedented cycle of activity within the party. The Liberals were neither unaccustomed to change, having undergone the reforms of Keith Davey early in the sixties, nor unfamiliar with broadened participation in party affairs, as witness the conferences in 1961 and 1966, but they were not ready for the approaching burst of democracy.

Political unrest in the United States and abroad in 1968 contrasted sharply with events at home, where a decade of campaigning through a string of minority governments had come to an end. The opportunity presented by a new majority government coincided with the need to demonstrate political stewardship in Canada. To the advocates of participatory democracy the way this should be done was clear: cynicism about traditional parties would be dispelled only when the public had freer access to those in power. According to Senator Stanbury, if the exercise was not to be a charade, then government when it made its decisions must be offered 'the countervailing force of public advice' along with the information and representations it normally received from the civil service and special interest groups.[5] Up to now, in the world of competing interests, the public had been poorly served by its chief spokesman, the member of parliament, who was handicapped in what he could do for the ordinary voter by his lack of resources and a low opinion of his own potential. It was here that the party, both in and out of Parliament, was now expected to play its crucial reform role in 'the development of the techniques whereby the expertise of the elite may be turned into wisdom through the alchemy of participation.'[6] A wealth of faith but little guidance lay in that medieval reference.

The techniques eventually adopted were informed by old as well as new ideas of participation. Federalism, whose cardinal feature – the limitation of power and specification of function – had long been evident in the Liberal party itself, ran counter to the expansive goal of participatory democrats. A compromise of principles had to be found. In the bad old days, harmony had been achieved at the expense of participation through the dominating influence of the federal cabinet minister, whose importance as time would tell was still unexpectedly crucial to any successful scheme of organization. The Davey reforms had favoured committees over individuals, but in the process of pressing the federal case had fomented intraparty rivalries. The problem was how to reconcile federalism's inherent concern to exclude with participatory democracy's equally strong desire to expand.

There was a further complication. Canadian federalism in the sixties and seventies was actually moving in the opposite direction to what the advocates of participation wanted. While there was considerable overlap in sympathy and personnel between Ontario and federal Liberals, such coincidence was nowhere else as evident or likely possible. In Quebec, separate party organizations in federal and provincial politics accurately reflected the state of the constitution as far as that province was concerned. And to some national observers, the Quebec separate-but-equal model appeared the more reliable harbinger than a continuation of a single Janus-like organization. Logistics, too, favoured separation, for the old practice of Liberals working, first, provincially and, then, federally for the party was no longer feasible because, in Senator Stanbury's words, 'once you start running a continuous party then you can't separate yourselves into pieces like that.'[7]

New structures had to be devised to assure a modicum of integration, thereby helping to promote greater participation than before but at the same time to permit provincial Liberals that measure of freedom coincident with a decentralized Canadian federal system. Attempts to reconcile opposites bode ill more often than they promise peace; the structures Senator Stanbury created did both depending upon where they were located and at what time they were being examined.

At the centre, the prime innovation was the creation of 'the political cabinet,' which brought together the cabinet and representatives of caucus and the National Liberal Federation to discuss, from their different perspectives, such problems as the place of the MP in the political system, the financing of elections, and the growth of regional discontent. Because political cabinet opened the door to any subject being discussed if it was judged sufficiently important to occupy the limited time of ministers, it constituted the principal assurance that the government would not again lose touch with people or party. In this way, it kept politics alive for those most susceptible to the malaise of power. On a day-to-day basis the health and welfare of the party was the responsibility of the National Advisory Group, composed of representatives of caucus, the Prime Minister's Office, the Federation, and regional caucuses who were supposed to meet frequently to monitor what was going on in the country. Its success in turn depended on the information gathered and handed on by advisory groups established in each province, which had as their respective chairmen a federal minister from that province (if there was one) and was composed of a delegate of the federal caucus, a representative of the provincial Liberals, and a member of the Ottawa party headquarters staff to act as secretary.

The advisory groups helped co-ordinate party activities in the province but, most important, they were intended to gauge the pulse of the individual ridings. The provincial advisory groups were the connectors, the synapses of the party, responsible for transmitting political messages. On their successful operation depended the co-operation and harmony which the whole structure was intended to achieve. While Senator Stanbury's hopes for the Ontario group were likely to be realized more quickly than elsewhere, the expressed objective was the same for each province:

I would like to see over the next year or so the Advisory Groups take complete charge of the oversight of all of the functions of the party within the province. They should be acting as the channel for the party's political input into Cabinet through recommendations to Ministers, the Prime Minister, or through attendance at political cabinet. They should be pressing Members of Parliament and party organization into completing the restructuring of the riding organization as a community agency. They should be looking forward to the next election ... in terms of candidates, the kind of material and support needed by candidates, fund-raising techniques, leader's tours, etc.[8]

Political cabinet and the provincial advisory groups were related reforms and neither would work unless both did. It became one of Stanbury's frustrating tasks to cajole co-operation from Liberals both at the centre and in the provinces. In his arguments the trump card was prime ministerial support for the reforms. Failure to make them work was therefore depicted as all the more dispiriting because it was due to the poor response not of those 'at the top' but of the rank and file, who had the most to gain from this expansion of participation. But the reasons for foot-dragging were not all that mysterious, being instead a combination of jealousy on the part of politicians and confusion all round. Nowhere did jealousy appear more unattractive than in Saskatchewan, where the quarrel between federal and provincial Liberals continued to boil. But there at least the dispute between two reigning parties (up to 1971 for the provincial Grits) made the jealousy intelligible if no less bitter, while in a province like British Columbia where provincial Liberals were excluded from power in the foreseeable future, the unco-operative attitude of local federal Liberals was plainly irksome:

The ridiculous thing about our present situation is that we finally have built channels at the top of the Party which make it possible for even a local problem to be brought effectively to the attention of the Cabinet Minister or even to the full Cabinet if the problem is serious enough. But we have not yet persuaded our riding associations to equip themselves to use those channels ... In fact, there is a blockage in B.C. because the Provincial Advisory Group has never been made to function. It seems to be because neither Arthur Laing nor the Caucus want the Party Organization to have a voice, and the Party Organization has not been insistent enough to see that the group is set up.[9]

The reasons for jealousy, however, were often more complicated than a quarrel over possessing the fruits of power. There was first of all the fact that some ministers and members of parliament disagreed with the interpretation Senator Stanbury gave of how the party should be run or how it had been run. Politicians who, in fact, thought they were doing a good job 'communicating' or 'representing' interests could not be expected to welcome proposals for change that would consume precious time and energy for inconclusive if not adverse returns. Moreover, no matter how one described the political system, the incontrovertible fact remained that it was the politician who put his neck in the electoral noose after the writs were issued. If he had to chance paying the full price, he could be excused for thinking he, too, was the most prescient and responsible judge of how to play the game.

The organizational reforms and, indeed, the whole idea of participatory democracy required a good deal of explaining before they could be understood and even when they were, they suffered the weakness, in the eyes of some, of seeming impractical, remote, and perhaps irrelevant to individual partisans. The advisory groups appeared to be, said one Liberal MP, 'a sort of nebulous thing to most members and they don't really understand their function and feel that it is pretty much a quiet operation locked up by those directly involved.'[10] Other Liberals compared deeds with words, on the latter score of which participatory democracy was particularly vulnerable because of its prolix and rotund theory, and found the whole enterprise wanting. Stanbury's defence that the obstacles to success were 'at the local level where the tradition of election-time activity only dies hard' and his analysis that 'the public will need a lot of persuading' were not acceptable to those who found the already lengthy appeals unconvincing.[11] Government solicitude for sounding out the public's opinion alarmed those voters who viewed the threat of continuous consultation an unwelcome possibility:

The present Government by white paper, committees and commissions, continually asks the electorate [sic] for his or her opinion on various vital matters and leaves the whole thing up in the air for too long a time. The understanding that the one who casts his ballot has for this kind of situation, is organized confusion. The voter justly expects his member to represent him in the Government and at times when he is home, to sense the pulse of the community, through his own methods.[12]

The proof of participation depended upon some grand achievement, one which would show rank and file and those at the top alike the benefits to be had from extending democracy. The ideal vehicle was a sophisticated program of policy development which would involve the party at all levels of its activity; ideal as well because it had been intended from the start that Liberals across the country should play an integral role in formulating public policy. Policy would, therefore, be the test of the new structure: it would help convert the riding associations into 'community-oriented organizations,' it would inject ideas and issues into party discussions too often preoccupied with immediate issues such as sharing spoils, and it would demonstrate through the projected three-phase program that the avenues were open to the seats of power. At the last stage, the national party conference, the government would have to take account of what the party said. Success at the riding and regional levels would be the party's authority when the national conference met.

In this complicated and sweeping exercise in democracy, the seeds of disillusionment could germinate along with those of confidence. Eventually conclusions had to be reached and decisions made. After such breadth of discussion, were the decisions any less likely to rend and divide? Was the danger of friction perhaps not greater? Senator Stanbury recognized this possibility early in his presidency:

One of the difficulties with a participatory programme is the danger that people will not be satisfied with their degree of participation unless their own view is accepted and of course everyone's view cannot be accepted, no matter how legitimate it may be. Someone always has to take executive decisions and executive responsibility ... What we are really trying to do is to increase understanding of the issues to see that Cabinet makes its decisions based upon not only the expert advice it receives from the Public Service but also from the democratic forces through the Member of Parliament and the Party. But they must eventually make a decision and they must be prepared to account for that decision both to the Party and to the public. The same is true at every level of the Party.[13]

The policy program took nearly a year and a half of party headquarters' time from the initial discussions about what kind of conference should be held to the implementation of the three-phase plan between November 1969 and November 1970.[14] Essentially, the three phases consisted, first, of a meeting of 'experts' who would talk about 'the vital issues of the seventies' confronting or about to confront the party, followed by constituency and regional meetings to debate and pass resolutions on the basis of the digested and circulated content of Phase I and, finally, a national policy convention where the collected and informed will of the party would be expressed directly to its leaders. Phase I, the experts' contribution, took place at Harrison Hot Springs, British Columbia, during a long weekend; Phase II sounded the broad and geographically dispersed opinion of the party in response to the experts over a matter of months; while Phase III, again of a few days' duration, left the experts and the resolutions behind and concentrated on producing 'a series of options for the delegates to consider' before they indicated their final preference.[15]

The planning that went into this mammoth undertaking was intense and to the near-exclusion of other activity. It coincided, for instance, with the heated debate that followed publication of the government's White Paper on Taxation in November 1969 and with demands from members of Parliament for assistance from the national office to meet the flood of constituency criticism. While headquarters did something to answer the requests, Senator Stanbury recognized that it was not enough:

All our limited resources have been taken up for at least six months now with preparations for the Harrison Hot Springs Conference, the preparation of material for the discussion of policy questions at the local level as part of Phase II of the Policy Development Programme, and the preliminary arrangements for the National Convention in November.[16]

The central office's commitment to the three phases of policy required secondment of staff to the conference committee and subcommittees, the allocation of office time and resources to circulate the mountainous stacks of pamphlets and papers made necessary in the service of 'communication' (half a million pieces of literature in Phase II alone), but most of all it preoccupied the attention and interest of the party's officers, for whom policy development was the centrepiece of participatory democracy.

The Harrison Hot Springs Conference was organized around task forces which doubled in number from an anticipated five in May 1969 to ten by the time the Conference assembled in November. They covered a spectrum of traditional concerns – agriculture, the economy, regional development, and the individual – while at the same time reflecting the particular interests of the immediate period – cities, poverty, student unrest, and communications. In terms of subject matter, task forces on international relations and industrial relations fell midway between traditional and new; they were not unheard-of topics for a conference to discuss but they had not been debated at length before and the discussion they now prompted was very much related to current events.[17] The task forces in the person of experts reported to the Conference via panels which were followed by small group discussions. Time and expense precluded the national office from having all papers translated, although summary translation was available. It was originally estimated that 415 persons would attend, the figure comprising 260 from the ridings (with provincial participation roughly in proportion to each province's seats in the House of Commons), another 140 from the media, the experts, cabinet, and caucus and the remainder party officers, Federation staff, and observers. In fact, just under 400 persons registered, with slightly over 300 coming from Quebec and Ontario and the remaining quarter equally divided between the prairie provinces on the one hand and British Columbia and the Atlantic provinces on the other.[18]

The response to this first stage of the new policy process was generally complimentary about what the conference had set out to do but qualified in commending the final results. 'Too abstruse,' 'too scholastic' were sample criticisms directed at the preponderance of experts, usually from universities, whose common characteristic was 'the unreality of [their] ... assumptions.'[19] When the press scored the participants, it was for their neglect of practical questions on the one hand or their absence of 'purpose' on the other. These contradictory criticisms were partly the responsibility of the press itself, whose coverage aggravated the complaint. In a survey of 210 articles in major Canadian newspapers, the central office compiled a list of conference topics that received coverage. For a federal political party, the results of the survey were less than reassuring: cities, student unrest, and international relations received inordinate attention (the number of articles varying between twenty-one and twenty-eight), while regional development received mention on only four occasions and agriculture just once. The explanation for the disproportionate attention was that each subject in the first group had produced a visible and voluble difference of opinion at the Conference and each was therefore 'newsworthy.' While this was no doubt true, it revealed a serious weakness in this first stage of policy development. Despite the extensive preparatory work and despite the objective of identifying medium-term problems, the Conference was susceptible, perhaps even disposed, to deviate from its appointed tasks. Purpose had succumbed to timeliness. Disturbing, too, was the ease with which federal diversities were ignored. Such categories of thought tended to be overlooked in favour of interests of immediate concern and in the context of the Conference, agriculture and regional development were minority interests while student unrest and the cities (especially the two or three very large metropolitan centres) were not. In any electoral calculation for the future, however, this balance of interest would require adjustment.

Continuity between Phases I and II presented a problem when the setting changed from the seclusion of a political retreat to the disordered atmosphere of hundreds of riding offices. Phase I specialist material had to be condensed but, at the same time, its appeal broadened if it was to act as an incentive for building strong constituency networks. Phase II was intended not only as an essential part of policy formulation but as the genesis of new party channels that would improve contact between community and government. For that reason, the imbalance of Phase I in terms of attention to subject matter had to be corrected with greater attention being paid to the disparities of federalism. How this might be done was suggested by Senator Stanbury: 'Because of the problem of finding ten subjects which will be equally topical in all parts of the country, you may find it necessary to consult with various advisory groups or caucuses or policy committees to be sure that there is some content of regional problems.'[20]

Even if subjects of local appeal could be found, Phase II depended on additional ingredients for success. Especially, it required active participation by the delegates who had attended Phase I as well as a receptive hearing by the local constituency executives. Stephen Clarkson, who has studied the response of the Toronto and District Liberal Association to the experiment with participatory democracy, concludes that in that metropolis Phase II proved a disappointment. The anticipated activity of the Phase I delegates hardly materialized, while the rank and file members of the party were anything but receptive when it did. The reasons for this, he suggests, can be reduced essentially to ignorance or scepticism of the grand design. The implications of the failure, however, extended beyond Toronto, for 'if the political culture of the party in highly urbanized Toronto was [not] "civic" enough to give Liberals a sense of power within their own organization, it was even more unlikely that the more traditional party system in the Maritimes and the Prairies could generate significant member involvement in party policy-making.'[21] Although it may be questioned whether civicism mounts the closer one draws to Toronto, there is no evidence that Phase II was any more welcome in its implementation in the prairie provinces than in populous Ontario.

The National Policy Convention in November 1970 marked the culmination of the elaborate process begun a year earlier. According to Stanbury, 150,000 people had taken part in developing the material that came before the Convention for discussion while at the Convention itself seventy per cent of the delegates voted on about 500 decisions. With that evidence of activity, the party believed it possessed a strong claim to a respectful hearing from government. It was understandable, therefore, why expectations then and for the future were so high: from this enterprise the nature of Liberalism in the new decade was to be revealed, the basis of the platform for the next election decided, and the party's guidelines (to use no stronger word) to government made explicit. Arguably, then, the single most important obstacle to placing 'the political system in the hands of the people' was about to be cleared.

Those most immediately familiar with the processes of government could not fail to respond, but the nature of their reaction proved unpredictable. They sought to brake the momentum of participatory democracy by reminding its enthusiasts that access to power was not power itself. 'I want to make very sure,' said James Davey of the prime minister's office, 'that no one is deluded about the amount of influence that can be exercised on the policy decision process.'[22] Rebuttal was made on several counts. Government was not some malleable creature ready to be shaped by every influence exerted upon it, even if the stimulus was a 'democratic' party. In the two and a half years since the last general election in 1968, government had experienced sweeping and sophisticated reforms which surpassed anything accomplished by the party, with the result that in expertise and thoroughness, the party's policy structure was no match for 'the effort and detailed work that goes into the development of major government decisions.' New committees in cabinet, caucus, and the House of Commons, new departments of government and reforms to the rules of the House exemplified the breadth of innovation. The problems these particular changes had been designed to meet were beyond dispute. In fact, there was 'a diminishing freedom of choice' as to what government could do and, therefore, what it did was no longer worth debating. The question that ought to concern the party was how did government go about dealing with a problem? 'If style is the man, then style is the Party. Methodology and approach will increasingly replace ideology as distinguishing party characteristics.' The role of the modern party was not to posit problems, less so solutions to problems, but to enunciate for the guidance of government 'the values that should be emphasized.'

How the role of the modern party, according to this definition, differed from that of the traditional party, the one participatory democrats were trying to replace, was less than immediately obvious and the identification of government with means not ends no more evident. But if the significance of the particular words was blurred, the implication of the rebuttal was not: the party was for amateurs and the government for professionals. Unpalatable though the suggestion might be, it rang true when the time came to implement the Convention's decisions. The prime minister might direct cabinet ministers to designate some official to see that relevant convention decisions were considered when discussing policy in departments, but that was surely less than participatory democracy had promised. In its defence, government might respond that convention resolutions were not always unequivocal and that even sympathetic ministers occasionally experienced difficulty in deciphering the will of the party. Open to question, too, was the representativeness and authority of convention decisions made by 'putting checks on a piece of paper' by people unacquainted with the facts, who may or may not have listened to the relevant discussion when the party was assembled. Finally, the individual minister responsible for deciding how much weight to give the respective preferences of the Convention, now that it had dissolved, experienced the frustration of being held accountable to an absent master with whom as likely as not he had had little opportunity to debate specific policies in the first place.[23]

The concern of participatory democracy was never solely with policy; electoral matters had always bulked large among the purposes of its new structures. But if amateur status were to be granted to policy which had only been of secondary interest to the party in the past, what chance was there that the heart of Liberal politics would be any more accessible? Here surely was the original 'accountability session' but, once again, Senator Stanbury recognized the problem the reformers faced:

One other item that troubles me is that, as the election approaches, the Cabinet and perhaps even the Leader seem to be losing interest in the normal programs of the Party. I can see this as being understandable but there is danger of us falling back into a traditional electoral role, rather than carrying through our reforms into the logical extension in the election process. If we allow this to happen we shall have to start back at square one after the election, and I am not prepared to see us put in that position. We have to define the implications in election terms of the new kind of party we have been building and then see that that definition is accepted and implemented.[24]

His appraisal summarized accurately the conflicting attitudes that government and party brought to the election campaign in 1972. To be sure, there was a community of interest – to see the Liberals successful at the polls – but not a community of motive. For, while the party expected as part of its new duties to play a vital, even determining, part in the campaign preparations, the government anticipated a more circumscribed contribution. The party would provide the leaven of popular opinion. The Liberal version of the Greek chorus was to be expressed through a committee on which party, caucus, and cabinet would be represented. From the government's perspective, the party's contribution must be limited to platform oversight because it possessed neither adequate machinery to evaluate formal policy nor constitutional responsibility to the electorate.[25] Instead, government must take the initiative because it was going to be held accountable.

In electoral terms, participatory democracy fared no better than it had as an innovator and determiner of policy. It failed to fulfil the expectations of all but its most sanguine promoters, although when compared to past practice some progress in expanded participation might be discerned. Yet how much was debatable, for in 1972 as in all but the most recent elections under Keith Davey's direction, the campaign was directed by a committee chaired by two cabinet ministers – Robert Andras and Jean Marchand. Participatory democracy had been anything but modest in its proposals; it was never more than that in its results.[26]

After the unfavourable returns were in (a drop of more than seventeen per cent in seats in the House of Commons and seven per cent of the popular vote), criticism of the campaign indicated how awry matters had gone. It was ironic in light of the theory of participatory democracy that the common complaint from Liberals across the country was the government's failure to maintain contact with its rank and file supporters. The alleged result was policies that were unpopular, usually misunderstood, and in either case attributable to a failure in the communications 'linkage' which the new structures were supposed to improve. The campaign itself was held up as a model of ineptitude in this regard. Government seemed distant and its members as remote from public opinion as had the St Laurent administration fifteen years before. In spite of all the talk of more responsive, open authority 'a government that began its life with a massive flowchart style [had] ended up ... one of the great ad hoc governments in the history of Canada.' And the misfortune was about to be compounded because of the lesson government seemed ready to draw from its electoral mauling: 'Those who interpret the western results as anti-French are, I think, grossly mistaken and do a disservice to the best interests of this country.'[27]

A combination of local lethargy and latent-to-active hostility explained the failure of advisory groups to prove themselves in most provinces, with the possible exception of Ontario, although even there the record, measured in seats and votes lost between 1968 and 1972, was scarcely creditable. On the prairies, the reforms introduced after 1968 aggravated rather than reduced tension. It is a moot point what form of organization other than one giving the provinces a clear hand would have found favour in Saskatchewan and Alberta. Fortunately, constructive alternatives are not a prerequisite to criticism: certain it is that while the Liberals were in power in Saskatchewan and for nearly a year thereafter, while they recovered from defeat and the death of Ross Thatcher, the advisory groups failed. The cause was indisputable – the premier. Although early in his presidency Stanbury sought to establish a harmonious relationship with Ross Thatcher, complimenting him as 'an extremely able and forthright man and one who has made a substantial contribution to the Liberal Party,' common cause with the Saskatchewan Liberals proved unattainable.[28]

In his battle with Keith Davey, the premier had successfully demonstrated that he would not co-operate with the federal Liberals unless he could dictate terms. Thus to integrate any party matters between the two levels of government was doomed to immediate failure because the provincial organization actively avoided involvement with the new Saskatchewan Advisory Group. The result of this refusal to participate was that the Advisory Group was deprived of one of its important 'constituencies.' At the same time, because the important provincial organization was absent, the federal cause directly suffered. Faced by this impasse, Ottawa Liberals had to create other channels of communication with the faithful in Saskatchewan and these structures were necessarily at odds with Stanbury's design for internal party democracy.

On a visit to Saskatchewan in 1968, the party's National Director met Otto Lang, now minister without portfolio in the Trudeau Government, and reported that

it was generally agreed that on the one hand we will attempt to strengthen the federal organization's presence in the Executive of the Saskatchewan Liberal Association, and on the other hand will move to establish a Federal Affairs Committee in the province so that political decisions in the province, respecting federal affairs, will be influenced more by the federal constituency Presidents and the defeated candidates rather than by the Premier.[29]

The Federal Affairs Committee was always considered a part, however tangentially, of the Saskatchewan Liberal Association's executive. Indeed, in organizational terms, it could be nothing else since there was no separate federal organization in the province, although the possible establishment of one was recognized by federal Liberals at least up to the time of the Saskatchewan Liberals' defeat in 1971.

The advisory committees for Alberta and Manitoba were no more successful than the Saskatchewan group, although the reasons for failure were different in each instance. In Alberta, by the end of the sixties, the provincial wing had ceased 'to be taken seriously by federal Liberals,' or by anyone else.[30] The spectacular revival of the Progressive Conservatives under Peter Lougheed coincided with the final collapse of the provincial Liberals as an electoral force. In 1967 the Grits had won eleven per cent of the popular vote and three of sixty-five seats, but by the time of the 1971 provincial election, a succession of short-lived provincial leaders had presided over the loss of all their legislative seats (two through by-election defeats and one through the defection of a Liberal MLA to the Progressive Conservatives) and the final disintegration of local organization. In that election, the new provincial leader, Robert Russell, encouraged interested Liberals in constituencies where no official Liberal candidate was standing to file nomination papers themselves. Few supporters followed his advice or even voted for the party, whose share of the total popular vote fell to one per cent.

For obvious reasons, therefore, Ottawa officials found the annual meetings of the Alberta Liberal Association 'dispirited.'[31] They also found themselves singled out as the cause of local Liberal malaise and although the charge was by now hoary with age, it did make impossible any successful operation of the provincial Advisory Committee. Invariably the indictment against them listed federal patronage as a prime grievance. There was little doubt that the subject demoralized and angered local Liberals and encouraged some of them to think of joining a separate provincial organization.[32] Although this did not happen, the provincial organization could never be depended upon to play the role assigned it in the integrated structure created after 1968. In Alberta, political content, which had never matched political forms, once again drained away. Therefore, the following response to a complaint by a local federal activist was as futile in its defence of communication as it was protracted:

We have been in steady communication with Bob Russell and Ches Tanner is a regular attender at National Executive meetings and we are in regular telephone and correspondence communication between meetings. As you know, our organization is a federation of provincial bodies and therefore we are obliged to work through the provincial organs. In spite of that, we have developed a number of direct contacts through the use of the Info. kit which goes to the executives' [sic] members of the Party every two weeks through the

Liberal newspaper which is available to the provinces bi-monthly, through the Consultative Council which gives delegates of the Party the opportunity of participating in the decision of current political issues on a regular basis. In addition to that the Provincial Advisory Group, which includes the Cabinet Minister named by the Prime Minister (Bud Olson), the President of the Party in the province (Ches Tanner) and the Chairman of Caucus for the province (Pat Mahoney) have the responsibility of consultation with the riding presidents and other interested Party people in the province and making representations to Ministers and, if necessary, to the full Political Cabinet which meets once a month. The National Executive meets every three months and the President of the provincial Party has the opportunity of raising any serious concerns about any of these matters on those occasions, or for that matter between times with me or with the Office.[33]

As before, the situation in Manitoba was hardly more encouraging but a good deal more complicated than in Alberta. The root of the problem was the old 'left-right' division within the Liberal party, which was reflected in the continuing tension between federal and provincial Liberals. However, because harmony was difficult to achieve when either the federal (as in Alberta) or the provincial (as in Saskatchewan) Liberal interest predominated, Manitoba, where the two groups were more evenly balanced, seemed to hold the most promise. The fact that the new integrative structure was unable to prevail over the philosophical differences of Manitoba's Liberals indicated how greatly organizational reforms depended upon sympathetic support from those directly affected. That truth was demonstrated at the national level by the stimulus Senator Stanbury personally provided to participatory democracy. In Manitoba it was confirmed, this time negatively, by the equivocal response of the federal minister, James Richardson, and by the failure to replace Gildas Molgat, who in 1969 abruptly moved to Ottawa, with a provincial leader equally committed to maintaining harmony between federal and provincial Liberals.

Richardson's disinterest might not have been so damaging had it not reflected a more fundamental weakness. At the end of the sixties, Manitoba Liberals had yet to adjust to the political changes introduced by Duff Roblin more than a decade before. Their Liberal-Progressive heritage of coalition ill prepared them to meet partisan competition first from the Conservatives and then later from the NDP as well. Refuting labels but reflecting their rural base, the party of Bracken, Garson, and Campbell had become the most conservative political force in the province. It was this background that explained why provincial Liberals in 1969 professed to see an unpalatable likeness in the social and economic goals of federal Grits and the triumphant provincial NDP: a judgment that seemed confirmed by Ed Schreyer's lone support among Manitoba politicians for the Trudeau Government's Official Languages Act. In the eyes of federal Liberals, the provincial party was in the unhappy position of finding its traditional political aspirations thwarted by successful local Tories and its opportunity to follow the 'progressive' precedents of its Ottawa brethren denied by a rejuvenated provincial NDP.

The Manitoba Liberals' lack of purpose was made the more irritating for federal observers by the local party's failure to remedy it. The national office looked in vain to the federal minister to provide direction. In the 'interminable' debates over the party's future, Richardson's contribution was 'not [to] rule out the possibility of a new party ... and this outside the present Liberal party!'[34] It was understandable, therefore, that suggestions for the complete separation of federal and provincial party organizations should be canvassed but equally clear why no decision could ever be reached. In provincial affairs, the selection of a former cabinet minister in the last Liberal-Progressive government to succeed Gildas Molgat, at a time when provincial politics had evolved far beyond the muted partisanship of that earlier day, demonstrated the distance that now separated Manitoba Liberals from electoral reality.[35] The integrated organization envisaged by Richard Stanbury required if not agreed ends at least defined goals towards which action might be directed. Without this minimal understanding in Manitoba, the bleak prospect presented itself of deteriorating fortunes for the federal Liberals, who had dropped to third place after the NDP came to power in 1969.

Faced by a perilous future at home and aligned against their federal counterpart on a range of issues including an electorally unwise and politically unnatural opposition to the Official Languages Act, the Manitoba Liberals grew paralyzed through loss of direction. Unable to summon the will to break with the federal Liberals, or the courage to join them, the Manitoba party became as ineffectual a servant of its own interests as of the public's.

In operation, participatory democracy was not a one-man effort, but at the beginning Stanbury was the spark and throughout the guiding spirit. He reignited interest in the traditional political party by making it less traditional and it was he who devised the means for broadened participation by channelling aroused interest into practical political forms. In time, enthusiasm moderated but not before a basic change was wrought in Liberal perceptions of party and policy. If Stanbury had to countenance ministerial opposition in some instances, he received support in others. Coming from a province which provided few philosophical Liberals, Otto Lang's interest in policy might be interpreted either as predictable or exceptional but, in any case, early in his federal career he pressed 'the question of involvement of people throughout the country in policy matters ... [so] that it may be possible to prepare and present to constituents proposals for study on many policy questions.'[36]

But it was Stanbury's consuming passion and tireless energy which inspired others despite substantial personal costs. Participatory democracy demanded constant activity as evidence of commitment and in fulfilment of duty: 'In this business of participation, you have to keep running fast just to keep from sliding back.'[37] In the end it became an effort difficult to sustain. At the time of his resignation as party president in 1973, Stanbury explained his past motivation by comparing himself to Keith Davey and suggesting that their longevity as 'the only two who have persevered out of the original [Toronto] group' was due to the fact that they 'just plain enjoy[ed] politics.'[38] The change of pilots (for despite their different titles, each dominated party affairs while he was in office) provided more than nostalgia; it signalled the coming of age of participatory democracy. From now on it would be on its own, independent of a guardian. Party organization had come full circle or, if one chose a linear symbol, had begun to backtrack: Stanbury's last political cabinet meeting was Davey's first.

Participatory democracy depended upon co-operation attained through agreement on ends. It assumed a community of interest which, between federal and provincial Liberals, proved difficult to achieve, especially at a time when the grasp of the provinces grew almost as fast as their reach. Participatory democracy depreciated the effects of federal-provincial rivalry, jealousy, and conflict. Where Liberals in the provinces, and particularly in the prairie provinces for reasons already discussed, wanted the partisan equivalent of Canada's increasingly decentralized federation, participatory democracy sought to bring them closer together. Local Liberals wanted greater freedom to manage their own affairs: a desire as basic to them as it was antithetical to those responsible for the health of the federal party.

In Alberta and Manitoba, Ottawa Liberals understandably might treat these arguments as special pleading by Grits with a vested interest in a status quo that contributed nothing to the federal cause. But in Saskatchewan, where Ross Thatcher's Liberals ruled, there was a strong local organization that might have been employed to federal ends had greater tolerance for diversity prevailed. Why it did not can be explained only by going beyond organization to policy differences between federal and provincial Liberals. One source of the problem that developed was indicated by Richard Stanbury when discussing the difficulty the party had appealing to the West and the East:

The basic problem is the narrowness of the matters which concern and appeal to the people depending upon primary industry for their existence. During the election campaign [1968], the Prime Minister managed to go over the head of that narrowness to appeal much more broadly on the basis of his own personality, and on the basis of a very real desire on the part of all Canadians to have a viable country...

But our experience should teach us that, under the umbrella of Canadianism, these people are tremendously and necessarily jealous on matters affecting the narrow base of their existence. One dare not be flippant about such matters...

If we are going to be successful in the primary industry areas of Canada, *we shall have to take as seriously as they do their legitimate interest in the narrow economic base of their existence*. We shall always have to show our *deep concern* about these matters even when there is nothing practical that we can do about them in the short run. (emphasis in original)[39]

6

The Contribution of Policy

The Liberal Party has failed to win support on the Prairies because it has failed to identify with agriculture and more specifically with the ordinary prairie farmer. (Hazen Argue, 11 January 1968)

Operation LIFT is ... discrimination ... The fellow who was fortunate enough to get a stockpile of wheat is definitely more blessed than one who hasn't got it ... No man can continue to violate God's laws and expect victory in his life. Neither can governments. ('Discouraged Saskatchewan Farmers,' letter to the editor, *Western Producer*, 28 May 1970)

Changes in party organization were internal and their electoral effect limited, party policy was external and its impact on the voter direct. After the defeats of 1957 and 1958 policy assumed a central and continuing significance in the life of prairie Liberals in a way not true before the deluge, when it had been synonymous with defending established programs and resisting requests for their extension. One of the reasons for this change lay in the example set by Progressive Conservatives, whose policies, for which the electorate repeatedly showed a strong preference, were thought by Grits to be responsible for Tory success. It was part of local Liberal wisdom that the Progressive Conservatives had no organization worthy of the name. Nor in the eyes of many Liberals was this necessarily a bad thing, since for some the intensive organization required by reformers in the sixties seemed more appropriate (as well as productive of results) in urban than in rural seats, while for others organization fell into disfavour because it had become a euphemism to disguise the squabbles over patronage.

But emphasis on policy grew in its own right and not only as a product of organization's dislike. Specific Liberal policies dealing with grain, taxation, language, and resources, which local supporters found hard to defend let alone promote, stimulated debate and dissent. Equally invidious but more general was the conviction that national Liberal policies had become too 'socialistic.'[1] The calculated flirtation between minority Liberal governments and the NDP after the elections of 1963, 1965, and 1972 provided some grounds for complaint, while the comity which maintained the liaison indicated an agreement on principles that westerners frequently found hard to accept. Officials in Ottawa were given a simple enough reason for the disapproval: 'Compared to Ontario and Quebec, a Prairie Liberal is a right-wing Conservative in terms of political philosophy.'[2] Observations about the westerner's 'innate Conservatism' and the pervasive influence of 'the Protestant ethic' were easier to state than to prove, especially as they failed to account adequately for previous Liberal success on the prairies or for the perversity of some western Liberals who professed to see their central Canadian counterparts as 'right-wing.'[3]

In answer to the first, the old bogey of ministerialism, when 'the habit [grew] of having all legislation presented in a Liberal package,' had to be summoned once more. By implication dissent had been muted because it lacked opportunity to express itself, while the impress of a dominating cabinet minister who was also a seasoned campaigner presumably had discouraged it arising in the first place. There was no satisfactory answer to the second query except to attribute it to ignorance or misunderstanding. Such confusion over who was left and right (and of what) might have been expected to raise doubts about the utility of the distinction itself. Unfortunately for Liberal unity, it did not and federal Liberals never understood that when a westerner said eastern Liberals were right-wing, he meant they did not serve the West's interests. By way of contrast, the Progressive Conservatives, particularly John Diefenbaker and Alvin Hamilton, were seen to be 'working for [westerners],' and therefore their critics stood accused as opponents of agriculture and the region.[4]

There were other reasons why policy grew in prominence. Concern among Liberal leaders to promote broader participation in its formulation offered opportunities for public dissent. Beginning with Walter Gordon and continuing through the Stanbury reforms, policy debates were encouraged as an activity appropriate to both followers and leaders. Western Liberals took advantage of the new structures to the chagrin of reformers like Walter Gordon, who had not anticipated blatant displays of regionalism: 'Carefully organized and voting in a bloc, the [westerners] rammed through a resolution in favour of a North American free-trade area.'[5] The culprits might reply that regional interests were no less respectable than those of economic nationalism nor were they less patriotic, but events like the 1966 Policy Conference widened the gulf which had originated in organizational differences and which already separated western Liberals from their fellow Grits.

Electoral results, too, promoted policy. The parliamentary caucus of the governing party plays a fluctuating but generally small part in the creation of policy. Normally it does no more than Bagehot's monarch: advise, counsel, and warn. But many people outside of Parliament think it is important and therefore, when the West virtually excluded itself from the ruling party's caucus, both government and the disaffected community sought alternative means of maintaining contact. It was understandable why the old farm organizations, which had once acted almost as deputies of the government, should believe that 'meaningful consultation with farm organizations must surely lead to the development of effective farm policies,' but newer organizations committed to preserving or changing the status quo in western agriculture accepted the Pool's premise as well.[6] Because the grain constituency had ceased to be identified with the Pools, the government faced a fragmented audience. No longer could it rely on reminding a single organization in each of the prairie provinces of past favours and expect them to help rally support. Instead, a variety of approaches had to be made and when, for reasons discussed below, government took the initiative after 1968 in reforming the grain industry, its policies were attacked and necessarily defended on different fronts. It was this dispersal of activity and the response it generated which occasionally brought about 'the unique situation where farm organizations worked as much with opposition parties as with the government, and where organized farmer commodity groups asked the opposite of general farm organizations.'[7]

Because the number of western Liberals in the House of Commons were few and fewer still possessed an interest in farming, defeated western Liberals who had gained sanctuary in the Senate were called upon to help. Hazen Argue, unsuccessful in two bids for election in 1963 and 1965, and Harry Hays, minister of Agriculture between 1963 and 1965 but defeated in the latter year, did for federal agricultural policy what Pierre Trudeau designated Earl Hastings of Alberta to do for government policy generally in that province – act as federal ambassadors.[8] It was an inversion of the intent of the Fathers of Confederation, who had mistakenly expected the upper chamber to become a house of the provinces. But it was necessary if substitute communications were to be created in place of an attenuated party organization.

Although parliamentary committees and independent commissions of inquiry have a tradition of useful service in modulating the conflicting demands of western agriculture, their contribution was never more significant than during this period when they helped communicate attitudes towards policy between governor and governed.[9] Nor should it be thought that the linkage was of interest only to the few individuals in positions of authority. The briefs and representations made by a host of organizations were first the subject of extensive study and discussion within their own ranks. Two of the best-known commissions of the seventies were the

Hall Commission (on Grain Handling and Transportation, appointed April 1975 and reported May 1977) and the Snavely Commission (on Costs of Transporting Grain by Rail, appointed April 1975 and reported October 1976). While their recommendations were unlikely to secure unanimous agreement, the Commissions helped satisfy the desire for consultation which westerners feared they might not receive from a government with sparse representation from the region.

Consultation, as used here, means providing a forum where a problem is posed, alternative solutions presented, and government and public learn more about each other's position.[10] In a region whose traditions of popular democracy included petitions, marches, and delegations, the act of consulting was as significant as the policy that resulted from it.[11] In 1969, when the glut of wheat depressed incomes and threatened to seize the grain handling system, the House of Commons agriculture committee made a tour of the prairies, holding two dozen meetings alone in Saskatchewan, attended by 18,000 farmers and their families. The *Western Producer* described the charged atmosphere that accompanied the Committee's progress around the province as 'reminiscent of the early days of the pooling movement on the Prairies.'[12] That comment referred not only to the conviction that 'something had to be done,' although what that something was remained undefined, but also to the breadth of feeling. As in the twenties with the formation of the Pools and in the thirties with the creation of the Co-operative Commonwealth Federation, the whole community became restive and traditional partisan and economic divisions blurred.[13]

Because the Liberal caucus contained so few prairie members, the government was easily depicted as unsympathetic to the needs and desires of the West. The opposition argument, made in and out of election campaigns for close on to a generation, had been that the Liberals 'write off the prairies' and sell the farmers 'down the river' because there is no electoral penalty: what have they got to lose?[14] Why the Liberals should want to do this, having learned that the difference between a minority and majority can be found in the West, is not altogether clear unless it is some form of retribution on an unco-operative electorate. The quality of Liberal rule in the West as in other parts of the country is open to criticism, an invitation few observers have refused, but claims that the region suffers neglect do not stand up to investigation, especially in the period after 1968. Arguably, the continuing source of Liberal unpopularity since 1968 has been too much not too little attention being paid to its basic industry. Mismanagement of affairs in the West during the Pearson years was partly due to this government's unhappy marriage of 'old' and 'new guard' Liberals. According to Walter Gordon, in the sphere of policy, as contrasted to organization, old guard attitudes survived. Habits of thought that encouraged deference to ministers on regional matters poorly served a region with the weakest possible contingent imaginable.[15]

Where the charge of insensitivity to western interests finds its mark is in policies of national dimensions, language being the prime example. On these subjects westerners might legitimately complain that theirs was a voice in the wilderness. The reason, however, was not that the government 'writes off the prairies' but that the region's representation is partial – geographically scattered, urban and professionally oriented. Claims to mediate what westerners feel can scarcely be made by a band of MPs rarely typical of those whose views they profess to express. Could it be otherwise when so few are expected to represent so many? The organizational disputes with provincial Liberals, which have already been discussed, accentuated the solitude of the few Liberal MPs, for it deprived them of that useful contact which ministerialism for all its faults provided federal members before 1957.

As the longest serving western minister since James G. Gardiner and with uninterrupted responsibility for the Canadian Wheat Board, even when his portfolio moved from Manpower and Immigration to Justice and then to Transport, Otto Lang was identified with Liberal party fortunes to an exceptional degree. Formal responsibility for the guardian agency of the wheat farmer fails to explain this prominence, however, as the history of the Board under the Pearson Government makes clear. Between 1965 and 1967 Mitchell Sharp, first as minister of Trade and Commerce and then as Finance minister, carried responsibility for the Board, an assignment his years as deputy minister to C.D. Howe made reasonable and the paucity of western Liberals necessary.[16] Despite record grain sales Sharp neither sought nor received accolades from the farmers. Believing the Board's autonomy to have been compromised by the Progressive Conservatives' taking credit for the big grain sales of the early 1960s, the Liberals were content to grant the Board its due. They believed, erroneously, that the farmers who had on occasion criticized the bravado of Alvin Hamilton would welcome this example of political modesty. Had some further indication of federal government understanding of the farmers' condition accompanied renewed fidelity to administrative norms, this expectation might have been realized in farm support. As it was, neither as individuals nor as a group did the Liberals establish themselves able to deal with grain problems.

Instead, from the outset the Pearson Government dispelled any claim to confidence through a series of false starts and ineffective measures. The Throne Speech of 1963 had promised to create a two-headed Department of Agriculture with responsibility divided between matters of eastern and western concern. Sensitive as they were to regionalism, prairie farmers were not unsympathetic with the intent of the proposal, although even they might take offence at its blunt expression by a Quebec member: 'Our [Quebec's] problems cannot be solved by westerners, that is asking too much of foreigners.'[17] But sudden change to the Department of Agriculture, by tradition and practice seen as the West's department of government, much as Interior had once been in the days of Sifton and Oliver, was unsettling, especially as it was not preceded by consultation. Discussion after the fact and even eventual abandonment of the idea did nothing to improve the new government's reputation in the region. Repudiation by Liberal ministers of major agricultural planks in the party's platform of 1963 were equally damaging. Leeway is granted parties in implementing campaign promises, but for the federal minister of Agriculture to describe policies the West had long sought and the Liberals had adopted as 'mistakes' raised doubt not only about party sincerity but competence as well.[18] Two-dollar wheat and a two-price system for wheat, the latter of which would mean a higher domestic than export price, had for too long been pressed by farmers to be shunted aside on grounds of expense to the treasury or consumer. But the issue that most disturbed prairie farmers and which was not resolved during the life of the Pearson Government or for that matter in the subsequent decade was the thorny question of railway branch lines.

The Pearson Government had inherited the recommendations of the Royal Commission on Transportation (the Macpherson Commission), among which were those relating to the abandonment or, in lieu of that, the subsidization of branch lines. Railroads had tied together the economic and social fabric of the prairies but changes in grain handling, such as the decline in number but increase in size of line elevators, demanded corresponding alterations to the transportation system. The subject was explosive for any political party (the Tories had done nothing to implement the Commission's recommendations) but the Liberals made an inept first attempt. In 1964 they introduced legislation which would have allowed railroads to apply to the Board of Transport Commissioners to close individual lines. Those lines the Board thought should remain open would be eligible to receive compensation for losses incurred. Both ideas were anathema to prairie farmers, who disliked the piecemeal approach towards their vital communication network and even more were displeased to see the railway companies receive extra money for purported losses yet to be proved to the farmers' satisfaction. The legislation, said the Pools, would lead railroads 'to tear up the tracks from all but a few branch lines in western Canada during the next fifteen years.'[19] Feeling was assuaged only slightly by assurances from the prime minister that lines would not be closed without a study of the economic and social consequences of such action. Nor was it mollified greatly by the legislation's withdrawal altogether or a later prohibition (until 1975) on closure of all but ten per cent of the prairie provinces' 17,000 miles of track:[20]

As far as the people of the Prairie provinces are concerned, they were amazed that the legislation in question should have made its appearance with as many glaring deficiencies as it contained. It was on a par with Finance Minister Walter Gordon's first budget in terms of workability and chances of accomplishment of the things it was supposed to do.[21]

The Pearson Government disqualified itself in prairie eyes because it never seemed confident of its own actions when dealing with the West. Although the Trudeau administration also suffered from inadequate regional representation, it possessed from the start a minister who while frequently a source of dispute could never be accused of lack of interest. Otto Lang was the first Liberal since Gardiner who could claim to share that legendary minister's sentiment that 'the interests of the people who grow wheat are my interests.'[22] But the methods the two had of going about this task could not have been more different. Gardiner saw agriculture as a way of life and the family farm its home. Years before he entered the government Lang had declared himself opposed to cosseting agriculture.[23] Agriculture was an industry which had to make its case on economic grounds. It could not expect to win converts to its special interests, which he like Gardiner recognized, by invoking Jeffersonian virtues. Western complaints about inequalities of the tariff and freight rates made no sense when embellished with homilies. Security for the farmer was important and necessary but only as part of a rehabilitated grain industry. Thus the minister responsible for the Wheat Board became one of the chief reasons for the preoccupation with policy which characterized political debate in the West for much of the period of Liberal troubles.

There is more to politics in the West than grain, although the discussion so far belies that assertion. The priority nonetheless is justified because between its production and sale grain affects the livelihood of more people than any other commodity or industry. At the same time it has spawned an extraordinary range of interest groups who articulate with great clarity the needs and wants of the different sectors of its constituency. Finally, in the period under review the volume of legislation and governmental activity devoted to grain surpassed that affecting all other industries or issues. Having said that, the federal government's policies with regard to language and resources constitute important explanations for the party's problems in the region and they too must be assessed. But that will follow a final examination of its grain policies which, because they have multiplied since 1968, will be considered in three categories: those intended to clear up the backlog of problems, those designed to stabilize the industry, and those directed towards making it efficient.

The legacy of unresolved problems the Trudeau Government inherited at the end of the sixties was acutely aggravated by a market slump which caused a drastic fall in farm income and the creation of an unmanageable and unmarketed surplus.[24] On all sides expressions of alarm were heard; the most notable, for shock value more than as a serious proposal, was the Saskatchewan Wheat Pool's secession resolution in 1969. 'If the federal government does not give due consideration to the problems of western Canada, we should consider the implications of seceding from the rest of the nation.'[25] Late in 1969 demands for action produced a consensus, itself rare among farm spokesmen, that the federal government should act to relieve the distress being experienced by a majority of farmers. The prairie premiers and the Pools for a time seemed to favour a scheme of acreage reduction combined with government payments to farmers which would redress the decline in income and at the same time grant some respite during which longer-term change might be considered. In this situation as in 1957, at the time of another huge surplus, the government becomes, in Stuart Garson's words, 'willy-nilly ... a guarantor of the farmers' position.'[26]

The government's response was a program for reducing wheat acreage by fifty per cent between 1969 and 1970 and for paying sixty-three million dollars to more than 100,000 farmers.[27] It was the first piece of Liberal agricultural legislation in years to secure its objective so completely; in fact its effectiveness guaranteed its obloquy. In the Canadian system the farmer produces all he can, the Wheat Board sells it, and any restriction placed on the activities of either is blamed on the government. Thus the greater was LIFT's success, the more roundly was it criticized as evidence of the Liberals' lack of confidence in farmers and in their own ability to make the grain system work. Finally, LIFT was an unprecedented break with previous government wheat policy. Faced by surpluses, the St Laurent Government had waited and then provided low interest loans to help pay storage costs; the Diefenbaker Government had also waited after giving cash advances on farm stored wheat, but the Trudeau Government did not wait. It legislated the surplus out of existence by curtailing production. For an industry whose structure and operation were still imperceptibly different from a half century before, LIFT was a portent that roused concern and even alarm.

Disturbing too was the publication in 1970 of the report of the Task Force on Agriculture that had been appointed in 1967. The report proposed fundamental changes in the production and marketing of wheat which included, among others, a more competitive pricing system, the return to exchange hedging for coarse grains, and a prairie grain price stabilization program. In spite of this last proposal, the fact that greater price fluctuations would inevitably follow upon the implementation of the study's recommendations guaranteed that the Report would receive meticulous examination by prairie farmers who sought more, not less, security. Perhaps most distressing was the implication throughout the report that the federal government saw itself playing a different role in western agriculture than the farmer had grown used to expecting. Essentially the new view amounted to the government's 'providing an economic climate in which agriculture can fight for its progress.'[28] As the report envisaged the disappearance of large numbers of small, inefficient and, while not so described, presumably 'family' farms, many occupants of these uneconomic units could be forgiven for seeing industrial progress purchased at their individual expense. According to the *Union Farmer*, the organ of the National Farmers' Union, the report was a 'chilling document.' One did not have to go to so unsympathetic a source, however, to discover unease among farmers at faint but favourable invocations of the free market. To all those who had fought for government support, arguments that existing programs were contradictory, expensive, and not always effective paled against the one incontrovertible fact that they were already on the statute books.

Both the Task Force report and the LIFT program betrayed a professionalism which threatened the vaunted consultation between farmer and government as well as making it seem old-fashioned. The Task Force actually proposed to institutionalize consultation through a new national agricultural advisory council. But the Saskatchewan Wheat Pool's rejection, on the grounds that 'this kind of council might dilute farmer organizations' access to government,' summarized the wariness of all established farm groups. Nor were they ready to take at more than face value government assurances of a new era in consultation 'employing white papers and press releases, then inviting comment, with the final decision coming after these comments.'[29] By 1969 the future of the grain industry was discernible, if not in detail, at least in the direction and pace of change. A body known as the Grains Group, made up of officials from the departments of trade, agriculture, industry, and transport, was created by the minister responsible for the Wheat Board to advise him on the development and co-ordination of grains policies. The weight of expertise had always been on the side of the minister, although as Charles Wilson has noted, 'when [he] formed the Wheat and Grain Division of the Department of Trade and Commerce in 1941, [he] provided the minister with a support staff of one.'[30] As LIFT made plain, the balance had tipped sharply and for those farmers who had missed the point, the Grains Group proceeded to demonstrate it again, and again, by producing policies which, for example, made quotas more flexible and deliveries as a consequence more efficient or by undertaking necessary yet until then postponed studies of controversial subjects like the elevator and transportation systems. With initiative coming from the centre, the nature of consultation changed. The new sequence of stimulus and response was exemplified in the minister's defence of the LIFT program: 'When it is understood by the producers that this plan is part of a total examination of where the agricultural industry stands and what must be done to put it into its proper state, there is general support and agreement for this approach.'[31]

The Throne Speech in 1968 acknowledged the difficulty government had when it came to sound out opinion in the grain industry. As a remedy, it proposed 'bring[ing] together the best brains in the industry.' With the help of federal funds, twenty-seven founding organizations, including the Pools, the United Grain Growers, and the Palliser Wheat Growers' Association, as well as the elevator companies and local government associations, set about creating a forum where the views of the industry's multiple parts might be expressed. However, the Council proved less than satisfactory to its participants, including the minister, because the interests they represented were so diverse. Differences that arose were less the result of conflict of purpose than they were conflicts of jurisdiction. In the grain industry the responsibilities of each segment abutted those of another. Thus time was taken in Council defending the CWB from real or apprehended depredations or squelching discussion because it touched on some policy allegedly reserved to one of the traditional farmers' organizations. This constellation of interests discouraged action, while the jesuitical skills needed to discuss substantive matters without trespassing on policy preserves encouraged a formalism and caution that frustrated the early hopes the Council had inspired.

In administrative terms the Council and the Grains Group were as much innovations as any of the technological changes they had studied. They were also perceived by the proponents of reform as essential additions to the policy process in the same way that hopper cars, new road beds, and an improved box car allocation formula were considered necessary practical improvements. They were all part of the new weaponry which would arm agriculture to compete efficiently and economically. Presuming the changes to be reasonable, Ottawa was ill prepared for the opposition encountered to policies designed to promote agricultural security. Experience with LIFT might have suggested a well of local feeling on matters touching grain which federal policy-makers ignored at their peril, but the strength of the criticism on that occasion had been explained away by the unorthodox solution proposed. Quite different was the Grain Income Stabilization bill, introduced late in 1970, which set out to realize the previously unattained goal of a comprehensive measure of income security for grain farmers. The breadth of its intent, unfortunately, was part of the explanation for the hostility it encountered. But a more vital reason for its eventual withdrawal after months of parliamentary combat was the, by now, all-too-familiar complaint that government was planning to withdraw its support from established programs. The scheduled disappearance of the Temporary Wheat Reserves Act roused particular criticism because federal commitment to pay a portion of storage costs for wheat was accepted as necessary and right. But the details of the bill were equally unpalatable, especially as they provided for gross income from grain to be maintained at a five-year average level. Because recent income had been exceptionally low but the costs of production had continued to mount, the farmers foresaw their net income inexorably squeezed. This was all the more probable since the scheme was not intended to secure the individual in any case but to iron out the peaks and troughs of the region's volatile income. The individual farmer therefore accepted the prediction that in the long run he would receive less rather than more help from Ottawa.

The protracted debate which followed the bill's introduction in 1971, during which Otto Lang charged Progressive Conservative and NDP members from the prairies with mounting a filibuster, took a dramatic turn when the government withheld payments to the Canadian Wheat Board required under the Temporary Wheat Reserves Act. Mr Lang argued that the Act would be repealed when the new legislation became law and that payments provided by the Bill under debate would be larger than the required transfer of funds to the Wheat Board. Nonetheless, the opposition was now able to focus on a single but easily understood issue – the government, they argued, was in breach of the law and in contempt of Parliament. Such Liberal arrogance, said one opposition MP, constituted 'anticipatory autocracy,' not participatory democracy.[32] An attempt to impeach the ministers responsible for breaking the law failed in Parliament, but when four Saskatchewan farmers succeeded in securing a writ from the Federal Court of Canada seeking the compliance of the minister of Finance with the terms of the Temporary Wheat Reserves Act, the stabilization legislation was withdrawn and the required payments were made to the Wheat Board.

In the avalanche of criticism surrounding the first grain stabilization bill, the subject that vied for attention with the Temporary Wheat Reserves Act was the demand for two-price wheat. Where the Bill would have provided a cushion to bad times in the region, two-price wheat would have improved individual income by giving the farmer a higher price for domestically consumed wheat than he received for wheat exported. A first step to a new, and this time successful, stabilization bill was taken in 1972 when the price for prime wheat milled in Canada was set at three dollars a bushel. This achievement was, according to the minister, 'the greatest victory of [his] career.'[33] The farmers had received a better deal than ever before and the federal government had at last recognized the justice of their complaint that they could live with either a protected or a free market but could not survive buying in one and selling in the other. Two-price wheat won grudging praise from the government's critics, but not for long. The farmers' advance was unfortunately checked by the unpredictable international market, where within a year the price of wheat shot up from two to six dollars a bushel and a policy meant to expand farm incomes now appeared to restrict them. Even when the domestic price was increased, criticism remained; for the federal government tried to keep bread prices down by offsetting what millers had to pay. The farmers' subsidy was eclipsed by a consumers' subsidy, with all that that implied. Mr Justice Emmett Hall made the point as neatly as any prairie spokesman might have wished: 'In the period from 1973 to February 1977, the Canadian government paid $276 million ... Two-thirds of that, of course, on the population basis was in Eastern Canada, not Western Canada at all.'[34]

Further attempts to balance agricultural interests within and between regions opened the government to more criticism. The policy which demonstrated this truth most accurately had to do with feed grains; a program whose complexity it fortunately is not necessary to detail before explaining its political implications. The point has already been made that the West sees the Wheat Board as its protector and the minister the Board's advocate. The question of feed grains (that is those grains used by livestock producers) and Board policy towards them cast a less benign light on the Board, especially as seen by eastern livestock producers, who depend on western as well as imported feed grains. The East has provided the main livestock market because, under the discriminatory freight rates, it was cheaper to send feeder cattle east than it was to send dressed beef. Therefore the complaints from Quebec and Ontario about feed grains represented those of a major industry.

Eastern livestock producers considered the Board a 'barrier' to freer trade between east and west and the Western producer a protected species who flourished because of his Crow's Nest Rates, two-price wheat, storage payments, and even LIFT. Because they 'controlled' it, Westerners could afford to take the view that government should leave the Board alone; the East had to argue for interference so that feed grains would be offered them at something approaching an equitable price. 'In the circumstances,' declared Albert Allain, president of l'Union des Producteurs Agricoles, 'We have no alternative but to demand policy arbitration.'[35] Accepting the proposition that 'prices and products should flow freely [because] part of our Canadian Identity demands that,' the government set about creating a new feed grains policy which would try to accommodate eastern and western interests.[36] Part of the change required an alternative market to that provided by the Board for feed grains, although grain farmers might continue to sell as before to the Board. Response was not universally hostile to the plan, but those opposed found powerful allies in the provincial governments, particularly in Saskatchewan, whose indictment of federal perfidy chronicled fresh attacks on 'orderly marketing,' 'price stability,' and the 'family farm' and concluded the list by labelling Ottawa a 'captive of eastern interests.'[37]

One of the political effects of inflation in the seventies was to add a new stratum to the accretion of western grievances – those policies designed to help the consumer. Support by the Food Prices Review Board for an open market in feed grains appeared, or so it was said, to confirm the suspicions of farm and parliamentary critics as to the location of the government's true interests.[38] It was a measure of the attraction of the new grain stabilization bill that despite strong opposition to these other policies, it passed through Parliament in 1975 and early 1976 relatively unscathed. In contrast to the previous bill it enjoyed the advantage of appearing while wheat prices were high so that the guaranteed five-year average was more attractive then than in the late 1960s. More important, it had been considerably improved over its benighted predecessor, particularly as it now dealt with net rather than gross incomes. The deleterious effects of a rise in the cost of production were thereby avoided and so too the opposition which had killed the previous bill.[39]

Policies to bring stability to the grain industry raised criticism and dissent, but no one seriously questioned their objective. The same could not be said of commitments to make the industry efficient. That was a goal whose meaning varied, according to speaker. For many farmers and their spokesmen the government's interpretation of efficiency involved unacceptable costs. As suggested in Chapter 2 and again in references to the Task Force on Agriculture, only the most dispassionate failed to see that the family farm was credited with being the bedrock of prairie life. Like the word 'efficiency,' the phrase 'the family farm' became a receptacle for all the sentiments, inarticulate and articulate, born in response to schemes to remake western agriculture. For those able to express their objections, the language used alternated between excess and platitudes, or else they forecast the wasting away of the family farm and with it the local community. Proponents of efficiency urged the farmer to accept technology and direct it to his benefit.[40] Their prescription, expressed with the confidence of scientific certitude, prescribed change and, as far as many westerners were concerned, ignored the social effects of what they advocated. Proposals to abandon branch lines or construct inland elevators at central locations would make obsolete dozens of local elevators and, if adopted, would accelerate the decline of rural communities just as the consolidation of schools and hospitals had before them.

The long, fluid, and often acerbic debate over the future of the prairie transportation network which had been given life by the Macpherson Commission's recommendation in 1961 but had faltered for nearly a decade thereafter was renewed with the appointment of the Hall Commission in 1975. Enough has been said about that Commission's report to suggest that despite a thorough examination of rail line abandonment, the controversy was not resolved. Nor from what has been said was this unexpected; by the late 1970s it was realized that the decision about the future of the branch lines must be a 'political' one in the sense that neither economic nor technical reasons made one course of action indisputable. That realization was in many ways the most important contribution of the Hall Commission. Finally, the subject was exhausted. The same could not be said of the Crow's Nest Rates, though they had been the subject of thorough investigation by the Snavely Commission. Even accepting that they were unprofitable, the alternatives – to keep them or replace them with some equivalent benefit – remained undecided despite Mr Justice Hall's tendentious claim that they were 'fundamental for the unity of the country.'[41]

The troubles the Pearson and Trudeau governments encountered in the West were not all traceable to wheat, nor were they the result of differences over economics. Yet it is true that a series of economic policies reinforced the unfavourable opinion westerners held of Liberals that had been conditioned by their handling of wheat more than anything else. In the 1960s the principal issue to excite prairie opinion was tax reform, as it took shape first in the recommendations of the Royal Commission on Taxation (the Carter Commission) and later matured in the White Paper on Taxation. The effect of this particular sequence of events was to prolong discussion for the sensible reason that the subject matter was contentious and public opinion had to have time to digest the proposals and align itself behind (or against) the different reforms. One effect of the drawing out of discussion for nearly a decade was to allow regional opposition to mount a campaign against the recommendations. While the West had never been happy with what it saw as the centralist assumptions of Canada's economic policies, it had not hitherto confronted Ottawa on tax policy. But by the end of the decade the prairie provinces did just that. Changes in estate tax, introduction of a capital gains tax, as well as the principle of all increases in economic gain being included in the taxable base were interpreted as threats to the family farm, which passed from generation to generation as a gift or through inheritance. Proposed changes in tax exemptions on mineral exploration raised the cry of regional discrimination, for Ottawa seemed ready to close the door to investors in western Canada now that Quebec and Ontario had their mining industries. That at least was the view of a number of prairie politicians, especially Liberals who had spent a good part of the decade fighting Walter Gordon's nationalist economic policies.

Relations between the centre and the western periphery changed during the period of the Trudeau Government in two significant respects: first, the area encompassed by the term 'the West' unquestionably came to include British Columbia and, second, while many of the old complaints remained, resources assumed (one might almost say resumed) a special prominence. Whether the West embraces British Columbia as well as the prairies is a bit like the question whether the office of Solicitor General before 1966 was part of the Cabinet.[42] The more correct answer would seem to be 'it depends,' in the case of the Solicitor General on what the prime minister wanted and in the case of western boundaries on the subject being discussed. The differences between British Columbia and the prairie provinces can be enumerated at length with economic, political, geographic, and even literary differences coming readily to mind. But similar differences exist to some degree between the individual prairie provinces themselves. Arguably there are several Wests, each having its own base in economics, or politics, or literature, and each having boundaries which overlap rather than coincide.

After the 1972 election in which the number of Liberals elected on the prairies was reduced to three from eleven in 1968, the Trudeau Government acted so as to bring about a united response from the four western provinces. The Throne Speech early in January 1973 called for a conference on western economic opportunities, which was eventually held in Calgary in July; as well it promised 'concrete programmes' in areas of finance, industry, and transportation and hinted at a general re-evaluation of the West's place in Confederation. That meeting and the expectations aroused in anticipation of it, such as Otto Lang's prophesy that it would 'alter the course of history in this country,' did more than anything else to encourage the new, enlarged, regional perspective.[43] It amounted to formal recognition that the old unity of the prairie provinces, based on similar though not identical ethnic, economic, and political traditions, was less notable when compared to the nation in the 1970s than it had been half a century before. But even if these characteristics were now less distinctive, to what degree did that fact make the prairie provinces more like British Columbia, or more like British Columbia than some other province? For federal-provincial relations the 'new West' was a convenient designation, however. As the decade progressed, it was without doubt a useful categorization for the provinces concerned as well.

The publicity that preceded and then surrounded the conference encouraged its depiction as an epochal event. The impression grew that the federal government rather encouraged this dramatic interpretation while at the same time the critics thought this atmosphere discouraged chances for progress on specific issues. In an example of unprecedented co-operation, the four western provinces drafted and then presented joint submissions on four broad topics: economic and industrial development, transportation, finance, and agriculture. In each, specific grievances were enunciated and particular changes to national policies advocated. The overall criticism was that national policies had discouraged diversification and impeded development. The federal government approached and left the meeting with far less clearly defined objectives. The premiers, the press, and the public agreed that the federal response was unsatisfactory and interpreted it as a product of unwillingness to recognize the legitimacy of western ambitions.

That explanation, while no doubt true in part, failed to recognize the distinctive problem the federal government faced once it had proposed the conference. Some general discussion of principles and goals among the leaders of the federal and provincial governments was one thing, but actual negotiation and bargaining was another. In Calgary, Allan Blakeney might claim that 'we meet as *Canadians* concerned above all with the well-being of Canada as a whole.'[44] But how was there to be that balancing of interests which passed for national policy when the forum was composed of participants from two-fifths of the country's provinces and the national government? To the absent premiers, WEOC must have appeared the most remarkable example of axe-grinding ever achieved by any group of provinces. To the federal government it proved an unpalatable alignment of forces but not necessarily an unprofitable one.

The prime minister had entered the conference convinced that it was essential 'to reduce the sense of apartness of the West.'[45] The conference therefore served a symbolic function by giving the federal government more visibility in the region on those subjects where it was traditionally most vulnerable to criticism. In 1973 there were three social democratic premiers and Peter Lougheed, all more recently placed in office than Pierre Trudeau. In all four provinces but most definitely in Alberta, the identification between provincial ambitions and provincial government competency was growing closer. Western alienation is an overworked term; certainly this was the case in the press of the period, but the general election results of 1972 had convinced policy advisers in Ottawa that the West was slipping away from the national government.[46] The prospect, in Arthur Laing's phrase, and in the opinion of many other national politicians, was that 'we are in danger of Lougheed of Alberta rising as a western leader.'[47]

WEOC had a more specifically partisan connotation as well, not in the paradoxical sense that partisanship hardly arose at the conference – this is not news, as Richard Simeon has already revealed in his work on federal-provincial relations – but for what it implied about the state of the Liberal party in the West. Immediately prior to WEOC, the Liberals had held their own Conference on Western Objectives in Vancouver. Forty-five papers, statements, and submissions had been presented, most of which dealt with specific subjects like Arctic energy or community livestock enterprises, along with the inevitable discussions about the tariff and freight rates. The purpose of the Vancouver meeting was less than obvious even to Liberals: some saw it as a preparatory step for Calgary, while others argued that it was a preliminary move towards creating a western Liberal platform. The latter view was probably the more realistic political judgment if only because in federal-provincial negotiations party, like other interests, bows before government and its leaders. But as a statement of party policy the Vancouver meeting could only be disappointing as well as prophetic. It was sparsely reported in western newspapers, attracting little attention or comment. Its impact on federal politicians at Calgary was scarcely discernible. The 'apartness' of the West which WEOC was intended to narrow if not bridge seemed to have widened as government moved farther from party, including its own.

International events far from the Canadian prairies conspired to give the Calgary conference a prominence never intended by its promoters. Action by the oil-producing and-exporting countries had the retroactive effect of making WEOC a first rather than a single occasion in which the federal government faced a resurgent West; however, not all four provinces approached later conferences with the confidence displayed in 1973. After Calgary the customary forum of the traditional federal-provincial conference prevailed, but within its confines a triangle of relations between oil-producing and -consuming provinces and the federal government was much in evidence.

Domestic affairs as much as foreign ones served to aggravate relations over energy resources. The year before the Calgary meeting the federal government had begun to implement in modified form the Carter Commission's proposals as they related to taxation of the mining industry. Several changes were enacted, but the one to which the provinces took greatest exception was the inclusion of provincial mining taxes in taxable income. The year after Calgary the federal government moved to make royalities non-deductible as well. It is no exaggeration to say, as have R.M. Burns and Wendy MacDonald, authors of two detailed studies of the mining industry, that these federal initiatives were 'at the centre of the [subsequent] conflict.'[48]

At issue was the price of oil, although throughout the remainder of the decade the exploration and development of new sources and the conservation of old also occupied attention. But as the international price soared, the two producing provinces, Saskatchewan and Alberta, were exhorted by federal Liberals to think of the national interest, have compassion for their less fortunate partners in Confederation (including Manitoba), and accept negotiated and staggered increases. To some extent regional fury, expressed at initial federal moves to prevent sudden escalations in price and to check exports of oil to the United States, dissipated as the severity of the energy crises sank home. The economic consequences of maldistribution of energy resources in Canada demanded the application of some equity. The problem was by whom and how? The federal government was the obvious candidate, but that possibility immediately put the resources of the provinces at risk. It was here that events in the seventies after WEOC aggravated relations between the West and the federal government.

Premier Blakeney of Saskatchewan expressed the concern of all provinces but most particularly those of the West, who once before had experienced at first hand federal control of their natural resources. In his statement to the first ministers' meeting in 1976 he charged Ottawa with a 'systematic and deliberate attempt to destroy ... the provincial rights to resource ownership.'[49] His language was not extreme, even to the ears of western Liberals like Arthur Laing who recognized that 'if you exclude International Nickel you will find most Canadian resources ["mines, forests, water, soil, and petroleum"] lie West of Winnipeg and in the Canadian North.'[50]

At mid-decade the argument over resources intensified as questions of jurisdictional competence were posed. When the Supreme Court of Canada, overturning lower court rulings, found for the federal government, the conflict reached a new level. As the final, non-political arbiter of the constitution, the Court's decisions symbolized the limitations the western provinces faced. One had to go back to the early years of Social Credit in Alberta for a comparable sense of enforced dependence and even then that dispute affected only one province.

At issue were two Saskatchewan cases.[51] One, *Central Canada Potash Co., Ltd et al.* v *Government of Saskatchewan et al.*, attacked the province's scheme to prorate potash production, which along with setting a minimum price for the mineral had had its origins in Ross Thatcher's attempt to guarantee a portion of the United States market to Canadian (mainly US subsidiary) companies. In this case the federal government actually joined the Company as a co-plaintiff. The issue in the second case, *Canadian Industrial Gas and Oil Ltd* v *Government of Saskatchewan et al.* (CIGOL), was a provincial royalty tax to limit windfall gains accruing to petroleum producers. Again, the Federal government attempted, this time unsuccessfully, to be joined as co-plaintiff. In the potash case the Supreme Court unanimously found the prorationing scheme *ultra vires* the provincial legislature, while in the CIGOL case the Court, with two dissenting voices, found the contentious mineral tax to be indirect and therefore beyond the jurisdiction of the province. In both cases Saskatchewan's legislation was seen to interfere with interprovincial and international trade and, as was said in the CIGOL judgment, 'provincial legislative authority does not extend to fixing the price to be charged or received in respect of the sale of goods in the export market.'

In her valuable monograph examining the effects of intergovernmental bargaining on an industry, Wendy MacDonald has usefully summarized the situation as regards the provinces and natural resources in the wake of the Supreme Court's actions:

The *Potash* and *Cigol* decisions have been attacked by some provinces as centralist and unjustifiably restrictive of provincial responsibility for the management of their resources. Certainly they are restrictive; whether they are unjustifiably so is still subject to debate.

The provinces can continue to manage their resources, through their control over access to resources, and their ability to impose, through leases, conditions regarding production and processing. They may not, however, manage them by attempting to influence export market conditions through price fixing or control of supply. Nor can the provinces justify policies on the grounds that they seek to preserve or improve the viability of the industry. This does not necessarily mean that these powers *ipso facto* accrue to the federal government. As a rule, it means that such policies must be made jointly.

Thus, in most instances, legal decisions have served to check the expansion of provincial powers, rather than to reduce them. The major exception is pricing. The decisions appear to restrict the legal rights of the provinces to sell their resources at the price they wish, and to give that right to the federal government. A further effect of the *Cigol* decision is to limit provincial powers to levy royalties and direct taxes.[52]

While the affected parties had every right to challenge legislation which they believed the offending government had no power to pass, the federal government's intervention, especially as co-plaintiff, was interpreted as an 'aggressive attack' on provincial resource policy.[53] There were good reasons for Ottawa to become involved in the litigation but they nonetheless called up once again the old charge that the central government coveted the region's resources. Coveting alone could be tolerated; what could not be accepted so resignedly was the growing belief that in jurisdictional conflict the rules of the game favoured one side and that they might be invoked by the federal authority to limit local autonomy.[54] In the latter part of the seventies the probability grew of this happening more frequently, for the federal government was increasingly concerned that its constitutional ambit, especially in the field of trade and commerce, be confirmed.

Although the 1979 and 1980 general elections fall outside the period under review in this book, it was clear in those campaigns that the Liberal party had assumed as its mantle defence of the national interest, by which it interpreted protection of those provinces deficient in energy resources. Against this position apparently stood the Progressive Conservative party led by Joe Clark, although the difficulty the short-lived Tory government had in reaching an accommodation on oil prices with Alberta raised the spectre of no national party being able to satisfy for long the interests of energy-producing and energy-consuming provinces.

Constitutional questions more generally had percolated through regional life ever since the Liberals had returned to power in 1963, with the most obvious effect being to irritate the prairie provinces. The response of westerners to the Report of the Royal Commission on Bilingualism and Biculturalism and to the Official Languages Act was never favourable; at best it could be described as latent acceptance, but on more than a few occasions it amounted to overt rejection and opposition. The search for a reformed constitution which would take account of the cultural ambitions of Quebec more adequately than the existing one was counted a waste of time and a confusion of priorities as far as most western politicians were concerned. Bluntly stated, by Thatcher, it would not sell more wheat. Phrased only slightly less belligerently, the complaint was that the 'Dominion-provincial fiscal arrangements were the main threat to national unity.'[55] Even Ernest Manning, a politician credited with some perspective, appeared unsympathetic, arguing instead that constitutional reform was a new version of central Canada's preoccupation with itself and another excuse for ignoring the West's problems.

Government language policy appeared, at least in its earliest manifestations, to be devised in terms of uniformity (there were two founding peoples: English and French) rather than diversity. Ethnic diversity, as suggested in Chapter 1, remained a root of western life. Part – large but still a part – of that diversity was English, a very small part French and the rest, excluding the native peoples, European and Asiatic. The West was not just a weaker version of Ontario or an enfeebled Quebec but a distinctive complex network of reinforcing social relationships, cultural values, institutional arrangements, and agricultural practices. The attitude towards the French was only bigotry when seen in national terms; regionally it was opposition to special treatment. To the extent that the western provinces extended French-language instruction but did not make comparable provision for other languages, they compromised their general position. Among prairie politicians Ed Schreyer was the only one to give public support to the Official Languages Act. His reasoning was also unique, at least for 1969: 'There is no future for minority cultures in Canada if we ignore the French fact.'[56]

The more general western view was 'unhyphenated Canadianism,' which was effectively transmitted through the ranks of the Progressive Conservative party as long as John Diefenbaker was at its head. After 1967, when Robert Stanfield, who was as committed to bilingualism and biculturalism as the government itself, became Tory leader, regional opposition to federal policies towards Quebec was converted into general harassment of parliamentary leaders with costly political results as a consequence. The breaking of party ranks on the passage of the Official Languages Act by Diefenbaker and sixteen other Tories, all but one westerners, thwarted Stanfield in his attempt to open wider the party's doors.

To counter the unpopularity of its language policies, the federal government sought to divorce them from bicultural associations and marry them to multiculturalism.[57] In the early sixties special efforts were made by the Liberals to reach ethnic communities and new Canadians. The work was directed by Andy Thompson, who later became leader of the party in Ontario, at which time the initiatives faded. Early in the seventies Senator Stanbury sought to revive contacts by using 'ethnic MPs' and keeping contacts alive with the ethnic press and ethnic associations.[58] Ethnic committees within local and provincial associational structures were encouraged. This was followed by the designation of a minister of state responsible for multiculturalism. As it turned out, that office was ministerially weak and financially poor. To westerners, multiculturalism in practice rather than theory seemed much like the old days when the Saskatchewan Liberals used to help finance local German papers and maintain ethnic leaders on the civil service payroll. Ethnicity arrived late in central Canada, after the Second World War; but in the West the 'ethnics' along with the British, American, and French-Canadian settlers were present at the creation. Their view of themselves and Canada could not help but be influenced by this long, in western Canadian terms, heritage.[59] 'These groups,' wrote one Albertan, 'are extremely anxious to be "formally recognized" by the high echelons of Canadian society as a completely integrated part of Canadian society and not just late arriving immigrant groups. Such an "Ontario Mentality" is not acceptable in Western Canada where these ethnic groups arrived on the scene at the earliest stage in the development of the Prairies.'[60]

It is not possible without more research to say to what extent the government's cultural and language policies contributed to the Liberals' unpopularity in the West. But it is reasonable to suggest that multiculturalism, which was formulated in the first place to meet ethnic opposition to earlier assertions about Canada's being a bicultural country, went only part way in assuaging criticism. Indeed, to the extent that it was promoted, multiculturalism posed a constant reminder that ethnic cultures were only partially recognized. Language must, as Wsevolod Isajiw has pertinently noted, be seen to operate on several levels: 'The heart of the problem is that language should not be seen as simply an instrument of communication. On the contrary, and often more importantly, it functions as an interactional symbol, by which people are included in or excluded from, social groupings, accepted as equals, or rejected as inferiors.'[61]

At first glance, multiculturalism appears eminently attractive to western Canada, the region of the country with the most heterogeneous population. But if one looks in generational terms at the country's population of non-British and non-French origin, then the policy is more applicable to the centre than to the periphery. Multiculturalism repelled as well as it attracted support. Its negative attributes were accentuated by this identification with the centre.[62] The reason for that extends beyond the subject of Liberal policies in the past quarter century and back to an earlier period.

The contribution of policy to the West's sense of separation from the rest of the country has redoubled in recent years. The traditional grievance has focused on economic policy whose errors, from the perspective of the region, have been those of omission as well as commission. The failure to meet western demands for improvement in status are as detrimental to the prestige of the federal government as are its policy initiatives which aim to rationalize the grain handling system. Indeed, potentially beneficial programs, such as two-price wheat or income stabilization, are made suspect by unpopular actions like LIFT or changes in federal taxation laws to curb mineral exploration. Cultural policy, especially language legislation, is totally new and, almost without exception, unwelcome. Substance aside, the formulation of policy antagonizes westerners, for it so often appears to have been conducted without regard to regional interests.

It is impossible to discuss these questions without raising the subject of centre-periphery relations and that opens the door to the wider topic of federalism. The change in focus is necessary if the third concern of this book, the nation, is to be considered. The intergration of region to nation which the national political parties and especially the Liberals in the West once accomplished is no longer evident. The reasons for the change have, as the last three chapters demonstrate, much to do with Liberal party organization and policies. But these are not the only explanations; the evolution of the federal system cannot be ignored. While that system has undergone a remarkable transformation in the period under review, there has been one thread of continuity as far as the West is concerned. That has been the region's perception that the centre maintains its dominance despite whatever other changes may occur.

PART III: THE NATION

7

The Hold of the Centre

A 3½ per cent solution may be very efficacious in medical practice but in the arena of the political conflict its effect is *nil*. (A. Bramley-Moore, *Canada and Her Colonies or Home Rule for Alberta* [1911])

Part One of this book examined the distinguishing characteristics of the prairie West and Part Two those characteristics of the Liberal party in the last quarter century which have made it unattractive to prairie voters. The discussion has centred necessarily on party politics. In view of the region's distinctive record of partisan choice, the emphasis is not misplaced. But it would be misleading in any study of Western Canada – of how it interacts with or reacts against the larger community – to limit the analysis to parties and elections. The attention, exceptional by Canadian academic standards, paid to the region's third-party tradition has had the unfortunate effect of diverting study from its culture or, perhaps more confusingly, of equating politics to culture. A broader frame of reference is needed and thus this chapter will focus, for want of a more concise description, on the region's attempt to loosen 'the hold of the centre.'

The nature of that hold and how it might be loosened have taken different forms. Most recently, in the period being discussed, the hold was identified with Liberal language and energy policies and with technocratic answers to the problem of the wheat industry. In an earlier time it was retention of the natural resources themselves. The West's response has alternated between seeking a more commanding voice at the centre and more provincial control over its own affairs. The quest for better terms followed the invidious treatment Manitoba received on entering Confederation and continued after autonomy was granted on similar but not identical terms to Saskatchewan and Alberta. This was the origin of Bramley-Moore's astringent comment above on Alberta's miniscule parliamentary representation and his recommendation that

Alberta might copy some of the tactics employed by the Irish. This would entail a change from the present pacific policy of sending seven members of parliament – three of whom vote one way, four the opposite – and a compact body would have to be sent, pledged to harass the Central Government on every possible occasion, to expose her perfidious practices, and to cheer any reverses Fate might have in store for her.[1]

This continuity of concern gives an historical cast to western politics unexpected in so new a region. It also limits the application of Rupert Brooke's lyrical description of the 'brisk melancholy of this land' without its 'dead.' An historical consciousness of a more prosaic world than Brooke had in mind, of politics and co-operatives, is a feature of western life newcomers soon learn.[2] The relations of the prairies to the centre are thus played against a backdrop of memory and, as a consequence, sequence and perspective become distorted as new complaints are joined to ancient grievances.

The expulsion of the Liberals from federal and provincial politics in western Canada, especially in Saskatchewan and Manitoba where they were until recently a viable electoral force, signifies more than prairie political pique. Whatever their future in the West may hold, the passing of the Grits in the third quarter of the twentieth century signals a triumph of regional over national or, if that term's meaning is now imprecise because of constitutional debate, at least extra-regional interests. Its significance could be ignored if it were seen as just another example of the West's political inconstancy. But it represents the severance of an historic tie between the national party with the greatest record of western electoral successes to its credit on the one hand and the region whose settlement constituted the realization of Canada's nationhood on the other. It should not be forgotten either that it was western support which provided the Liberal party with the hegemony it enjoyed for most of this century.

For some decades the Liberals were able to transform the tension inherent between region and centre into strength. In fact, during Sifton and Gardiner's time, the centre was far from being generally unpopular and, in contrast to the 1970s, few westerners sought changes that would weaken the federal government. The example of Sifton, whose personal control over immigration and settlement policy was absolute and who created a department in his image, is proof to the contrary. The Department of the Interior has been described as 'the largest and perhaps the most dynamic of all government departments' of its day and the administration of public lands as the most 'far-reaching activity' in this century except for the prosecution of the wars.[3] Gardiner and his Department with its program to rehabilitate the farmer and protect his livelihood exerted similar authority. Neither of these strong ministers was free from criticism, indeed each was at the centre of it for most of his career, but no one wanted to nullify the activity of the central government. The Canadian Wheat Board, the creature of the Bennett Government but subject to Liberal tutelage, replicated the short-lived board at the end of the First World War which the Americans labelled as 'communistic' but which the farmers actually wanted given more power.[4] The absolute power of the Board, like that of the Tudor monarchs, was welcomed because it guaranteed an effective and efficient arbiter of the West's interests.[5] It is no coincidence that critics of Liberal wheat policy today are the most vociferous defenders of the Board. Nor should it be overlooked that Otto Lang never commanded a department of government like Interior or Agriculture identified unequivocally with the West. Rather, responsibility for the Wheat Board as well as the experts assembled to redesign the wheat industry accompanied Lang as he moved among his different portfolios.

But if the advantage once lay with federal ministers in posing as defenders of the region's interests, events since the Second World War have undermined that claim. Where in the past provincial governments did little because little was expected of them or because they were financially embarrassed, post-war prosperity and a new appreciation of their potential – to a significant extent itself a by-product of the evolution in federal-provincial fiscal relations since 1945 – have transformed the situation. Provincial expertise and bureaucracy grew apace with ambition and confidence and the region emerged a rival to the federal government at the very time the centre showed itself unresponsive to local feeling.[6]

Structural changes alone did not explain this contrast in development between the two levels of government. Social factors played a part as well. Many years ago Walter Scott, later to be the first premier of Saskatchewan, remarked to a correspondent who had opposed sharing patronage with newcomers to the West, that 'we were all Eastern men ourselves once.'[7] This was an exaggeration, since the majority of Saskatchewan residents were never easterners but Americans, British, and Europeans, but the generational and geographic links to the East, which the comment expressed, were a real enough feature of western life. He might have noted as well, had he been speaking only a few years later, the shared federal political experience of many western leaders. Three-quarters of a century afterward, however, the reverse was true: current prairie politicians arise within their own political systems and sedulously avoid inducements to leave them. On this point the contrast between men like Charles Dunning and Peter Lougheed is instructive. Half a century ago Dunning condemned the sectionalism of Canadian political life evident in the self-satisfied comment by the premier of Ontario, Howard Ferguson, that he need not consider succeeding Arthur Meighen as federal Tory leader because 'Ontario has always dominated in the field of Dominion politics and always would.'[8] Although they would not like the comparison, western politicians now act as Ferguson did and consider that there is enough political opportunity for them in their home provinces without looking to Ottawa. This attitude has helped to separate even further the federal and provincial realms. It has also made the relations between federal and provincial politicians of the same party, and not necessarily just in the Liberal party, more strained.

The explanation for the change is economic as well. The old dependency the prairies complained of remains but it is less debilitating than previously. Bruce Hodgins has described how once the skein of dual mandate, dual franchise, and the rest was untangled, provincial political life began to develop independently of the centre. He also showed how that freedom was qualified, for 'although one side of the Macdonaldian system, the centralist role in preserving "constitutional" liberty, had a short life, another side, the economic imperial side, with Ottawa as the joint agent of rival Toronto and Montreal élites, lived on.'[9] Even this aspect of the hold of the centre is less pervasive than before. The provinces have formed their own élites who, while not necessarily anti-federal in orientation, devote their energies in the first instance to promoting provincial aims.[10] As so often is the case, Harold Innis foresaw and recorded the change in memorable fashion: 'The hatreds between the regions in Canada have become important vested interests ... A native of Ontario may appear restive at being charged with exploitation by those who systematically exploit him through the charge of exploitation, but even the right to complain is denied to him.' He traced one source of the conflict to provincial control of the schools, which was responsible for fomenting 'regional ideologies ... built upon adult education and the universities.' At a time when the hand if not the visage of local political scientists, historians, and economists is seen at a succession of federal-provincial conferences and at the round of inquests into the state of Canadian federalism, the contribution of higher education to regionalism is more apparent than ever.[11]

One of the most important consequences of these changes has been the emergence of a new sense of community in the West. For Sifton the development of prairie agriculture through massive settlement and an efficient transportation network had as its ultimate objective the advancement of a strong national economy. For those less economically minded, the populating of the empty North-West was thought of in social terms – the promotion of Anglo-Canadian values. However ethnically blinkered the latter view may now appear, this too was seen as a national enterprise; the new nation in the West was to be the culmination of Canada's destiny. After the First World War and with Sifton and his European preferences behind them, westerners talked increasingly of acculturating the immigrant and attention was devoted to those most easily incorporated into Canada – the British. The British were seen as eminently desirable immigrants for another reason: they would add weight to the Anglo-Saxon balance reputedly threatened by the thousands of non-English. British immigrant behaviour thus became 'the norm of successful immigration.'[12] By the late 1920s some doubt was being expressed whether federal Liberals, under conflicting pressure on the one side from Quebec Liberals and on the other from Progressives, upon whom they depended for parliamentary support for most of the decade and for whom foreign immigration was an inflammatory subject, could be depended upon to promote British immigration. In one notable instance when Ottawa might have given a boost to British immigration – under the Empire Settlement Act of 1922 – and at reduced cost to itself, the federal government responded coolly to the scheme.[13]

This regional frustration over the ethnic make-up of the prairies ended as did immigration itself in the face of the economic upheaval of the thirties and the war in the early forties. It only reappeared in similar tone in the sixties and seventies as the Liberal government pressed its language policy and first a bicultural and then a multicultural program. The West, which had sought to foster British values in the twenties and received hesitant support from Ottawa, had emerged half a century later not as a multicultural society, less so a bicultural one, but as a community where ethnicity had ceased to have relevance. This was not to say that ethnic groups and ethnic cultures were not visible; they were and they thrived through local activity and enthusiasm. But western society because it was 'an integrated community [did not] see itself in terms of an ethnic group.'[14] Because it did not, policies that promoted French were resisted, as were those that married bilingualism to multiculturalism. Central government policies brought home to westerners the irrelevance of language and ethnicity to their modern experience.[15]

If ethnicity had disappeared as a characteristic of western identity, the region's rural past had not. In the debate between centre and region, in governmental and non-governmental circles, it was agrarian metaphors which studded the rhetoric: not of the lone farmer against the elements but of groups of farmers binding together to protect and promote their interests before an outside world – one which might not be hostile but where no quarter was given those who failed. Where the federal government was once seen as protector of the grain industry, the volume and magnitude of the reforms proposed in recent years had translated it to the 'outside' as well. Rather than guarantor it must be guarded against. The potential of the West's resources, like its rural past, is another part of this identity. Again the federal government has posed a threat to western ambitions. The uncertainty that the federal government represents only adds to the uncertainty that is endemic to prairie life. Where once the wheat industry gave rise to local co-operatives and united associations to provide a buffer between the farmer and the outside world, so the resource industry now looks to the provincial government to do the same thing.

But the hold of the centre today is as much psychological as it is economic or political. The good fortune enjoyed by Saskatchewan and Alberta in particular as a result of their energy resources has produced the most cautious response. No longer is there the spirit of adventure and self-confidence which before 1930 spawned a series of regional appraisals with titles like *Go West, Go Wise, When the West was Young*, or *The Land of Open Doors*.[16] The experience of the thirties, when the work of two generations was wiped out by drought and depression, has left the West permanently chastened: 'But how long can it last? In my view, not very long; perhaps a decade at the most ... when oil and gas no longer provide such a large number of our jobs, when production begins to decline, and resource revenue falls off.'[17]

The seriousness with which these provinces approach their promising future is explained by the jealousy and suspicion they feel towards the federal government. The belief that Ottawa covets their resources is not easily dispelled in light of recent history: the centre kept the resources of these provinces only, the three opposed the decision as unjust and inequitable and, eventually, but only after 'the purposes of the Dominion' had been fulfilled, the resources were handed back. It is difficult to imagine a more powerful symbol of central control and only the least observant observer would have trouble appreciating its significance for westerners.

As long as federal control of natural resources lasted, the prairie provinces were reminded of their inferior status in Confederation. There were other reasons why they should see themselves as different from their fellow partners in Canada, the principal one being that Alberta, Saskatchewan, and Manitoba were creatures of the federal Parliament. Unlike the other provinces, they had no legal existence as self-governing colonies before they entered the union and, as a result, 'none of them ... was ever in a position to register objection to the denial of resource control until after it came into being, and by that time it was without control.'[18] Nor did they ever have a voice in administering these resources. For decades the provinces argued, more or less vociferously depending on the party complexion of the governments in Edmonton, Regina, Winnipeg, and Ottawa, for the transfer of resources and for compensation for those already 'alienated.' It is a paradox of the English language that of the several meanings of that verb two of them – to transfer ownership and to estrange – should be used so frequently in prairie political discourse at different times in this century.

Between 1870 and 1882 Manitoba received no financial assistance in lieu of federal retention of its resources. But on achieving provincial autonomy Alberta and Saskatchewan each received a fairly generous grant, the modified formula of which was applied to Manitoba in 1912 and made retroactive to 1908.

Even when the federal government agreed, in 1922, that the resources should be transferred and compensation paid for those which had already passed into private hands, the negotiations dragged on for many years. So long in fact that in the case of Alberta and Saskatchewan the Rowell-Sirois Commission could note in its Report of 1940 that 'no agreement has yet been reached and the payment of compensation in respect of the natural resources of Saskatchewan [and Alberta] remains unsettled.'[19]

That having been said something more needs to be added. It is a cardinal feature of Canadian federalism that the provinces possess the resources within their boundaries (s. 92(5) of the BNA Act) – a constitutional provision of comparative political interest since the practice in the Unites States is just the opposite. The distinction is fundamental not only for the individual provinces and states but for the operation of the respective federal systems. The contrast between the two is discussed most extensively by H.V. Nelles in his study of the development of Ontario's resources.[20] From the perspective of the West the crucial difference was not that natural resources in Canada rested with the provinces and in the United States with the federal government but that until 1930 they rested, as far as the prairie provinces were concerned, with the federal government, too. Thus Canada had a dual system and the United States a unified one and in Canada control of resources or expectation of control instilled a set of rivalries with the central government never found to the south.

The 'public domain,' as it was known in the United States, grew out of the cession of unalienated land by the original thirteen states to the new federal government at Washington. This initial conveyance was vastly increased by conquest and treaty to over two and a half million square miles. American practice, which appears inconsistent with the states' rights orientation of the rest of the Constitution, had historic and geographic explanations. On the one hand, according to Harold Innis, when the United States 'withdrew from the first empire they were compelled to substitute for the centralized control from Great Britain a federal constitution ... which provided ... control over land outside the states as a basis for revenue and expansion.'[21] Opposition to Parliament thus forced them into support for the central government. On the other hand there were the practical difficulties a central government faced trying to control the trade of states strung along the seaboard. Land thus became the preferred source of revenue. The contrasts with Canada are striking on both counts: parliamentary supremacy allowed for the manipulation of resources in the national interest, while the principal trade route, the St Lawrence, was comparatively easy to control. But dependence on land in United States threatened the tariff and aggravated north-south relations.[22] This last factor probably more than any other distinguished the republic from the Dominion, for within the American union vertical tensions conditioned the horizontal thrust of the frontier. No such compromise troubled western development in Canada, although the Maritime provinces might complain, to no avail, about 'taxation without remuneration.'[23] A century after

Philadelphia and with economics, not independence, uppermost in its framers' minds, Confederation was accomplished with a new government at Ottawa acting as the engine of national development to a degree never imagined nor found necessary by the government in Washington.[24]

Canada had the benefit of American experience, where in 1802 the first public land state, Ohio, was created. Use of public lands to support education, roads, canals, railroads and, much later, settlement proved too potent an example not to be copied, although as Chester Martin at length demonstrates, Canadian variations on the model were almost as significant as the original itself. Moreover, the fact that there was a dual system meant that those provinces created out of the 'Dominion lands' felt exploited in a sense foreign to the American states. Discrimination did not end there; they were asked to contribute disproportionately to the nation's development as well: 'The total area alienated in railway land grants in Western Canada was about 32,000,000 acres, almost exactly the area of the kingdom which King Richard was ready to give for a horse at Bosworth Field.' From that kingdom 3600 miles of railways were subsidized, of which approximately 24 per cent were in Saskatchewan. Yet Saskatchewan contributed nearly half the land grants. In Alberta the respective figures were 22 and 41 per cent.[25] The sacrifice was tolerable only if benefits followed. With agriculture the fulcrum promoting investment, employment, and national prosperity, the plea was for people. As one Nova Scotian recently arrived in Alberta eloquently phrased it:

I am dead in love with Canada, anyway. I include all the Provinces, even Quebec ... It is to your interest as well as ours. You send us a thousand men, and in a few years we will send you back $50,000 for commodities that it is impossible for us to provide ourselves – commodities which you will control and in which we will not be likely to come into any serious competition with you.[26]

Sifton's success is well known. After 1896 immigrants arrived by the hundreds of thousands and the federal coffers began to fill not from land sales but from the revenues accruing to the government as a result of economic expansion. But there was another benefit: central control of the western lands and the hunt for suitable settlers by sending Canadian agents abroad made Canada known to the world. Western settlement became a great nationalizing event of which it is no exaggeration to say: 'The impressive fact to the mind of the man contemplating immigration, is that a well known and recognized Government holds unfettered in its own hands the lands which it offers free.'[27] It was a nationalizing event as well in the sense that it engaged the federal government to a degree never surpassed in peacetime. The government had to become involved because immigration 'was never a self-perpetuating, self-increasing movement, the pump worked well ...

but only with constant priming ... The masses, when they came, were at so much a head.'[28] The contrast with the experience of the United States again is revealing. If the American government was slow to become a party to westward expansion, leaving the job to private business, it was equally uninterested in seeking immigrants. Family and friends and private shipping agents did the job which in Canada governmental agents performed. Important too was 'the convenient congregation of foreign groups on [the United States's] eastern seaboard, rather than in [Canada's] Prairie Provinces.'[29] If the location of new arrivals influenced the subsequent flow of immigrants, it also directly affected the transmission of values between generations of immigrants. Canada insisted on its immigrants being agriculturalists, the United States did not. As a result the Canadian immigrants moved West immediately, while the American ones stayed in the East. The impact of immigration on established Canadian society before the First World War was minimal; in the United States it was direct and disruptive. Immigrants to Canada in the first quarter of this century quickly learned at first hand the isolation and regionalism that are the country's abiding characteristics.

Overseas immigration was not identified with the public domain, as it was with the Dominion lands. The 'purposes of the Dominion' and the policies formulated to realize them had no equivalent in the United States. In Canada national priorities took precedence over provincial priorities, although since both levels of government wanted growth conflict was not inevitable in this hierarchical relationship. Federal land grants in the western and mid-western states created a different relationship between centre and periphery: 'Virtually every major governmental function in the public land states benefited from federal land grants directly or indirectly.' State funds and state officials thus became involved as a consequence of federal initiatives. The most significant effect was that 'the public domain came to serve as an integrating factor in the development of co-operative action between the federal government and the states.'[30] Collaboration and co-operation between Ottawa and the prairie governments was not unknown, and indeed where the same party was in power in both locations usually easy to arrange. But the essence of the relationship was that of adversaries, not partners. When the demand was not renewed for control of the natural resources, then it took the form of pleas for more money as compensation. The principal purpose of the Dominion was to populate the West, yet on that subject, presumably of more immediate relevance to the region than any other, the prairie provinces adopted a hands-off attitude, arguing that without local control of the resources there could be no provincial responsibility. The provinces warded off local criticism of the policy, but at the cost of having less influence over a subject of great importance to them.[31]

Comparisons between Canadian and American systems can be helpful but they can also be dangerous because the experiences may be so different. In the one, three provinces are the bases of discussion and in the other, thirty states. Any one of the provinces is equal in territory to several of the states and each of the provinces embraces a vast tract of northern wilderness administered in imperial fashion from the south, while by comparison the American states are homogeneous and compact. The boundaries of the Canadian provinces as originally drawn and later extended have never received the attention they deserve.[32] Nor have the implications of the size of a province been discussed, with the possible exception of Sir Richard Cartwright's gloomy pronouncements on the postage stamp province Sir John A. Macdonald created in Manitoba, which Cartwright blamed for the West's late and slow development. Although his *Reminiscences* ring with partisan phrases, the 'danger' he described as 'inherent in the federal form of Government, where the several States ... differ very widely in wealth and population,' is not one of them.[33] This was a sentiment shared by another Liberal minister, W.F.A. Turgeon of Saskatchewan, who was Attorney General of that province for nearly two decades before moving to the bench and then to the diplomatic service. Turgeon, who was close to those responsible for creating two prairie provinces in 1905, later described the decision as a mistake. He gave credit to Sir Frederick Haultain, the territorial premier, who got it right the first time when he pressed for a single province in the North-West, although for his pains he was 'taxed with local megalomania.'[34]

As important as the discrepancy in the components of the two federations is the crucial difference in their political systems. According to Daniel Elazar, 'statehood came to mean the right to participate in national policy formation as much as the right to manage one's local affairs.'[35] In Canada, too, the desire on the part of territorial politicians and officials to mould or influence federal policy as it affected them was an element in the march to autonomy. But as evident was the ambition to borrow on the provincial credit and to charter railways within the boundaries of a new province. These were powers denied to the territories. Thus on the road to provincehood, acquisitiveness was the predominant motivation.

The perennial complaint of the western provinces has been to point to inadequate or ineffective representation at the centre and the preferred response to influence executive action, thereby recognizing the locus of power under the constitution which prairie governments understand as well as any organization or institution in Canada. The strength of the executive under cabinet government has been expanded even more by the growth in its responsibilities and when combined with the vast distances of Canada adds weight to the old fear that 'power more and more [will pass] into the hands of the permanent civil servant, and a mild form of the Family Compact will be the result.'[36] Western irritation at the decisions and immunity of federal regulatory bodies is frequently vented, as are proposals to limit their authority or barring that to give a greater say to the provinces over their composition and deliberations. In 1969 when the House of Commons was considering the need for a Statutory Instruments Committee, one of the proofs of an undesirable expansion in regulatory authority was the evidence of John Turner, then minister of Justice. He suggested that removing contentious matters to independent bodies, while it might reduce friction could also increase it; for it frequently meant delegating political decisions to non-responsible people. In other words, wherever there is a choice, there is politics.[37] The western provinces have echoed this sentiment with regard to agencies like the Canadian Transport Commission, the National Energy Board, and the Canadian Radio-Television and Telecommunications Commission. On occasion it is even, if somewhat surprisingly, said of the Canadian Wheat Board: 'We have no control over the [Board]. It is appointed by the national government and the national government is controlled by Eastern Canada.'[38]

Criticism of the centre and the way the region is treated is as old as the settled West itself. It is the explanation given for much of its distinctiveness, including third-party experiments that have received so much academic attention. Where there seems to be a difference today is that the hold of the centre is depicted as a grasp which has grown perceptibly tighter in recent memory. To quote Bramley-Moore once more for the accuracy of his prediction: 'Being allowed to send representatives to Ottawa causes them to imagine that they are governing themselves. To keep them in good humour the East prophesies that the West will one day predominate at Ottawa; should that day come, and should the West introduce legislation benefiting Western interests but disadvantageous to Eastern interests, be assured then that the East will abandon Confederation.'[39] The nature of the domination need not be reflected in the House of Commons for it to be evident in federal-provincial discussions in certain areas. Once that is understood, then the implication of the word 'abandon,' to mean give up rather than separate from, becomes clear. To cease to work for Confederation is one meaning that can be taken from the phrase and it is one which western provinces increasingly feel applies to the treatment meted out to them. Allan Blakeney, as the senior socialist politician of the provinces, could be expected to resist concentrations of economic and political power wherever he found them, but he spoke as a westerner first when he asserted that 'some of the same forces that threaten the family farm have acted to weaken the regions of Canada and centralize more and more power.'[40]

There is an apparent contradiction in talking of the hold of the centre as stronger while at the same time saying that the region is more autonomous. The explanation is that as provincial activity grows, the hold becomes more onerous. The result is the same, however: the grip is felt and the provinces seek ways of loosening it. Now, much more than at any time in the past, they look at constitutional reform as a means of reducing potential conflict: 'The effect of [the CIGOL decision] will be to weaken the provinces further just as resentment against the further levels of power is reaching dangerous levels elsewhere.'[41] And the Senate, the institution which occupied more time than any other at the Charlottetown and Quebec City conferences and which has preoccupied a legion of reformers ever since, returns to centre stage as the House of the Provinces or of the Federation. The attraction of the Senate has never been its power or prestige but the recurring, even continuing, belief that the Canadian constitution lacks balance. Canada might have national institutions but they are not federal or federal enough to accommodate sufficiently Canada's diversities. The parlous undertaking of constitutional review in the last dozen years throws in doubt that certainty as well.

The reason for concern is cabinet government, whose past virtue and present weakness is concentrated authority. Political styles change and with them the reputation of constitutions. The American Constitution with its balance of institutions and threefold representation of district, state, and nation in the two houses of Congress and the Presidency and with the Supreme Court to interpret its tested principles is currently very attractive to Canadians. It is also radically different. To give a federally reconstituted second chamber in Canada more regularized and effective checks on the executive is not a modest proposal. Abuses of power are not being remedied by such suggestions; that could be done by distancing the House of Commons further from the cabinet. To remove the current imbalance in the constitution as it relates to federalism, a new imbalance – this time giving the provinces an entrenched power to nullify – is favoured.

The concern about the amount of regional participation at the centre illustrates and enforces the conclusion that the political party has declined as integrator. Decisions at the centre in an increasingly wider area are no longer seen as valid or sustainable. Parties at one time helped create an atmosphere in which decisions were accepted and thus conferred validity upon them. The Liberal party most assuredly can no longer do this in the West. It remains to be seen whether fifteen years of federal-provincial change will qualify the authority of an alternative government. The Progressive Conservative members of Parliament from the prairie provinces embrace a diversity of views on a range of issues only explainable in terms of V.O. Key's rich hypotheses on the one-party south.[42] The strength of regionalism is the strength of the economic and cultural factors within its geographic boundaries. These will remain potent regardless of the complexion of the central representatives because, for example, whoever governs a province 'owns' its natural resources. This is a neutral fact in any discussion of partisanship. But it is 'basic to the problems of federal finance, for it is largely the difference in resources that accounts for the differences in the capital income. It is usually taken for granted and is less frequently challenged than the unequal operation of national policies of which it is the condition.'[43]

It was this fundamental truth that led Sir Richard Cartwright to label Canada as peculiarly unfortunate 'because the difference in wealth among her provinces is enormous and the temptation to the poorer provinces to sell themselves to the party in office is always very great and is certain to be traded on by practical politicians on both sides.'[44] The deleterious effect that a sense of dependency has upon provincial integrity might be questioned. Prominent Liberals from east and west have argued on opposite sides. It probably is not unexpected that the public position, as opposed to the private one, is that obligation can be reconciled with independence. This was the view of Stuart Garson, then premier of Manitoba:

Since we Manitobans have been widely misrepresented as being federalist in our leaning and therefore unconcerned about provincial rights, I am glad of this opportunity of explaining our position ... Do not forget that the people of the prairie economic area have always been and by present prospects, always will be, politically a minority in such vital matters as the tariff, freight rates, and fiscal policy, all controlled by a federal Parliament in which we of the prairie provinces only at long intervals can hope to hold even a balance of power. Therefore, to say or to imply that we are not interested in protecting provincial rights which we need so much is a poor compliment to our intelligence.[45]

The defence of provincial rights is parochial, although it can be respectable. However, it confounds the hopes of those, like Lord Carnarvon, the shepherd of the British North America Act in the House of Lords, who confidently predicted that 'as the sphere of action is enlarged ... larger questions will be discussed' with consequent benefit for leaders and led.[46] Without some perception of a larger purpose, change is as difficult to accept as it is to reject. The problems which language legislation has created have been almost as insuperable as those it has tried to solve. To make bilingualism part of Canadian self-identity, whether or not the individual Canadian speaks both or even one of the two official languages, is the nature of the change required. But while the need for reform, in the eyes of the government, is radical, its full appreciation in the West, in particular, has been slow: 'Sometimes I wonder,' said Pierre Trudeau in 1977, 'if in far-away Saskatchewan you think that [Quebec separatism] is real or is just a fantasy.'[47] Allan Blakeney, more than any other prairie leader, has taken on the job of reinforcing the federal message. He has argued that western Canadians must understand the bargaining that will eventually take place if Canada is to survive and that they can only do that if they know themselves better.[48] It is a measure of the seriousness of the problem as he sees it and of the attrition in federal authority that the senior prairie provincial politician has come to the aid of the Liberal party.

Northrop Frye has said that by contrast with the United States 'Canada ... had no eighteenth century.'[49] Americans knew themselves early and fully in a sense that Canadians never did. Timing and geography have conspired to limit and contain. It is to overcome those restrictions that the centre works so hard to make its hold secure. The Liberal party has been accused of identifying itself with national unity. This has been, say its critics, the party's monumental arrogance. Arrogant or not, the Liberals have argued for a national policy to combat Quebec separatism and it is this policy as much as anything which has driven westerners from them. The raising of language to a fundamental proposition for survival forces the belief that 'not only ... is there an older Canada and a newer, an eastern and a western, but between the two there is a very definite belt of barren land; not a line but a zone of separation.'[50]

The West has rejected the hold of the centre as intolerable but without it the unity of the nation grows tenuous. If there is any comfort, it is that in the four decades since Stephen Leacock described Canada as turning into 'a sort of confederate league, a union of commonwealths, a hyptarchy,' it has not as yet done so.[51]

8

The Lost Liberal West

The political party originated as a basic unit of parliamentary government. Its invention permitted dissent without violent retribution. (Richard Stanbury, 'Why the Party?' [1970])

Western Canada's attempts to break 'the hold of the centre' have taken a form not anticipated by Senator Stanbury in his description of the origin and function of political parties. Rather than acting as a vehicle for dissent, the Liberals have become its object. Pan-Canadian structures aimed at maximizing electoral support for the federal cause proved insensitive to regional grievances where the regions embraced comparatively small numbers of voters. Despite its name, participatory democracy offered no alternative, capitalizing as it did on popular strength to the detriment of minority interests. Traditionally western concerns such as agriculture attracted little comment, while natural resources, which were to assume so much prominence later in the seventies, received only scant attention at the beginning of the decade. Policies that emerge from a government controlled by the Liberal party reflected the same priority of concerns, even though that government was careful to assert its independence from extraparliamentary dictation. In the competition that grew between a party committed to democratic liberalism and a government enamoured of technology and administration, western Canadians believed their interests to be poorly served.

To these reasons for unpopularity must be added the Liberal party's commitment to bilingualism. The party was identified with a view of Canadian society which was foreign to that held by large numbers of westerners. As events in Quebec were to prove, it was an interpretation large numbers of Québécois could not accept either. To western critics Liberal failure at the centre, evidenced in the rise of the Parti Québécois, as well as on the periphery demonstrated the party's inability to control either a divided society or a sectionalized country. Many westerners never saw the Quebec problem as more than a regional issue and, as a result, disputed the prominence the Liberals gave it. But even accepting the government's own evaluation of the magnitude of the issue, the Liberals hardly fared any better in regional estimation. Bilingualism was a policy which could never win but only lose votes in the West. Indeed, to the degree that the government encountered reverses in realizing its objective, to that extent it fired even more opposition from the prairies. Failure, as well as success, fed the fissiparous tendencies of federalism.

The regional weakness of the Liberal party signalled the decline of a national institution whose contribution to integrating the country, if not unequalled, was never surpassed. Ronald Rogowski has written that 'political competition and adjudication in societies where the segments are few and large are always a matter of *negotiation*, not of voting and dictation. The negotiators are segmental organizations or representatives, and only through them does the individual participate in politics.'[1] For the history of the West up to the point in the fifties when this study begins, the predominant organization that facilitated regional representation was the Liberal party. The political élites shared a common (though not the same) provincial background; the exception was always Alberta, where the Liberals appeared for part of the time as a spent force but never so completely moribund as the Progressive Conservatives. With former provincial premiers like James G. Gardiner and Stuart Garson holding federal portfolios, it was natural, though an oversimplification, to see them as extensions of the provincial political élite. In any event, that perception could not go unchallenged, even within party ranks, once provincial Liberals were out of office. In the quarter century since 1955, the decline of the Liberals in federal politics has only been matched by their eclipse provincially as well. In their stead as segmental negotiators has appeared not another national party but the governments of the provinces. Vertical provincial worlds have extended even further into the horizontal federation.

The actors may have changed but the singleness of politics remains. It is the political élite who define the problems and seek answers to them; the natural resources issue of the seventies and federal-provincial conflict surrounding it is only a current example. Canadian politics, or at any rate, western Canadian politics, is a picture that lacks relief. It could never be said of the West what William Hesseltine once remarked about his own country: 'The dynamic force in American history has been the struggle of rival groups for the control of their regions.'[2] The prairies were never diverse enough for rival groups to become established. Such changes as occurred came sequentially and in each instance centred on resource exploitation or staple production. At all stages, the government played a crucial role. As well, until the end of the Second World War, the overlap of farmers and governments testified to the dominance of agriculture, so much so that in Alberta and Manitoba the organized farmers had actually become the government. In Saskatchewan, under the Liberals and until the formation of the CCF, the grain growers accomplished the same feat without actually entering politics as a party. But there is another, constitutional, reason for the dominance of government: 'The Cabinet system of responsible government ... stresses the position of leaders and in turn of organizations which respond to leadership.'[3] Rivals to leaders, or factions generally, are the exception within Canadian parties, notwithstanding the experience of the Progressive Conservative party in the sixties. The leader, indeed the same leader for long periods of time, dominates federal or provincial politics. Voluntary associations and economic organizations take their cue from politics in the manner of their formation and in the nature of their strategy.

The dominance of government is indisputable; the shift in its locale during the twenty-five years with which this book is concerned remarkable. The swing of the pendulum away from the federal leadership of the war years and post-war decade towards the provinces has been catalogued and measured by a number of authorities. *The National Finances* and *The Provincial and Municipal Finances* record, first, the explosion in provincial revenues and expenditures, in public employment in the provinces, and in provincial policy initiatives as compared to any past period or to similar federal measurements today and, second, the absolute growth of government at all levels. The explanation for this dramatic turn in Canada's federal evolution must touch on events in Quebec and the federal government's response, especially its fiscal adjustments, during Lester Pearson's years as prime minister. In its broad outline this is a familiar story which does not require repeating here. But its implications for development in the West will need to be considered.

The West was a federal creation. Its immigrants were there because of policies set down in Ottawa, while the land they occupied was surveyed and administered by officials ultimately directed from the national capital. The myth of 'the West' should have become (as it did in the United States) the myth of the larger federation.[4] But it did not. Except for Manitoba before 1900, the prairies were not an extension of settled Canada. 'The West was not,' says one writer, 'a catalyst of self-definition.'[5] The majority of migrants were not Canadian and those who came from central Canada and the Maritime provinces carried a mixed cultural legacy. Even if most of them were British in origin, the culture of their homeland was by now diluted. In a comment of wider implication than the subject about which he was speaking – Orangeism – A.R.M Lower once remarked that 'a second transplantation has been rather too much, and consequently in the newer parts of the country it does not fluorish as it does in Ontario.'[6] This was his explanation for the virility of the Ku Klux Klan, 'another alien importation,' in the West. It is an observation that makes intelligible that peculiarly virulent expression of prejudice which seized Saskatchewan in 1929. But it also suggests a reason why contact between an extended (and perhaps attenuated) Anglo-Saxon culture and a brace of directly imported European cultures should have given rise to the ethnic rivalry and insensitivity for which the English-speaking West was so long criticized.

The conquest of one race by another at Quebec in the eighteenth century and the influx of Loyalist and British settlers in the next did not create the harmony which would permit a second conquest, this time of the new country to the west. Socially and politically, but less so economically, the settlement of that region was perceived as tantamount to the founding of a new society. The taming of the West was a mild affair, if the two rebellions are excluded, which they must be: however the outcome of those battles was viewed a century ago, in this century they have until very recently had little hold on the consciousness of westerners. The central figure and act of western settlement was the immigrant turning the sod. The creation of farms, the use of land, and the establishment of governmental and social institutions were the subjects that monopolized attention.

While at their birth most of the institutions and practices might share features of, and even replicate, those found in the east or in Great Britain, invariably they assumed provincial or regional characteristics or were replaced by distinctive local institutions: the Torrens land title system was not invented in the West but it was used only in that part of Canada; Saskatchewan to this day does not have counties, while Alberta has had a modified county system for twenty-five years; and the founding and organization of the provincial universities illustrated the adoption of eastern precedents accompanied by important local modifications. Except for the CPR, with its original, legislated, immunities and monopolies, few private institutions did not face some local challenge and even when success fell short of the grain growers' victory over the private grain trade, it nevertheless strengthened the fibre of regional sentiment. Where the region gained least ground, with the significant exception of the reintroduction of statutory rates on grain by 1925, was in its attempts, after the First World War, to influence federal government policy on the marketing of wheat and on the tariff and freight rates.

If the settling of the West and the exploitation of the soil created a distinctive region, the 'unsettling' of the West three-quarters of a century later has reinforced it, although in contradictory ways.[7] Urban growth and rural decline are part of regional migration patterns which have seen Alberta and British Columbia gain population at the expense of the rest of the prairies (and Ontario).[8] The disparity in growth rates between the two eastern prairie provinces and Alberta and British Columbia fragments the former cohesion of the prairie region. Yet because the vast majority of migrants are retained within the four provinces the region has expanded, at least for some purposes, rather than dissolved.

More important about the migration is its direction – from rural to urban, in particular to a few major cities – and its direct or indirect relationship to the fortunes of the provincial economies. Because unfavourable federal policies prevented the perennially anticipated secondary manufacturing condition from materializing, the economic prosperity of the western provinces has been linked to the exploitation of mineral and natural resources: potash and uranium in Saskatchewan, oil and natural gas in Alberta, hydro-electric development and timber in British Columbia and, to a lesser degree, in Manitoba. The eclipse of agriculture, especially grains for which the federal government had a special responsibility, and the renewed dependency on local resources intensifies the identification westerners have made with provincial governments as protectors of their interests. It goes a long way, too, towards explaining the resentment at federal institutions and leaders which thwart provincial initiatives.

If provincial initiatives can spark a federal response in the economic sphere, the reverse has been true in the field of culture. The federal government's apparent obsession with what in the West is seen as a regional issue – bilingualism – has created a provincial cultural response. Federal language policy enhanced the West's real or imagined disabilities in the federation.[9] In its origin and operation it was a potent reminder of the region's peripheral location, while it presented practical difficulties for implementation even for those sympathetic to its purpose. Essentially, bilingualism was a simpler tune than westerners wanted to hear. The plural ethnic base of the West, which had survived the Anglo-Saxon's enthusiastic Canadianization policies of the 1920s, could not easily be fitted into a bicultural interpretation of Canadian society. Even when the federal government moved towards a multiculturalism policy in 1971, by the creation of a ministry of State, that policy in application appeared too little, too calculated and, often, too remote from the life of those it was intended to serve. On the other hand, in the same period, since the passage of the Official Languages Act, the prairie provinces have moved with determination into the same field. Whether or not intended, the result has been to identify the provincial governments even more than the federal government with multiculturalism policies but, coincidently, to defuse the opposition to the federal bilingualism policies.

Because of provincial government control over education policy and administration, the federal government has been able to do very little with regard to promoting instruction in the French language beyond making special projects grants through the office of the Secretary of State, to provincial ministries of education, to finance French immersion classes. The provinces may use this money, as most have during this decade, to establish a French stream in their elementary school curriculum. In all three provinces, where once there was violent objection recorded against languages of instruction other than English, and where, in 1969, the premiers of the time (Thatcher, Strom, and Weir) threatened to challenge the constitutionality of the Official Languages Act, toleration has advanced. What is remarkable in the same period is that while French instruction has been permitted in the schools, instruction in languages other than English, or French, has also been permitted. The relevant legislation is the Education Act ([Saskatchewan], 1978, cap. 17, s. 180[2]), the Alberta School Act (1971, cap. 100, s. 150), and the Public Schools Act ([Manitoba], cap. P250, s. 258[2], as amended SM1978, cap. 38, s. 6). In each province, Ukrainian has appeared as a language of instruction, albeit at kindergarten and elementary levels. This use of languages other than French and English is not directed at reaching new Canadians, as one might find in night schools in Toronto, Hamilton, or Montreal but to Canadian-born children. The prairie experience is therefore the obverse of that discovered in Toronto, where 'the work group on multiculturalism decided not to recommend third language programmes for elementary schools because of the general lack of community and school support for them.'[10]

Canadian experience has demonstrated that education is one of the most sensitive areas of public policy. In the past, disputes over schools, and particularly separate schools, have sparked some of the most bitter debates in the country's history. The decline of religious fervour in recent decades has helped make the introduction of languages other than English easier because it has reduced the anti-Roman Catholic dimension of the conflict which invariably used to appear. One by-product of the calmer atmosphere is that provincial government initiatives with regard to language and education have enhanced provincial prestige in the area of multiculturalism and, invidious as the comparison may be in light of the constitutional limitations placed on federal intervention in educational matters, made the provinces appear more genuinely sympathetic to the non-English and non-French segments of the population. At the same time provincial educational policies confirm and strengthen the view most prairie residents have of themselves as neither English nor French. The principal exception to this generalization would be Manitoba's French population, whose future dramatically changed late in 1979 when the Supreme Court of Canada found the province's unilingual legislation (The Official Language Act of 1890) *ultra vires* the language provisions of section 23 of the Manitoba Act.

Provincial multicultural activities, however, have not been restricted to formal educational policy.[11] In each province agencies within their respective departments of culture, youth, recreation, and tourism have been created to promote multicultural activities. The pattern has been to appoint an advisory council (in Alberta it is composed of representatives of fifty-two ethnic groups including spokesmen for English, Scottish, Welsh, Irish, and French-Canadian organizations) among whose terms of reference is usually a directive, such as in Saskatchewan, 'to encourage diversity as a broadening, rather than a fragmenting, influence to unify and enrich the people of the province.' In each province the emphasis has shifted from an early concern to reflect, through annual festivals, what Saskatchewan calls its 'multicultural and pluralingual society,' to a policy to promote individual and collective demonstrations of that ethnic pluralism. All three provinces make grants to ethno-cultural organizations who provide second language instruction outside the school system; Saskatchewan is typical in requiring, as a condition for financial support, a minimum of eighty hours' instruction. In addition, summer language camps have been established across the prairies, while the councils have also established programs that allow individuals and groups to return for brief stays to their ancestral countries, where they may study at first hand languages, crafts, or the arts. Grants, as well, are made to local municipal authorities and private groups to stimulate an awareness of their province's ethnic heritage. An illustration of the breadth of activity which these funds support is to be found in the Public Accounts of the Government of Saskatchewan for 1977 8, where grants totalling $690,000 are listed as having been distributed among approximately seven hundred individuals and public or private organizations.[12]

Of the three provinces, Saskatchewan has formalized its response more than the rest by passing, in 1974, a Multicultural Act which extends 'official recognition to the reality of multiculturalism.' Manitoba, on the other hand, has recognized the distinctive place of the French Canadians in its society by creating a Secretariat on Federal-Provincial Cultural Relations within the Department of Tourism, Recreation, and Cultural Affairs. Through this agency a special set of programs link the province with France under the umbrella of the France-Canada Cultural Agreement. While the incidence of interest may vary, the prairie provinces have recognized in a deliberate, substantial, and highly visible way the variety of ethnic groups within their boundaries. In so doing they have blunted the impact of the federal government's multicultural policies. Because the federal program from the first was restrained and indirect, the provincial response received more attention. But for the federal government there was at least one benefit from this competition: it lessened the probability of objection to federal bilingual policies which might have developed had they not coincided with an expansive multicultural program. The timing was not deliberate; rather, interest in culture and cultural matters grew at both levels of government in the seventies. It was no less fortuitous that they should complement one another.

The reason for provincial interest in multiculturalism requires further study. No doubt the B and B Commission acted as a prod to cultural sentiments generally. But the reasons why provincial governments and the populace they serve have come to accept multiculturalism still is not explained. Again, one can look to Harold Innis for a possible answer. Innis suggests that modern communications can act as a countervailing force to urban influences. Speaking of the 'levelling influence' of radio, he noted that it can produce a 'powerful effect of country on city.'[13] Although this effect is the reverse to what is often implied by the term 'urbanization,' one can speculate that multiculturalism may be a response to the arrival of a large, rural (and, on the prairies, ethnically heterogeneous) population whose interests are now reflected by governments through the communication resources at hand.

The reciprocal influence of federal and provincial activities in the realm of culture reaches beyond the bounds of this study: but before leaving the subject, the influence on regional identity of related federal activity should at least be suggested. The period covered by this book almost coincides with the history of the Canada Council, founded in 1957. Although a study of the formation and implementation of the policies of that remarkable body has yet to be undertaken, when it is, one of its concerns must surely be the influence the grants program has had on the performing and visual arts in the regions of the country. Arguably, it is to the Canada Council that painters, musicians, and actors owe their freedom to choose not to move to central Canada. There is every reason to believe that federal policies have been responsible for the burst of regional artistic activity that has marked the seventies, although it is still the case that artists wanting to work in some areas have to go to the centre for galleries and markets for their acting and singing. The same might also be said about changes in federal taxation laws which encouraged the proliferation of Canadian publishers. While it is true that the costs of commercial publishing promote concentration and that the two official languages of Canada make Toronto and Montreal the obvious locations, nonetheless the growth of regional periodicals and publishers has provided further opportunity for local identities to become manifest. The Canadian Broadcasting Corporation, which is now into early middle age, has done less with respect to regional culture than might have been expected. Its mandate, American competition, and the costs of production have discouraged anything more than token regional sensitivity. Provincial interest in cable and closed circuit television indicate one avenue that might be followed in making this area of communication sensitive to regional concerns. But except in Saskatchewan little governmental initiative has been displayed.[14]

In the flowering of provincial culture, the governments of the provinces have been slow to take part. In none of the provinces has there been a counterpart to the federal Royal Commission on National Development in the Arts, Letters, and Sciences (the Massey Commission), which reported in 1951. While it is generally agreed that the provinces have undisputed authority in the field of culture and that the federal government must tread warily over the same ground, the provincial governments have been loathe to do anything constructive in the area until very recently. A change in attitude coincided with the legalization of government-controlled lotteries, a subject which itself became embroiled in a federal-provincial dispute. Regional lotteries have proved a boon to provincial governments and the athletic and artistic recipients of government largesse. They are also a milestone in the West's history. Once outlawed everywhere because they offended Anglo-Saxon puritan morality, they now are welcomed on all sides as a ready source of wealth which can be used for a number of purposes including, on the prairies, the pursuit of multiculturalism.

The distinctiveness of the West is explained in part by its ethnic heterogeneity, but also by the historical experience of founding a pioneer society within the lifetime of some of its residents. The provinces of Alberta and Saskatchewan celebrated their fiftieth anniversaries in 1955 when there were still sodbusters among the population. Even by Canadian standards, the prairies are a young region. The major cities, with the exception of Winnipeg, have been revitalized as a result of their phenomenal postwar growth, while the land is marked by the ceaseless migration that has characterized it since the turn of the century. The farms of the prairies appear anything but solid or even prosperous when compared to those in rural southern Ontario or the eastern townships of Quebec. Unoccupied, decrepit buildings only add to the air of impermanence which the depopulation of the countryside creates.

There has hardly been a time when the farmers were not moving onto or away from the land. In the thirties the migration was north as well, to the fringes of the Shield, to escape the worst conditions of the drought found near the CPR mainline. The shared experience which demography, history, and the economy gave westerners has been reinforced by the unsympathetic response of those from outside the region. Federal policies continued to feed the sense of grievance even when the circumstances occasioning it had changed. For this reason objective measurements to demonstrate the West's prosperity become irrelevant in stilling the criticism. It is because the West is more unhappy than unfortunate that the physical boundaries of the region – the Shield, the Rockies – frequently assume greater importance to understanding prairie attitudes than the political boundaries within. For other purposes the internal, provincial, boundaries can be meaningful, as Larry Pratt and John Richards have demonstrated in their comparison of Alberta's and Saskatchewan's natural resource development since the war.[15] On this matter, different interpretations of the provincial good as well as different conceptions of the proper role of government in provincial society explain the contrast in policies.

Where once the Liberal party paid slight heed to those boundaries and thus transcended the divisions of federalism, it has ceased to do so. The disability of the Liberal party is symptomatic of a more general, regional, even national, phenomenon which compartmentalizes provincial and federal politics. For a long time in this century, up to the mid-fifties, Liberal leaders from the West moved with impunity between the two levels of governments. To some degree this was true of other parties: T.C. Douglas's entry into federal politics in 1962 would be the most obvious and, perhaps, last example. Today such crossing of political boundaries is avoided, even frowned on. In fact, politicians now pay a penalty when their party is in power in Ottawa as well as in the provincial capital. Whatever benefits may come their way through the exercise of restricted patronage are outweighed by the criticism they are asked to bear for federal actions. The refusal of strong and attractive premiers, like Lougheed of Alberta and Blakeney of Saskatchewan, to enter federal politics reiterates the point. The reasons vary according to individual, but in each instance it is clearly more satisfying to maintain a provincial base than to enter the larger and, traditionally, more challenging federal ring. Their reluctance denies the country the service of some of its most experienced politicians, while it also underlines the decline in the status of federal politics.

Western Liberals can pose no rival of the calibre of Lougheed or Blakeney. Otto Lang is the only minister from the region in two decades to have gained a national reputation, a distinction none of his colleagues in cabinet from the West could claim.[16] The comparison between James G. Gardiner, the last great western Liberal minister, and Lang is inevitable and the contrasts striking. Gardiner's reputation was made initially in provincial politics, from the backbenches through to the premiership, and his forte lay in party organization. He was pre-eminently a party politician whose talents Mackenzie King recognized and wished to place directly in the service of the federal government. Lang's political origins were emphatically not provincial and, as long as Ross Thatcher led the Saskatchewan Liberals, Lang was portrayed, even by Liberals, as hostile to their cause when it conflicted with his policy objectives.

While he recognized the importance of organization in party affairs, his first and continuing interest was to develop policies which he thought would strengthen the party and Liberalism. His contribution to the Trudeau Government therefore was measured not in terms of the legion of Grits he commanded but according to his ability to mount a convincing argument. In this regard he was not untypical of that government in which seasoned politicians were conspicuous by their absence. James G. Gardiner was a passionate and untiring advocate of his region and, while he had political opponents on the prairies, no one of them doubted his commitment to the region's interests. Otto Lang's most vocal critics came from the prairies, where it was believed that the long-term benefits he claimed for his grain and transportation policies would, in the short term, disrupt and maybe destroy the traditional society and economy.

Although a number of other contrasts between the careers of the two men might be suggested, the final one of interest relates to Gardiner's campaign for the leadership of the party in 1948. In an era when dissent was less prevalent than now, he ran against Louis St Laurent, Mackenzie King's chosen successor, as well as against Chubby Power, and although he lost, he nonetheless won 323 votes to St Laurent's 848. Not only did Lang never run for leader, but no westerner ran in 1958 or 1968. With its secret ballot and individual voting, the leadership conventions depreciate federalism to a remarkable degree for a country otherwise so federally conscious. The conventions would therefore seem to offer a rare opportunity to escape those fetters of regionalism long resented in western Canada. Yet at rallies of the faithful, for policy as well as leadership purposes, western Liberals appear to play a pro forma role of negligible influence. Not only was there no western candidate in 1968 but none of the eight articulated any of the West's concerns. Pierre Trudeau owed nothing to delegates from the region for his selection.[17] (By way of contrast, Joe Clark may have become leader of the Progressive Conservatives in 1976 because of the support he received from western delegates, but that support did nothing to help him, an Albertan born and bred, make his way as a westerner in Saskatchewan and Manitoba. Between the 1979 and 1980 elections his party lost five sets in those provinces.)

Even where western Liberals organize in support of a position, as at the 1966 Policy Convention when they sought to defeat Walter Gordon's anticontinentalist policies, and where their view prevails, it has made little difference to the direction of government policy. Western criticism of the federal Liberals therefore remained unassuaged even on the few occasions when intraparty wrangles were resolved in favour of the West. The lesson of these years was clear: whatever the region might want, whatever the extraparliamentary party might decide, the region's wishes could only be fulfilled through sympathetic parliamentary representation. It is to that subject that the discussion must turn.

The central question is why the party has remained impervious to western interests. The answer W. Burton Hurd gave half a century ago, that 'the East is prone to see the West through home-made spectacles,' correctly gives geography and distance their due.[18] A distortion in perspective is only part of the problem; political recruitment is another. The organizational changes described in Chapters 4 and 5 established not only new structures and procedures to further the federal cause but revealed as well preconceptions about what kind of candidate could best promote it. Because the primary qualification was sympathy for the federal purpose, this often favoured those with 'Ottawa connections.' Whether currently useful elsewhere or at another time in the West, it was a libellous designation on the prairies in the sixties and after. The disdain that greeted such candidates was best summarized by a *Winnipeg Free Press* columnist: 'England had its village Hampdens, and here we are in Manitoba with our village Trudeau.'[19]

The local organization, which was the one body that might have righted this tendency, found its voice ignored within the party and, even when in covert rebellion against the federal leaders, suffered at the hands of its opponents. Those who wanted to break free could not. Without the internal recruitment that the integrated structure had once provided, the provincial Liberals were set apart, appearing to have no function in federal politics other than to complain about their share of the spoils or to rally to the federal standard in a campaign. When the fate of all Liberals had depended on co-operation, each was free to participate, to challenge, and to compromise. Now that their statuses differed, with the provincial Liberals in the role of dependents, criticism was less easy to accept or offer. The Liberals were an easy mark for their provincial opponents: 'Try as it might,' said Ed Schreyer in his acceptance speech as the new leader of the NDP in Manitoba, 'the Provincial Liberal party cannot disassociate [sic] itself from the federal party with its "shabby regional bias." Provincial Liberals must be tied to it.'[20]

If the compartmentalization of politics demoralized the party, it had practical consequences as well. The period being discussed opened with a crushing defeat for the Liberals in 1958. So total was it that George Marler, then a vice-president of the party, talked about developing 'substitute communication' while the pieces were put back together.[21] The separation between federal and provincial Liberals which followed the organizational reform and the coincident decline of the party in provincial politics enfeebled the local constituency organization. In Manitoba and Alberta the process antedated John Diefenbaker's electoral successes but those victories accelerated it, while the dominance of Ross Thatcher and the rift between him and the federal Liberals pushed the Saskatchewan party a long way in the same direction as the other prairie Grits.

Knowledge of constituency organization, especially for a party out of power for so many years in Manitoba and Alberta, or even when in power, as in Saskatchewan between 1964 and 1971, is extremely difficult to come by except for the most obvious gross data. Yet it is here where in the short run the damage is irreparable. It was at this level, for instance, that the disruption of long contact between the Pools and the Liberal party had the most detrimental effect. Indeed, the ties between a multitude of associations and the political élite, maintained for a long time through the good offices of the local Liberal party, were loosened. The integration of politics which the Liberals accomplished was not to be duplicated by one successor party, however. The Progressive Conservatives and the New Democratic Party shared the inheritance, but studies of federal and provincial elections suggest that depending on the level of election a significant transfer in allegiance takes place between these two parties.

The decline of the Liberal party is most evident when results are matched against intent. In 1970, in a speech entitled 'Why the Party?,' Senator Stanbury presented six tests the party would have to meet before it would be capable of 'fulfilling the needs of society.'[22] By the end of the next decade the Liberal party, at least in the West, had failed to meet any of them. The first was that the party should be 'in continuing and effective existence,' a requirement so basic as to be redundant but in retrospect also prescient. The federal Liberals were frequently criticized for not caring about the West, for abandoning local supporters or ignoring local interests. Moreover, from the arguments that arose between provincial Liberals in the three prairie provinces and their federal counterparts, the public could be forgiven for concluding that the impact of the federal presence was as often detrimental as it was beneficial. As a second requirement, Senator Stanbury argued that the party should be 'open and democratic.' If openness meant the party should receive all comers, then the Liberal party remained an open organization welcoming supporters from wherever it could find them. This did not mean that those most active in provincial politics might not feel ill at ease with federal activists, and vice versa, but at neither level did the party discourage adherents. 'Democratic' was another matter and its presence or absence the subject of debate. Despite the concern for promoting 'participatory democracy,' one of the persistent objections raised against reformers was their self-imposed set of values and attitudes to which others must conform. Alberta, Saskatchewan, and Manitoba Grits all resented the assumption of federal infallibility, while at the same time they charged the national officers with that most heinous of partisan crimes – the creation of a party within a party.

The third test, that the party should be representative of the profile of the community, became a frequent cause of complaint. Prairie Liberals were viewed as middle and upper middle class, increasingly professional in occupational make-up and more and more urban in habitat. Aware of their rarefied, and reduced, profile, the Liberals made heroic attempts to attract 'successful' farmer candidates. But here they faced a problem unknown to earlier prairie Liberal politicians: the farm organizations had themselves begun to fragment as their interests ceased to cleave and the Liberals found themselves exposed to the hostilities that became evident between the pools, the National Farmers' Union and commodity specialists like the Palliser Wheat Growers' Association. A fourth test the party had to meet was that it be 'competent in the techniques of involvement.' For a section of the country long familiar with the processes of intraparty democracy as practised, first, by the CCF and, then by the NDP, the Liberal party's experiment was viewed as neither new nor remarkable. Rather it was suspected that the Liberals would not be able to make the scheme work and the party's unresponsiveness to western issues seemed to confirm that suspicion.

The fifth requirement, and the one where the Liberals failed most completely, was in providing 'the mechanics for effective, two-way flow between government and community.' Here was the Liberals' most critical weakness; despite the plans and promises of effective communication, westerners concluded that it was all pretence. It was not that hundreds, maybe thousands, of Liberals did not strive to make the system function as it was supposed to, but that in spite of their labours the system did not work. Or, that it seemed to work only partially well in one direction – from the centre out – which from the perspective of the constituencies was from the top down. Seen in that light, the party appeared to serve self and not others. The final test required the party to be 'made up of people whose motive is public service, not patronage.' Of the six requirements, this is the one the federal Liberals tried most hard to follow and the one provincial Liberals found equally hard to understand. Despite what the federal Liberals might say, they indulged in patronage, not all of it high class. Their basic reform was to place its distribution in the hands of a committee. Whether this was an improvement on the past practice of personally dispensing favours depended on what criteria were used in making the judgment. There is no reason to disbelieve the claim that many Liberal activists were motivated by a public service ideal. On the other hand, there is no reason to doubt that the 'new politics' aggravated federal-provincial relations more than the old. 'Public service' like 'merit' is a principle it is difficult to oppose publicly, especially when the alternative is 'patronage.' In fact it is so loaded with good sentiment that it is impossible to define. To prairie residents, what it appeared to mean in practice was a passionate disinterest by party leaders in their affairs.

The long period of Liberal rule and the equally long rejection of the party by the region worked to the detriment of the West and Canada. Parliamentary government is weakened when one area of the country places itself in permanent opposition to the dominant party, while political parties work best – that is perform their liberating function most effectively – when there is competition. Parties organize choice by opposing. When one great party is lost to a region or a region to a party, then the alternatives are narrowed.

Because the prairies as a region have chosen to oppose the governing party, the dwindling numbers of prairie Liberals who are returned find themselves powerless within the ruling caucus. A quarter of a century ago Stuart Garson clearly explained the predicament of those few in the ranks of so many non-western Liberals: '[They] find themselves in the position of urging a colleague from Ontario to support a measure that will be of benefit to the West and of receiving the reply: "why should I support it when the West doesn't, since it sends mainly opposition members to Ottawa".'[23] Having declared their allegiance, western voters nonetheless resent their exclusion from power. And they criticize. But the criticism reflects their impotence; first issues, that is the subjects of economic and political autonomy, remain continuing issues, modified only by persistent recrimination.[24]

Politically, this is an unhealthy atmosphere for the West and for the nation.

'Federalism,' says Daniel Elazar, one of the twentieth century's most perceptive observers of that demanding form of government, 'must be a public thing, that is to say, a federal polity must belong to its public and not be the private possession of any person or segment of that public and, therefore, requires public participation in its governance.'[25] Not everyone can govern all of the time. Equally sure is it that no area of the country can continually not govern without detriment to the polity as a whole.

Parliament may be weakened by its friends as well as its enemies. It is commonplace to hear that Parliament is handicapped because of an electoral system that makes it unrepresentative. So much is now made of this that it is possible to forget that Parliament has other jobs to do than represent party support on one day, polling day. It is also easy to overlook the fact that for much of an MPs constituency work (eg, help with pension applications, visas, immigration, and so on) party affiliation is irrelevant. Parliament must give or refuse approval to what government does. The validity of parliament rests upon its acceptance. And it should be remembered that at Confederation, and for eleven decades since, what Parliament has decided has been accepted by the country. So familiar is the litany of complaints that the prairie provinces are apt to forget their interests are partial and their combined populations equal only 43 per cent of Ontario's, 55 per cent of Quebec's, and 24 per cent of the two central provinces combined. (If British Columbia is included, then the percentages are 72, 92, and 40.)

Convinced of the rightness of their old causes and now emboldened by strength of new wealth, westerners may make unrealistic claims and proposals:

As far as western Canada is concerned [it] has always been and still is ... near[ly] impossible to obtain a proper voice and a strong voice in the Ottawa government. If we elect a number of members in one of the parties they are relegated to the back benches where we seldom if ever hear anything from them. If one of them is selected as a cabinet minister he often turns out to be either a kook or an egg-head or forgets he ever lived in the west.

A partial answer to all this would be for each elected member west of the Great Lakes to be legally given two votes and secondly for all votes in parliament to be free votes, whereby no government can be defeated by losing a vote ... In this way our members, having two votes each, would be able to vote with a clear conscience in a way they considered best for western Canada irrespective of party lines...

Such changes would, I believe, go a long way toward breaking the monopoly votes of Quebec and Ontario, something which is long overdue.[26]

More than on the House of Commons, proposals to reform Parliament concentrate on the Senate. Suggestions that the provinces should appoint or elect some or all of the senators need to be studied very carefully. On these issues there is no western position, only positions. No single province or organization can speak with authority for all of western Canada. Yet, in all of the proposed reforms as well as in the proposals themselves, there is a theme which can best be summarized as a preoccupation with the authority of place. The implication in each is that the anointment that accompanies election or appointment must come from a chalice held in provincial hands.

It would be too much to blame the decline of the Liberal party in the West for all of this. But that it has contributed in a major way is beyond question. The evolution of federalism in the last two decades has created strains that have reduced the elasticity of that system. The passing of the Liberals from the region has done the same for the operation of the party system. Parliament, it would appear, must bear the burden and pay the costs of both.

The general election of 1980 saw the popular vote decline for the Liberal party in British Columbia, hold its own in Alberta, and rise in Saskatchewan and Manitoba (in the latter province it increased by almost 4.5 per cent) It also brought about the loss of the one seat the party held west of Winnipeg – in Vancouver Centre, which it had won by a margin of 95 votes in 1979. From that modest performance a vigorous debate ensued about the merits of proportional representation, the admission of Senators to the cabinet, and even their appearance as non-voting members in the House of Commons. Interest focused on how Trudeau would create a 'federalized cabinet' when three provinces were unrepresented in the Liberal caucus. Saskatchewan had survived without representation in the cabinet between 1963 and 1968 and Alberta for much longer. The difference this time was British Columbia, which in living memory had had at least one member in the cabinet, and in recent years several. The popular criticism of the single-member plurality system is that it accentuates electoral strength while it punishes electoral weakness. It would be ironic if the loss of one seat formerly held by a margin of .2 per cent of the vote should lead to such fundamental changes as were being proposed.

9

Conclusion

'Grain Problem Growing Critical' (*Western Producer* [19 December 1968]1) 'Compulsory Language Courses Proposed' (*ibid.*)

The Liberal party has been the author of its own demise in western Canada. By virtue of the policies it chose to pursue – from C.D. Howe's refusal in the fifties to make cash advances on farm-stored wheat, through LIFT in the sixties, to bilingualism in the next decade – the Liberal party assured itself of widespread unpopularity. Each action revealed an insensitivity to western opinion which apologists found difficult to explain and which voters interpreted as further cause for distrust. To the repeated defence that these policies were in the public interest, westerners concluded that the public interest (for which they read central Canada's) and their own conflicted and that the federal government, at least when the Liberal party was in power, invariably was the servant of the one and not the other.

Liberal party reorganization, first under Senator Davey and then under Senator Stanbury, seemed to support this conclusion. Ministerialism, especially that aspect of it which saw cabinet ministers under Louis St Laurent play a key role in organizational matters, was blamed for the routs of 1957 and 1958. In its place appeared a new emphasis on pan-Canadian structures which, it was predicted, would circumvent the provincialism of the old structure. The provinces could not be dismissed altogether, but the penchant local Liberals displayed for 'the narrow perspective' had to be checked. Notwithstanding the vocabulary of reform, the political leaders still saw the prairies as a unit, distinct from the regions to the east or the west. Only in the 1970s did this perspective prove deficient and then only for the limited purposes of intergovernmental negotiations between the four western provinces and Ottawa. For most of the period covered by this book, the Liberals approached the prairie provinces with an image of the region scarcely different from that described by a visitor many decades before:

The Canadian West has been likened to a big-bellied bottle, whose narrow neck lies between the lakes of Manitoba on the one side, and the Great Lakes and the American border on the other side. In the bottleneck Winnipeg has established herself, and everything has to pass through it – the wheat and the cattle being shipped across the lakes to the east coast and on to Europe; machines, implements, and all the supplies that the young farm country has to obtain from the outside. The opening at the bottom of the bottle facing British Columbia (which is not usually included in the term 'western Canada' or 'the Northwest') has so far played only a minor role and the smaller outlets toward the United States to the West of Winnipeg are of even less importance.[1]

While this description would require some amendment to take account of the opening of the Panama Canal, which allowed grain destined for Europe to be shipped westward, the completion of the Hudson Bay Railway to the port of Churchill, which permitted brief seasonal shipments via the short route to Europe, and the growth in the last two decades of trade with the Pacific-rim countries, the simile of the bottle – of contained space – still depicts the single most important charactristic of these isolated plains which stretch for over eight hundred miles from the edge of the Shield to the Rocky Mountains.

And just as it is difficult to judge distances on so vast a plain, so is it difficult to devise policies for such an immense territory, or anticipate their impact, when the decisions are made outside the region. Yet this is what the Liberals have had to do as their partisan base has disintegrated. In the first half of this century the Liberals benefited from the vertical communication which their integrated structure based on the provinces allowed. For much of the same period, as the provinces moved only slowly to a merit-based civil service, the interpenetration of party and bureaucracy contributed to the clarity of communication. It helped avoid, or at least moderate, those conflicts which inevitably arose from concurrent, overlapping, or disputed jurisdictions. In retrospect and in comparison to politics today, the federal system appears then to have possessed an elasticity which it has lost and which is explainable only in part by the increased demands more recently placed upon it. On that point it is worth remembering, however, that had the Grits had their way in the thirties, there would have been no Wheat Board, certainly none with monopoly powers as came about during the Second World War, and, consequently, no federal responsibility for wheat. But depression and war saw that this did not happen; wheat became a federal responsibility and, except for the six years of Tory rule between 1957 and 1963, a Liberal responsibility.

While the farmers shared in the prosperity that came with war and after, they never received from the Liberal party those assurances of security they continually sought. The exception to that generalization was, of course, James G. Gardiner, whose labours to protect the farmer were legendary but whose ability to influence his cabinet colleagues on this subject waned in the post-war years. The Liberals never saw the western grain producer in collective terms, as a class, but instead they looked to the individual farmer to take responsibility for his own future. It was a view reminiscent of Sifton but consistently held from Howe through Otto Lang, and just as consistently rejected by many farmers as well as attacked by the Tories, and the New Democratic Party, who depicted the Liberals as the scourge of the family farm and the local community.

Liberal agricultural policy more than anything else earned the party its reputation as 'right-wing.' Although the left-right spectrum can be abused when describing party systems, there seems little doubt that on these matters western Liberals were perceived (and, indeed, perceived themselves) as being to the right of their NDP and PC competitors. It is equally clear that by adopting this stance the Liberal party incurred a major electoral disability in the West.[2]

The Liberals were unsympathetic to the proposition, which even 'responsible' farmers shared, that grain policy could not be evaluated according to textbook economics: 'Producer decisions are not necessarily based on the same factors as would be considered by the economist, who is seeking the most "economic" operation. The producer is a "businessman" but his decisions may be based on factors which are not apparent to other "businessmen." '[3] However, it was not tradition or sentiment only that explained Liberal resistance. Under Pierre Trudeau the party became enamoured of new techniques and structures which would provide for more responsive and sensitive policy: 'By transforming the control function and the manipulation of information,' Trudeau told the Harrison Hot Springs policy gathering in 1969, '[we] will transform our whole society. With this knowledge, we are wide awake, alert, capable of action; no longer are we blind, inert pawns of fate.'[4] The Liberal government's purpose and determination were reflected in the succession of white and green papers, task forces, and special study groups which were intended to broaden the base of consultation, and, at the same time, make government policy more efficient and effective. To the western farmer, who traditionally saw his interests in need of protection, the new orthodoxy of public administration constituted a threat; for the test Liberals in Ottawa now applied to determine the worth of a program was not the measure its beneficiaries traditionally used.

The role of the federal bureaucracy as an instrument of political integration in Canada needs study, both as a means of reconciling conflicting demands between and within regions and as one of the vehicles for promoting the recruitment of personnel from the regions. What is clear, even from this brief study of prairie politics, is that from the minister at the top to the staff within, the West looked to the mainline departments (Sifton's Interior, Motherwell's and Gardiner's Agriculture) for solicitude and protection. Despite the descriptions of him as ' "small-c" conservative,' the westerner was not opposed to government per se. The farmer accepted a strong minister in control of his department; on occasion he even demanded it. But he remained suspicious of the delegation of power affecting his interests to civil servants. And the Trudeau Government, in its determination to modernize administration, seemed ready to do just that. Even organizations normally sympathetic to the Liberal challenge to the status quo in agriculture expressed alarm at the government's willingness to relinquish power to the bureaucracy. The response of the Palliser Wheat Growers' Association to the proposed reforms to the Canada Grain Act (that descendant of another 'magna carta' of the farmers, the Manitoba Grain Act of 1900) demonstrated the concern:

Acceptance ... usually came to pass after considerable debate in the House and after investigation and the giving of evidence before Committees ... When the process was finished at least everyone vitally concerned had [had] a chance to contribute ... and Parliament exercised and accepted the responsibility for the reconciliation of interests that took place. But, if Bill c 196 is passed without appreciable amendment, it appears that a non-elected, non-representative, and, in the Constitutional sense of the term, an irresponsible body – public servants – are to have this power.[5]

The farmers remembered how politics was supposed to work even if the government did not. The explanation for this oversight on the part of the Liberals was not only their enthusiasm for system analysis, PPB (Planning-Programming-and-Budgeting), and cybernetics. It could be traced as well to their limited view of how the party was supposed to function, at least in the West. If there was one fact beyond all others which stood out in the election returns from the prairie provinces during the 1960s and 1970s, it was that the Liberals hardly ever elected anyone. The results are so evident as not to require comment; and yet the Liberals in Ottawa seemed to forget them. In a remarkable demonstration of just how the Liberal party became caught up in its own organizational reforms and how, as a result, it became detached from electoral reality, it would be hard to improve on the speech made in Regina, Saskatchewan, in 1971 by Marc Lalonde, then principal secretary to the prime minister, to the annual meeting of the Institute of Public Administration of Canada. In a paper entitled 'The Changing Role of the Prime Minister's Office,' he explained how the system, described in Chapter 5 of this book, was supposed to work:

An additional method of maintaining liaison between the prime minister and the cabinet, on the one hand, and the extra-parliamentary party, on the other hand, is the various provincial advisory groups sometimes referred to as 'troikas.' Each advisory group is composed of a minister from that province, the chairman of the federal Liberal caucus from that province, and the chairman or representative of the Liberal Party organization for that province. They meet from time to time to discuss a variety of subjects ranging from the consideration of government decisions affecting the region to the evaluation of political strategy. To ensure that the prime minister's point of view is known and that discussions of the advisory groups are communicated to the prime minister, a representative from the PMO (the regional desk officer) usually attends each of these meetings.[6]

His remarks were noteworthy not for the description they contained, which was accurate enough as far as the theory of participation went, but for what they ignored. Two months before he spoke, the provincial Liberal leader, Ross Thatcher, had died suddenly at the age of fifty-four; a month before that the only Liberal government west of the Ottawa River, in the only province in that vast area to elect a straight Liberal government since Mitch Hepburn in Ontario, had been soundly defeated; earlier still the president of the Saskatchewan Liberals had been killed in a plane crash during the election campaign, and, finally, for the whole period from 1963 to 1971, all of Saskatchewan's members of parliament together would have failed to form a 'troika' for want of numbers.[7]

From the perspective of western Liberals, the Davey and Stanbury reforms did not open up decision-making within the party; instead, they limited it. For those who already felt excluded, the new mechanisms of participation in the extraparliamentary party appeared unhappily similar to the mechanisms that controlled the intraparliamentary party. Westerners had for decades resented the discipline that the old parties enforced in the House of Commons. Therefore, when western Liberals meeting in Edmonton in 1970 decried the limitations on regional expression of opinion within Parliament, they were echoing an ancient (in western Canadian terms) complaint.[8] Their problem, however, had less to do with the operation of parliamentary government, as it is practised in Canada, or even with the imposition of the party whip, but a lot to do with the fact that they had no power to influence party officials before the whip was laid on. For the West to have its interests adequately articulated and respected required more weight than the strongest minister could carry in caucus. In their feeble condition, western Liberals might flirt with Senate reform, or even with electoral reform in the House of Commons. But while both, in whatever form they were implemented, would no doubt result in more Liberals from the West in Parliament, they would not improve the network of political communication, which begins in the constituency and through which is transmitted most directly the inputs and outputs of government. It was exactly here where the Liberals performed so poorly and it was also here where the party's rejuvenation would have to begin.

The Liberal party's decline in the prairie provinces accentuated the decentralization that has been so marked in the Canadian federal system since 1960. The ties of federalism have been loosened even more in this region than elsewhere, although all provinces have benefited from the change, because while 'they are not the ideal size ... they include enough territory to make viable systems possible; the political and administrative structures already exist, and the constitutional authority is there.'[9] With the party in power nationally for most of the intervening years but out of power in the region, the West has looked upon itself as excluded. While this is an exaggeration, as well as the consequence of the western voters' own action in rejecting the Liberal party, it nonetheless reinforces the regional perspective that geography and history have helped create. Liberal policies, discussed in Chapter 6, increased the sense of separation, for demographic and economic trends in the seventies encouraged the belief that they were both dated and misconceived. The confidence which has come with prosperity not only leads some westerners to believe that in this region lies the economic future of Canada, but also to see their experience as the authentic Canadian one.

This change in condition has encouraged an aggressiveness on the part of some of the provinces which is directed at checking the exercise of traditional federal authority. Saskatchewan's fight to protect its resources from federal intrusion has already been mentioned. But in 1978, at the Alternatives Canada Conference sponsored by the Canada West Foundation, the premier of Alberta, Peter Lougheed, proposed as well that the provinces appoint forty per cent of the members of federal regulatory bodies. It was the Alberta government which also proposed reorganizing the Canadian Transport Commission into four regional agencies, with only conflicts between the regions being settled by a national panel selected from the regions.[10] It would be a mistake, however, to exaggerate this assertiveness. Saskatchewan, at any rate, recognizes its limits: 'We need to be part of Canada because for future generations the most important problems for Saskatchewan will be world problems.'[11]

The Liberals have passed this way before, a hundred years ago, when they were then seen as eastern-oriented, Quebec-obsessed, and small-minded. Following the gloomy returns of those elections came Sir Wilfrid Laurier, and a western expansion only rivaled by the predictions of what is to come in the 1980s. There were many reasons for Laurier's success, but one explanation was that he echoed the optimism of the West and his administration realized its potential. Canadian political parties are liberating institutions, for to prosper they must be tolerant. They fail when they exclude, and they exclude when they become captive of a few interests and fewer ideas. The Liberal party in the third quarter of this century sought to break from its past, to adopt new ideas, and to incorporate new interests. It succeeded in becoming identified with the promotion of a dualism as old as Canada and an array of interests rooted in the heartland of the St Lawrence. In the bargain, it lost the support of a region which under Laurier had become for the world synonymous with Canada and which had acted as one of the two pillars of Canadian liberalism in the first half of the century.

Notes

INTRODUCTION

1 Donald J. Mills, 'The Occupational Composition of the Prairie Provinces: A Regional-National Comparison,' *Transactions of the Royal Society of Canada* VI Series IV, Section II (June 1968) 243

CHAPTER ONE: 'NOTHING LESS THAN A "NEW NATION"'

1 Lambeth Palace Library, Papers of R.T. Davidson, Archbishop of Canterbury, 1903–28, Special Subjects: Canada No. 1, 1903, 1909–10. B.K. Cunningham to J.V. Macmillan (secretary to the Archbishop), 28 July 1911. The chapter title is from a letter in the same series; italics are used in the original. For a judicious appraisal of the Canadian imperialists, see Carl Berger, *The Sense of Power: Studies in the Ideas of Canadian Imperialism, 1867–1914* (Toronto 1970) esp. Chap. 5
2 Sifton Papers, Sifton to W.W. Buchanan, 15 Feb. 1899, Letterbooks, vol. 230/859–60. All quotations from the Sifton, Laurier, and Grey Papers in this chapter are taken from the Papers of Mabel Timlin, University of Saskatchewan Archives, Saskatoon. Dr Timlin transcribed hundreds of pages of PAC records during her researches. For her evaluation of Clifford Sifton and his policy, see 'Canada's Immigration Policy, 1896–1910,' *Canadian Journal of Economics and Political Science* XXVI (Nov. 1960) 517–32.
3 *Ibid.*, Sifton to Hon. Charles Fitzpatrick (minister of Justice), 18 Dec. 1902, Letterbooks, vol. 249/748–53
4 Harold Troper, *Only Farmers Need Apply* (Toronto 1972) 14–15
5 USA, Timlin Papers, 'W.T.R. Preston and the London Emigration Office, 1899–1906,' incomplete manuscript, 27 pp at 2
6 For more on the NATC, see *ibid., passim*, and Laurier Papers, James A. Smart (former

deputy minister of Interior) to Laurier, 5 July 1905, 99330-7. See, as well, AS, IBR, 2.627, J. Lowe (deputy minister of Agriculture) to A.M. Burgess (Department of the Interior), 8 Apr. 1892, for reference to problems faced by agents on the Continent

7 Laurier Papers, unsigned memorandum on bonuses, dated 14 Mar. 1908, 137572-81; AS, IBR, Reel 2.627, Tupper to John Carling (minister of Agriculture), 21 July 1890; and Tupper to Daly, 29 July 1893

8 Sifton Papers, Sifton to W.W. Buchanan, 11 Feb. 1899, Letterbooks, vol. 230/787–9

9 See, for example, John W. Dafoe, *Clifford Sifton in Relation to His Times* (Toronto 1931) Chaps 6 and 15

10 The migration of the American farmers from the mid-west is discussed by Troper, *Only Farmers Need Apply*. The Canadian agency system, which closed finally in 1931, is described by Colonel Laval Fortier (deputy minister of Immigration and Colonization), 'Keynote Address to the Catholic Social Life Conference' in *Immigration and Land Settlement: Proceedings and Addresses* (Canadian Catholic Conference, London, Ont., 26–8 Sept. 1954) 30–53.

11 The figures and quotations in the foregoing paragraph are from R.H. Coats and M.C. MacLean, *The American-Born in Canada: A Statistical Interpretation* (Toronto 1943) 14 (figures); 20, 34, and 109 (quotations). For a comparison of various estimates of migration to and from Canada between 1851 and 1951, see William Petersen, *Planned Migration: The Social Determinants of the Dutch-Canadian Movement*, vol. 2 (Berkeley, CA 1955) 162.

12 USA, Timlin Papers, compiled from *Journals of the House of Commons*, 1907–8, XLIII, App. 2, Pt II, 360–3. Pages 323–408 of this particular issue of the *Journals* are devoted to evidence regarding 'Canadian Immigration' taken before the Select Standing Committee on Agriculture and Colonization.

13 Edmund H. Oliver, 'Saskatchewan and Alberta: General History, 1870–1912' in Adam Shortt and Arthur G. Doughty, eds, *Canada and Its Provinces* (Toronto 1914) XIX, 273

14 Dominion of Canada, Dominion Bureau of Statistics, *Origin, Birthplace, Nativity and Language of the Canadian People* (Ottawa 1929) 91

15 Sir Richard Cartwright, *Reminiscences* (Toronto 1912) 217. For an outsider's observations on the contrasts between country and city, see E.B. Mitchell, *In Western Canada before the War: A Study of Communities* (London 1915) 15.

16 Sifton Papers, Sifton to Col. S. Hughes, 11 Feb. 1904, Letterbooks, vol. 255/809–10

17 Marcus Lee Hansen, *The Mingling of the Canadian and American Peoples* I (Toronto 1940) 232–3. See also Laurier Papers, 'Memorandum on Continental European Immigration' by Paul Wiallard to Laurier, undated but between Jan. and Apr. 1896, 4067–73: 'Now, the immigrants, who are most likely to stay here, are rather the foreign farmers whose languages are not currently spoken on the other side of the border, and who, in arriving here, go and settle where their countrymen are already established.' Looking at it from the other end, Coats and MacLean, *The American-Born in Canada*,

comment: 'That the United States requires its native-born of whatever race to learn English has a meaning for Canada too in the assimilation of such as pass through that crucible.' (p 21)

18 Sifton Papers, Sifton to Col. S. Hughes, 11 Feb. 1904, Letterbooks, vol. 255/809–10. See also memorandum to W.D. Scott (Superintendent of Immigration), 9 Mar. 1904, Letterbooks, Vol. 256/389 and letter to Sir D.H. Macmillan (Lieutenant Governor of Manitoba), 5 May 1904, Letterbooks, vol. 258/339–40.

19 Sifton Papers, Sifton to John W. Dafoe, 11 Nov. 1901, Letterbooks, vol. 246/137–40

20 Berger, *The Sense of Power* 149–50. Some imperialists were alive to the evolution of prairie society. Compare Sir Robert Falconer's horticultural metaphor of eastern seeds and western fruit in 'The Unification of Canada,' *University Magazine* VII (Feb. 1908) 4 with his later recognition that 'the west will soon possess a marked individuality and ... the older influences will become fainter' in 'The Quality of Canadian Life,' *The Federation of Canada, 1867–1917* (four lectures delivered at the University of Toronto in Mar. 1917 to commemorate the fiftieth anniversary of the Federation, Toronto 1917) 124.

21 'Ethnic Settlers in Western Canada: Reminiscences of a Pioneer,' *Canadian Ethnic Studies* VIII, 2 (1976) 13

22 Petersen, *Planned Migration* 217

23 George Thomas Daly, *Catholic Problems in Western Canada* (Toronto 1921) Chap. 11

24 Grey of Howick Papers (Governor General of Canada), Grey to James Bryce, 30 Jan. 1911, 002795-802 at 01 from USA, Timlin Papers

25 See Troper, *Only Farmers Need Apply* 152 for a discussion of the statistical problems. See also, AS, IBR, Reel 2.600, W.J. White (Inspector of US Agencies) to Alex Cance (Special Agent, Kewaunee, WI), 10 Nov. 1909, for numbers of immigrants 'from the United States to Canada during the eleven years ended March 31, 1915 showing states of last residence' beginning with Minnesota (118,204) and extending down to Hawaii (34).

26 The 'Hamlet's ghost' of Canadian politics, as the school question was described, appeared rarely and then only briefly in Alberta. 'The School Question in Alberta,' *Willison's Monthly* II (July 1926) 66–8. The absence of a 'school question' in Alberta is noted in several sources. 'French and English in Western Canada' in Mason Wade, ed., *Canadian Dualism: Studies in French-English Relations* (Toronto 1960) 329; Canada, *Report of the Royal Commission on Bilingualism and Biculturalism* (Book IV: *The Cultural Contribution of the Other Ethnic Groups*, Ottawa 1970) 104–5 and George M. Weir, *The Separate School Question in Canada* (Toronto 1934) 96–7.

27 For a discussion of the West's party system from the perspective of class and cultural cleavages, see Jane Jenson, 'Aspects of Partisan Change: Class Relations and the Canadian Party System,' unpublished paper for Conference on Political Change, Saskatoon, Mar. 1977, 14–19.

28 Laurier Papers, Father J.A. Thérien to Laurier, 18 Mar. 1907, 122561–8
29 AS, IBR, Reel 2.599, James A. Smart (deputy minister of Interior) to Sifton, 8 June 1897.
It should be noted that this activity took place before the extensions to Quebec's
northern boundary in 1898 and 1912. Provincial legislation had appeared in 1875 'to
encourage Canadians in the United States, European immigrants and inhabitants of the
province to establish themselves upon the wild lands of the Crown.' J. Mercier,
'Immigration and Provincial Rights,' *Canadian Bar Review* (Dec. 1944) 856–69
30 AS, IBR, Reel 2.599, Benjamin Davies to W.D. Scott, 13 June 1910
31 AS, IBR, Reel 2.618, *Rapport du Congrès de la Colonisation* (tenu à Montréal, les 22, 23
et 24 novembre 1898, La Société Générale de Colonisation et de Repatriement de la
Province du Québec, Montréal 1900) 291–2. See, as well, A.I. Silver, 'French Canada
and the Prairie Frontier, 1870–1890,' *Canadian Historical Review* L (Mar. 1969)
11–36 and Albert Faucher, 'Explication socio-économique des migrations dans l'his-
toire du Québec,' *Transactions of the Royal Society of Canada* Fourth Series, XIII
(1975) 91–107.
32 Laurier Papers, J.K. Barrett to Most Rev. D. Falconio, 1 Mar. 1911, 182330-4 at
182331
33 The statistics are from Robert Painchaud, 'Les Origins des Peuplements de langue
française dans l'ouest canadien, 1870–1920: Mythes et réalités,' *Transactions of the
Royal Society* Fourth Series, XIII (1975) 109–21. The suggestion was made in an
unsigned and incomplete memorandum, AS, IBR, Reel 2.627, 26 Mar. 1904.
34 'Canada in the Making,' Canadian Historical Association *Annual Report* (1944) 14
35 Mitchell, *In Western Canada before the War* 5
36 The first reference is quoted in Northrop Frye, *The Bush Garden: Essays on the
Canadian Imagination* (Toronto 1971) 241; the second in E. Thomson, 'What Will the
West Do with Canada?' *The University Magazine* (Montreal) VI (1907) 7.
37 The idea of the immigrant being 'freed' is discussed by Henry Nash Smith, 'Mark
Twain as an Interpreter of the Far West: The Structure of *Roughing It*' in Walker D.
Wyman and Clifton B. Kroeber, eds. *The Frontier in Perspective* (Madison 1957) 216.
38 The two accounts of the origins and operation of the Empire Settlement Act are: John
Thomas Culliton, *National Problems of Canada: Assisted Emigration and Land Settle-
ment with Special Reference to Western Canada* (No. 9, McGill University Economic
Studies 1928) and G.F. Plant, *Oversea Settlement: Migration from the United Kingdon
to the Dominions* (London 1951). For its effects on western Canada, see David E.
Smith, 'Instilling British Values in the Prairie Provinces,' *Prairie Forum* VI, 1
(forthcoming)
    This paragraph is based on a reading of the records and correspondence of the
Oversea Settlement Committee, who administered the Act, Public Record Office,
London, CO721 series.

39 Herman Ganzevoort, introd. and transl., *A Dutch Homesteader on the Prairies: The Letters of Willem de Gelder* (Toronto 1973) 24

40 R.O. MacFarlane, 'Manitoba Politics and Parties after Confederation,' Canadian Historical Association *Annual Report* (1940) 53

41 AS, Martin Papers, *Mail and Empire*, clipping, 18 Dec. 1920, 44484

42 AS, IBR, reel 2.588, *Canadian Handbook with Maps* (London: Emigrants' Information Office) 48. The plaintiff was J. Obed Smith (Commissioner of Immigration, Ottawa), 20 May 1901. The complaint about misinterpretation was of long standing as well as deeply felt, for good reason: 'The critical evaluations which were to shape the future of the region were made by outsiders.' John Warkentin, 'Steppe, Desert and Empire' in A.W. Rasporich and H.C. Klassen, eds, *Prairie Perspectives* 2 (Toronto 1973) 121. See also Basil Stewart, *'No Englishmen Need Apply': or Canada as a Field for the Emigrant* (London 1909): 'If the Colonial Office and the Board of Trade of the British Government were represented in the West by a man who understood local conditions … there would be less misunderstanding.' (pp 80–1)

    The settlers invariably remarked on the vastness that surrounded them: 'Have you any idea what 125 miles mean in the winter through a rough country, about 35 hours of travelling,' Ganzevoort, *A Dutch Homesteader on the Prairies* 24. See also 'The Diary of a Barr Colonist Describing the Journey and the Settlement,' Appendix to Edmund H. Oliver, 'The Coming of the Barr Colonists,' Canadian Historical Association *Annual Report* (1926) 75–87.

    It was rare to find the contrary view of the prairies: 'as if the traveller were in the outlying parts of an old English park, too far from the house to receive particular attention.' The Rev. William Newton, *Twenty Years on the Saskatchewan: North-West Canada* (London 1897) 163

43 Henry Hawkins, 'They are All Progressives in the West,' *Canadian Courier* XXII (23 June 1917) (3)–18. Not everyone agreed: 'With them Christianity is nothing more than social welfare inspired by a vague philanthropy.' Daly, *Catholic Problems in Western Canada* 83

44 Frye, *The Bush Garden*

45 See W.T. Easterbrook, 'Recent Contributions to Economic History: Canada,' *Journal of Economic History* XIX (Mar. 1959).

46 'A Conversation with Margaret Laurence,' in Robert Kroetsch, ed., *Creation* (Toronto 1970) 63 as quoted in Eli Mandel, 'Ethnic Voices in Canadian Writing' in Wsevolod Isajiw, ed., *Identities: The Impact of Ethnicity on Canadian Society*, Canadian Ethnic Studies Association, V (Toronto 1977) 59. Elsewhere Mandel has said of Kroetsch's statement that it 'is not paradoxial but tautological … identity is fictional; it exists only in stories, in dreams, in fantasy.' *Another Time* III, *Three Solitudes: Contemporary Literary Criticism in Canada* (Erin 1977) 67

CHAPTER TWO: ECONOMIC OPPORTUNITIES

1 The isolation from American influence increases dependence on central Canada. Except for Winnipeg, cable television is a relative newcomer to the region; it appeared in Saskatchewan only in 1978. Residents have watched television originating almost exclusively from Toronto. News, too, has emanated almost solely from major metropolitan centres, with the effect that the image of the prairies held by other Canadians has been distorted. According to a recent study, 'Saskatchewan [is] practically unknown on the network except for the occasional report appearing in "Country Canada".' Canada, *Report of Inquiry into the National Broadcasting Service* (established by the CRTC, 14 Mar. 1977) 57. Long ago, A.R.M. Lower noted that while Toronto shared with Montreal the domination of the West's trade and finance, 'it was much more successful than Montreal in building up a human connection.' 'Geographical Determinants in Canadian History,' in R. Flenley, *Essays in Canadian History Presented to G.M. Wrong* (Toronto 1939) 229–52

2 Saskatchewan is unique in having been both a 'have' and 'have-not' province at different times in its history. In the 1970s, however, future prosperity was assured with its oil reserves and the discovery of rich uranium deposits in the north. But up to the time this study was written the distinction between the two sets of western provinces held true. Compare, for example, percentage change of population for the four since 1951:

	1951/56	1956/61	1961/66	1966/71	1971/76
Manitoba	9.5	8.1	4.5	2.6	3.4
Saskatchewan	5.9	5.1	3.3	−3.0	−0.5
Alberta	19.5	18.6	9.9	11.2	12.9
British Columbia	20.0	16.5	15.0	16.6	12.9

SOURCE: *Canada Year Book*, 1976–7, Table 4.4, 186

3 The amending formula treated the four western provinces as one region and required for successful passage the approval of at least two provinces having at least 50 per cent of the region's population. The most recent redistribution formula divides all provinces according to population into three categories (small, medium, and large) and provides a different calculation of the population quotient for each. Alberta and British Columbia are classified as 'medium' (with the latter expected to join Ontario and Quebec after 1981 as a 'large' province) and Saskatchewan and Manitoba as 'small.'

4 The conflict of interests that besets co-operation among the three prairie provinces is suggested by Norman Ward, 'One Prairie Province: Historical and Political Perspectives,' in David K. Elton, ed., *One Prairie Province?: A Question for Canada*, Conference Proceedings and Selected Papers (Lethbridge, Alberta 1970) 183–94.

Premier Strom of Alberta opposed the idea of one prairie province but spoke warmly of the union of his province and British Columbia because both of them had 'a fine record of making use of the great opportunities which we have in the West.' Thatcher dismissed the idea of any union as 'academic,' claiming 'it isn't going to sell any more wheat.' *Globe and Mail* (12 May 1970) 4. For an example of recent western co-operation, see Report of the Western Premiers' Task Force on Constitutional Trends (May 1977). Thirty-one of its fifty-three pages are devoted to an 'Inventory of Federal Intrusions.' See Richard Simeon, *Federal-Provincial Diplomacy: The Making of Recent Policy in Canada* (Toronto 1972) 240–1, for an account of W.A.C. Bennett's 'personalized leadership' in federal-provincial negotiations.

5 The percentage of Canadians who lived in rural areas declined between 1930 and 1967 from 46 to 28 per cent. Agriculture's contribution to the Gross National Product quadrupled, but as a share of the GNP it was more than cut in half from 11 to 5 per cent. Of Canadian exports, agriculture's share declined from 43 to 15 per cent. *WP* (26 Aug. 1971) 24

6 George Thomas Daly, *Catholic Problems in Western Canada* (Toronto 1921) 146. For John Diefenbaker's dictum about wheat, see Dalton Camp, *Gentlemen, Players and Politicians* (Toronto 1970) 187.

7 Vernon Fowke, *The National Policy and the Wheat Economy* (Toronto 1957) 72

8 Charles D. Tarlton, 'Symmetry and Asymmetry as Elements of Federalism: A Theoretical Speculation' in J. Peter Meekison, ed., *Canadian Federalism: Myth or Reality* (Toronto 1968) 30–6

9 P.J. Thair, 'Agricultural Development on the Prairies' in Proceedings of Seminar: Development of Agriculture on the Prairies, University of Regina (Jan. 1975) 137. The percentage of rural population in each of the three prairie provinces for selected censuses was: 1941 (Manitoba 56; Saskatchewan 67; Alberta 61.5), 1951 (Manitoba 50.5; Saskatchewan 55; Alberta 48) and 1971 (Manitoba 30.5; Saskatchewan 47, Alberta 26.5).

10 An exception is G.E. Britnell, 'Perspective on Change in the Prairie Economy,' *CJEPS* XIX (Nov. 1953) 437–54.

11 *WP* (25 June 1953) 1

12 *Ibid.* (3 Dec. 1970) 1

13 C.F. Wilson, *A Century of Canadian Grain: Government Policy to 1951* (Saskatoon 1978) 501; House of Commons Debates (17 Feb. 1970) 3677. See, as well, *WP* (27 Sept. 1962) 8.

14 *Report of the Grain Handling and Transportation Commission*, 2 vols (Ottawa 1977) I, 273–4

15 Although he had no responsibility for its contents, Thatcher had to fight fierce criticism of the report of the federal task force on agriculture published in 1969. That report envisaged a large number of non-viable farmers entering other areas of the labour force.

16 Wilson, *A Century of Canadian Grain* 680, 596
17 Anthony G.S. Careless, *Initiative and Response: The Adaptation of Canadian Federalism to Regional Economic Development* (Montreal 1977) Chap. 5
18 Quoted by Thair, 'Agricultural Development on the Prairies' 144
19 Reference to mandarins is in Commons Debates (3 May 1977) 5257. The other references are in *WP* (14 Jan. 1971) 8 and (11 Nov. 1971) 3. Concern about Ottawa bureaucrats and their injurious effect upon the West is far from new; see J.W. Dafoe, in Shortt and Doughty, eds, *Canada and Its Provinces* (Toronto 1914) 291–3, quoted in Wilson, *A Century of Canadian Grain* 20–1. The evaluation of the policy under Otto Lang is Wilson's. Interview, Jan. 1977
20 Hall Commission Report, 70
21 Trudeau had informed the House of Commons that he intended to make his first tour of the prairie provinces as prime minister at the time of an acrimonious debate over rules changes in the House: 'A Trip to the West Better than a "stupid filibuster".' *WP* (17 July 1969) 1
22 *WP* (22 May 1969) edit. (6 and 13 Dec. 1956) edit., 6
23 Hall Commission Report 23. See also, Lloyd Axworthy, 'Administrative Federalism and the West,' paper presented to Liberal Conference on Western Objectives, Vancouver, July 1973.
24 National Farmers' Union Submission to the Grain Handling and Transportation Commission, presented at Regina, Saskatchewan (23 Oct. 1975) 3. In a later brief, the NFU stated that 'every dollar farmers pay in freight costs represents a direct transfer of wealth from the prairies to the railway companies.' *Free Press Report on Farming* (15 Sept. 1976) 3
    After the Winner decision (*A.-G. Ont.* v. *Winner* (1954), A.C. 514) provincial boards acted as Ottawa's agents regulating inter- as well as intra-provincial highway traffic. In Saskatchewan in 1977 and 1978 this led to the local board threatening to prevent CP Transport from entering the province if, in the opinion of the board, it did not continue to serve local communities adequately.
25 A.W. Currie, 'Freight Rates on Grain in Western Canada,' *Canadian Historical Review* XXI (Mar. 1940) 40–55 at 54. In 1978 at the Alternatives Canada Conference, sponsored by the Canada West Foundation, the premier of Alberta, Peter Lougheed, proposed that the provinces appoint forty per cent of the members of federal regulatory bodies. Alberta also proposed reorganizing the CTC into four regional agencies with only conflicts between the regions being settled by a national panel selected from the regions. Saskatoon *Star-Phoenix* (16 June 1978) 1
26 See Hall Commission Report 273, for reference to being 'victimized by discriminatory freight rates'; Commons Debates (13 June 1977) 6618 for reference to 'betrayal of the whole principle of orderly marketing' (Les Benjamin, Regina-Lake Centre) and (28 Oct. 1976) 542 for reference to 'sacrificing the producers of this country for the

consumers' (Arnold Malone, Battle River). The language may be less emotive in committee but the meaning remains the same; see Minutes of Proceedings and Evidence of the Standing Committee on Transport and Communications (15 June 1978) 37: 57.

27 Northrop Frye, *The Bush Garden: Essays on the Canadian Imagination* (Toronto 1971) 226. The immunity of the Wheat Board is amply demonstrated: 'When I said … that I thought the Wheat Board had done a magnificent job, I did not mean by that that I expressed approval of the way the government had managed the wheat situation in the west this year.' Minutes of the Standing Committee on Agriculture and Colonization (6 May 1954) 143 (J.W. Blackmore, Lethbridge)

28 *The Progressive Party of Canada* (Toronto 1950) 157

29 Surendra N. Kulshreshthna, *A Current Perspective on the Prairie Grain Handling and Transportation System* (Saskatoon: University of Saskatchewan, Transportation and Extension Division, Sept. 1975) 16

30 Hall Commission Report 288

31 Lang's proposition is stated in Commons Debates (29 Oct. 1974) 837–40 and repeated nearly four years later in Minutes … on Transport and Communications, 37:72. The response of the Saskatchewan Pool members is in *WP* (28 Nov. 1974) 1 and 2, and (7 Nov. 1974) 3 respectively. The province of Alberta described the Rates as 'an inviolable commitment' in a brief to the Hall Commission. *Free Press Report on Farming* (15 Sept. 1976) 1

32 Wilson was the first director of the Grains Division in the Department of Trade and Commerce in 1943 and secretary to the Wheat Committee of Cabinet from 1943 to 1952. His study was prepared for the Grains Group in the office of the minister responsible for the Wheat Board.

33 The Progressive party had no wheat plank in its platform and Crerar, once president of the United Grain Growers, remained suspicious of government intervention all of his life. NLFP, Crerar to J.J. Connolly, 1 Mar. 1958. See also obituary in *WP* (15 May 1974) 4.

34 Wilson suggests in his analysis of this period that there was an element of pique in the government's decision occasioned by irritation at the Winnipeg Grain Exchange, *A Century of Canadian Grain*, 454 ff.

35 King Papers, 25 June 1936, quoted in *ibid.* 527.

36 *Ibid.* 683–7

37 *WP* (24 May 1956) 6, edit.

38 Saskatoon *Star-Phoenix* (6 Nov. 1954) 1–2; *WP* (16 and 23 May 1957), edit., 6

39 Following the Bracken Report, the Wheat Board was instructed to ensure as far as possible that producers were allowed to deliver to the elevator of their choice. In 1969 the delivery system was overhauled by dividing the prairies into fifty blocks, each of which was to be allocated box cars according to market requirements. The purpose of the change was to make the system more responsive to international demand for different grades and varieties of grain.

40 As far back as 1953, John Diefenbaker (with ten other Progressive Conservatives, eight of whom were from Ontario) had bolted his party and supported a Social Credit amendment advocating acceptance of sterling to promote trade. See Commons Debates (3 Dec. 1953) 592, 596. For more on the wheat sales, see Peter Stursberg, *Diefenbaker: Leadership Gained, 1956–62* (Toronto 1975) Chap. 8.

41 Liberal leaders like to juxtapose narrow regionalism against the national interest: '[Howe] raised the question as to whether we could expect special treatment in Western Canada. Did we know that the fishermen at the Eastern Coast may be worse off than the wheat growers of the West.' *WP* (3 Dec. 1953) 1 (magazine). Some years later Trudeau reminded aroused farmers of the same fishermen. *Ibid.* (31 July 1969) 5. The problem of balancing interests was ever present in Mackenzie King's calculations. See Wilson, *A Century of Canadian Grain* 600–1.

42 The National Farmers' Union described Otto Lang's suggestion of flexible hauling and handling tariffs as 'a strategy in concert with the international grain trade and the railroads to change the national transportation policy from one of community service to one of service to the industries involved.' *Free Press Report on Farming* (26 July 1976) 2

43 See Palliser Wheat Growers' Brief to the Grain Handling and Transportation Commission, submitted 25 Nov. 1976 at Regina, Saskatchewan, 93 pp. The Palliser group organizes excursions to Vancouver to acquaint farmers with the antiquated facilities and cumbersome procedures which delay the shipment of wheat from Canada. Side trips are made to Seattle for the purpose of invidious comparison with American techniques. The author accompanied one excursion of twenty-two farmers in October 1976.

44 Two changes have particularly concerned the NFU: rail line abandonment and the construction of inland elevators. Both, if carried out, would, in the eyes of the Union, undermine local communities and the rural way of life. Atkinson has noted that because of consolidation and rationalization in other areas of social and economic life 'the Prairies are lonelier now than in years gone by.' Saskatoon *Star-Phoenix* (22 May 1970) 32

45 The provincial governments must be included in this spectrum. Wilson notes that R.B. Bennett found the three premiers a great help in a time of emergency. *A Century of Canadian Grain* 490

CHAPTER THREE: NON-CONFORMIST POLITICS

1 The partial exception to this generalization is L.G. Thomas, *The Liberal Party in Alberta 1905–21* (Toronto 1959). Alberta and British Columbia are the only provinces not to have been studied in the Government of Canada series, published by the University of Toronto Press. Compare the entries in Alan F.J. Artibise, *Western Canada since 1870: A Select Bibliography* (Vancouver 1978). For Sasakatchewan, 21

per cent of the entries deal with the 'government and politics'; for Alberta, the
comparable figure is 14 per cent.

2 2nd ed. (Toronto 1962) 24

3 S.M. Lipset, *Agrarian Socialism: The Co-operative Commonwealth Federation in
Saskatchewan* (Garden City, NY 1968) xi–xx

4 *The Canadian Forum* XXXIV (Nov. and Dec. 1954), and 'Radicalism in North America:
A Comparative View of the Party Systems of Canada and the United States,'
Transactions of the Royal Society of Canada (1976) Fourth Series, XIV, 19–55

5 Maurice Pinard, *The Rise of a Third Party: A Study in Crisis Politics* (Englewood Cliffs,
NJ 1971) and Denis Smith, 'Prairie Revolt, Federalism and the Party System,' in Hugh
G. Thorburn, ed., *Party Politics in Canada* 3rd ed. (Scarborough 1972) 204–15

6 The magnitude and speed of the change may vary, however. Compare the dozen years it
took the CCF to come to power in Saskatchewan with the overnight sweep of Social
Credit in Alberta.

7 The contribution of the press in defining the prairie region needs investigation. Accord-
ing to Willem de Gelder, all paper and magazine subscriptions before the First World
War cost only a dollar and because they were delivered postage free 'practically
everyone [gets] a good selection of papers.' *A Dutch Homesteader on the Prairies: The
Letters of Willem de Gelder 1910–13* (Toronto 1973) 30, 40. See as well, Wilfrid
Eggleston, *The Frontier and Canadian Letters* (Toronto 1957) Chap. 10.

8 Norman Lambert, 'Dunning Came Up Through,' *The Courier* XXI (17 Feb. 1917),
5–6. A different relationship was depicted between Henry Wise Wood and members of
the UFA; he was an 'evangel' and they were 'fanatics.' John Nelson, *The Canadian
Provinces: Their Problems and Policies* (Toronto 1924) 61

9 See D.S. Spafford, '"Independent" Politics in Saskatchewan before the Non-Partisan
League,' *Saskatchewan History* XVIII (Winter 1965) 1 9 and Paul F. Sharp, *The
Agrarian Revolt in Western Canada: A Study Showing American Parallels* (Minne-
apolis 1948) Chaps 5 and 6.

10 The dilemmas of the Progressives are extensively chronicled in W.L. Morton, *The
Progressive Party in Canada*, rev. ed. (Toronto 1967).

11 *Ibid.* 292

12 Vernon C. Fowke, *The National Policy and the Wheat Economy* (Toronto 1957) 200

13 The best single explanation of the theory of group government is in Macpherson,
Democracy in Alberta 2nd ed. (Toronto 1962) Chap. 2.

14 Walter Young, *The Anatomy of a Party: The National CCF, 1932–61* (Toronto 1969)
15; David E. Smith, *Prairie Liberalism: The Liberal Party in Saskatchewan 1905–71*
(Toronto 1975) 213

15 W.L. Morton, 'The Bias of Prairie Politics,' in Donald Swainson, ed., *Historical
Essays on the Prairie Provinces* (Toronto 1970) 300

16 Larry Pratt, 'The State and Province Building: Alberta's Development Strategy,' in Leo Panitch, ed., *The Canadian State: Political Economy and Political Power* (Toronto 1977) Chap. 5

17 On ethnicity, see Thomas Flanagan, 'Ethnic Voting in Alberta Provincial Elections, 1921–1971,' in *Canadian Ethnic Studies* II (Dec. 1971). See, as well, Peter Stursberg, *Diefenbaker: Leadership Gained, 1956–62* (Toronto 1975) 95 for comment by Michael Starr on importance of ethnicity in the 1958 campaign.

18 *My Discovery of the West: A Discussion of East and West in Canada* (London 1937) 258

19 M.S. Donnelly, *The Government of Manitoba* (Toronto 1963) 58

20 AM, Maybank Papers, File 88, 'Political Memoranda of 1926–27,' 46–50

21 Ministers and the party organization are discussed in the next chapter. The most extensive published account is in Reginald Whitaker, *The Government Party: Organizing and Financing the Liberal Party of Canada, 1930–58* (Toronto 1977).

22 *Leader-Post* (Regina) (24 July 1953) 38

23 'Of 7237 townships in the prairie provinces, 79 per cent lost population during the period 1941 to 1956.' Thomas R. Weir, 'Population,' in J.R. Smith, ed., *The Prairie Provinces*, published for 22nd International Geographical Congress (Montreal, Toronto 1972) 96. Weir concludes his survey by saying: 'The farmer who lacks managerial skill, who regards farming as a way of life rather than a business, is sure to be eliminated in time.' (p 97)

24 '"Old Albertan," Prairie Revolt,' *Saturday Night* (28 May 1938) 1, 2

25 John G. Diefenbaker, *One Canada: The Crusading Years, 1895–1956* (Toronto 1975) 126–7 and 141

CHAPTER FOUR: DEFEAT AND RECONSTRUCTION

1 The shift to the Progessive Conservatives in 1957 was most dramatic in the Atlantic provinces and Ontario. The comparable surge in Quebec and the prairie provinces came nine months later.

PC victories

Election	Atlantic Provinces	Ontario	PQ	Prairies*	BC
1953	5	33	4	6	3
1957	21	61	9	14	7
1958	25	67	50	47	18

* Five of the eight seats gained on the prairies in 1957 were in Manitoba.

In four of the five elections that took place in the decade 1962–72, more than 48 per cent of the seats won by the Progressive Conservatives in the prairie provinces (when measured by the winner's margin of vote) fell in the top quartile of all Tory victories. The exception was 1968, when only 43 per cent of the prairie victories fell within the top quartile.

2 See Joseph Wearing, 'Mutations in a Political Party: The Liberal Party of Canada in the Fifties and Sixties,' unpublished paper presented at annual meeting of the Canadian Political Science Association (June 1975) 14–15.

3 'Ministerialism' is most fully discussed in Reginald Whitaker, *The Government Party: Organizing and Financing the Liberal Party of Canada, 1930–58* (Toronto 1977). Its effects are described by Richard Stanbury, President NLF, 'Liberal Party in Canada: An Interpretation' (5 June 1969) 49 pp ms.

4 The 'new politics' meant 'maximum involvement and maximum party communications,' NLF, vol. 728, Keith Davey to John Nichol, President NLF, 'Final Report of National Organizer,' 31 Jan. 1966 (unless otherwise noted all sources in this chapter are NLF); see, as well, *ibid.*, Davey to Pearson, 4 Feb. 1964. See, too, L.B. Pearson, *Mike: The Memoirs of the Right Honourable Lester B. Pearson* III, 3 vols, ed. J.A. Munro and A.I. Inglis (Toronto 1975) 150.

5 Vol. 881 (NLF, Committee on Political Organization, Suggestions), Summary of Suggestions on Party Organization, made to Sub-Committee on Political Organization (met 13 Jan. 1959)

6 *Ibid.*

7 Vol. 698 (National Executive Committee Meeting, Dec. 1959), Pearson to A. Bruce Matthews, President NLF, 18 Feb. 1960

8 Davey, Stanbury, and a group of prominent young Liberals were credited with rejuvenating the local Toronto riding associations. It was they who formed the nucleus of the reformed Ontario structure and who, in turn, acted as a spur to federal reform. Walter Gordon associated himself with the group in 1960. Denis Smith, *Gentle Patriot: A Political Biography of Walter Gordon* (Edmonton 1973) 81 ff.

9 Pearson's 'lack of elementary organizational sense' is recounted by Smith, *ibid.*

10 Claxton Papers, vol. 79 (Liberal Assn, material and drafts) undated typescript (post-June 1957) re: 'What should the Liberals do.'

11 *Ibid.*, vol. 83 ('Political Comments'), memo. 'Some observations on how to improve the present position of the Liberal Party,' Draft No. 2, 21 Sept. 1957, 12 pp at 3.

12 *Ibid.*, Walter Gordon to Claxton, 'Draft Memorandum for Discussion,' 4 Dec. 1957

13 The dimension and definition of the 'national community' depended on the subject being discussed. Different perspectives were evident, for example, in the negotiations during the sixties on constitutional reform and the pension plan. See Richard Simeon, *Federal-Provincial Diplomacy: The Making of Recent Policy in Canada* (Toronto 1972).

14 Vol. 850 (Hon. J.J. Connolly–H.E. Kidd, Correspondence, G.E. 58), Memorandum to J.J. Connolly (signed 'DKM'; D.K. McTavish was NLF President) 27 Feb. 1958. The author reported a conversation he had had with Walter Harris and A. Bruce Matthews.

15 The Liberals followed the Progressive Conservative example at a time when Tory strategy was about to change: 'The strategy ... of the hierarchy of the Conservative party ... was to gain seats in central Canada ... where the majority of seats are, and then take their chance on the Atlantic provinces and western Canada. Even as early as [1953], I [Gordon Churchill] had raised the objection that it was quite wrong for the party not to give more attention to western Canada.' Peter Stursburg, *Diefenbaker: Leadership Gained, 1956–62* (Toronto 1975) 42

16 Relevant to this latter consideration was Senatory Stanbury's comment in 1969: 'Davey made valiant efforts to stimulate the surge of democracy ... but his success was limited.' Stanbury, 'Liberal Party in Canada' 3–4

17 John A. Stevenson, 'Ottawa Letter,' *Saturday Night* (13 June 1953) 16 and Regina *Leader-Post* (22 July 1953) 3. See also vol. 652, article from *Farm and Ranch Review* (July 1953): 'The West can't service its interests by electing these bumps on logs.'

18 Winnipeg *Tribune* (12 Nov. 1955) 6 (edit.) and Saskatoon *Star-Phoenix* (12 Nov. 1955) 2. In the election campaign, the reaction of prairie audiences remained unfavourable. See John Meisel, *The Canadian General Election of 1957* (Toronto 1962) 184–5.

19 Vol. 654, H.E. Kidd, General Secretary, to P.S. O'Dwyer, Publicity Director, SLA, 21 Nov. 1955. This attitude changed after the fact: 'How very odd CD who was responsible for winning a good many elections, general and by, was perhaps the chief cause of defeat in 1957.' Maybank Papers, File 134, Maybank to Mr Justice J.H. Sissons, 2 Dec. 1960

20 The NLF has been described as a 'clearing house' but it never seemed to have much knowledge of the prairies. Kidd's comment that 'we don't get much news from Saskatchewan here apart from reports appearing in the Saturday edition of the *Globe and Mail* (vol. 654, Kidd to A.H. McDonald, 18 Aug. 1959) was true of all three provinces throughout the decade. McDonald, who was provincial leader in Saskatchewan from 1954 to 1959, grew frustrated at federal incomprehension; 'It seems almost unbelievable to me that Ottawa are not prepared to take a more realistic approach to this problem.' Vol. 654, McDonald to Kidd, 24 Oct. 1955

21 *WP* (1 Dec. 1955) 6 (edit.)

22 The title changed to national organizer the following year. The metamorphosis of the position through its various titles and occupants is described most completely in Whitaker, *The Government Party*. Davey's immediate predecessor and the first occupant appointed after the 1958 collapse was James Scott, who had resigned because of poor health. His successor in April 1966 was Allan O'Brien.

23 Vol. 765 (Saskatchewan, 1960–2), Davey to Pearson, 21 Sept. 1961

24 Tom Axworthy, 'Innovation and the Party System: An Examination of the Career of Walter L. Gordon and the Liberal Party' (MA thesis, Queen's University, May 1970), 203, quoted in Smith, *Gentle Patriot* 371

25 Vol. 640 (Election Statistics), 'Liberal Organization in the 1957 Campaign' (Draft), nd

26 Walter Gordon, quoted in Axworthy, 207–8 and cited in Smith, *Gentle Patriot* 83.

27 From the perspective of reformers, Thatcher's antediluvian obsession with 'power,' expressed in terms of control of patronage, was regrettable but not unexpected. Patronage had a long lineage in Saskatchewan and 'had been used with devastating effect ... by federal Liberals (the Jimmy Gardiner machine), federal Tories and the provincial CCF.' Vol. 1038 (Saskatchewan Campaign Committee), Davey to Pearson, 'Western Trip, November 22–November 28, 1963: Saskatchewan,' 2 Dec. 1963.

28 Whitaker, *The Government Party* Chap. 6, at 236

29 Smith, *Gentle Patriot* 87

30 Vol. 704 (Campaign Clinic), Minutes of Campaign Clinic Committee (Ontario), 19 July 1962 and 10 Aug. 1962; and *ibid.*, vol. 1038, Walter Tucker, former Saskatchewan Liberal leader, 1946–52, to Davey, 6 May 1963

31 Vol. 704, Minutes of Campaign Clinic Committee (Ontario), 19 July 1962 and 10 Aug. 1962; and vol. 696, *Campaign Clinic Scripts*, Ontario Liberal Association, Lecture 1

32 Vol. 728 (Federal Organization), Davey to Walter Gordon, 30 May 1963, and 'Confidential Memorandum Re: Continuing Operation of NLF,' 'A.B.M.' 7 May 1963

33 *Ibid.*, Davey to Pearson, 9 May 1963

34 *Ibid.*, John Lamont to J.J. Connolly, 10 May 1963

35 *Ibid.*, Davey to Pearson, 4 Feb. 1964. In one specific instance of ministerial obduracy, Davey noted: 'It will take time and patience and our understanding, in order to make [the minister] more useful to us, to the Party, and I suspect, to himself. Meanwhile, I must try to spen[d] more time with him ... A sense of latent hostility, borne out of lack of political knowledge, has been replaced by a more positive type of uncertainty.' Vol. 1037 (Alberta Campaign Committee), Davey to O'Brien, 18 Mar. 1964

36 Vol. 728, Davey to John Nichol, NLF President, 'Final Report from National Organizer,' 31 Jan. 1966

37 *Ibid.*

38 Vol. 1029 (Alberta Liberal Association), David McDonald at Western University Liberal Federation Annual Conference, Banff, Alberta, 4 Dec. 1965

39 Acting as 'political sounding board,' the FCC in Alberta invited provincial agricultural spokesmen to meet Mitchell Sharp at the end of 1962. The former deputy minister to C.D. Howe found himself on the receiving end of western criticism. Mr Hamilton, the minister of Agriculture, was depicted as 'working' for the farmers and 'listening' to them while the Liberal party was seen to place obstacles in his path. Vol. 763 (Alberta, 1961–2), Jim Coutts to Pearson, nd (15 Dec. 1962)

40 Vol. 715, Keith Davey to Gordon Keith, 3 July 1963; and vol. 728, Davey to John Nichol, 'Final Report ...' 31 Jan. 1966

41 Vol. 728, Davey to Nichol, 31 Jan. 1966, and Davey to B.D. Stanton, 21 Apr. 1964

42 *Ibid.*, Davey to Nichol, 31 Jan. 1966

43 Vol. 652 (Constituency Association–Bow River, 1949–60), Francis Olson to NLF, 15 June 1959

44 *Ibid.*, Oct. 1959

45 See L.G. Thomas, *The Liberal Party in Alberta: A History of Politics in the Province of Alberta, 1905–1921* (Toronto 1959) and Norman Ward, 'Hon. James Gardiner and the Liberal Party of Alberta, 1935–40,' *Canadian Historical Review* LVI, 3 (Sept. 1975) 303–22.

46 Vol. 651 (Alberta Liberal Association, 1951–6), Helen A. Grodeland, 'Liberalism in Alberta,' 11 pp ms (1951) and Hugh John MacDonald to Kidd, 19 Feb. 1954; vol. 715, 'Political Tape: J. Harper Prouse' [sic] (1963)

47 The labyrinthine world of patronage rends more than it mends the Liberal party in Alberta, according to Nick Taylor, leader and past-president of the ALA. Interview, Dec. 1976. The papers of John James Bowlen (MLA 1930–44 and Lt Governor 1949–59) in the Glenbow-Alberta Institute illustrate in one decade the tangled world of pressure and counter-pressure: letters from MacKinnon soliciting names from Bowlen for appointments to federal boards; letters supplying the same. Letters from others to MacKinnon with copies to Bowlen volunteering names for Senate appointments because 'the seat has always been regarded as belonging to the cattlemen'; because 'the South has never done very much for us but an appointment such as this ... would be helpful'; and the replies from Ottawa stating that the appointment has been 'made from a racial standpoint; it was not religion.' The inexactness of the enterprise was revealed in the request to Bowlen for more information as to a contract: 'I wish you would write and give me all the details as I am not quite clear about it. If I remember right, it was [x rather than y] that you ... wanted to help out but maybe it was the other way around.' All of the correspondence may be found in Files 94, 95, and 102, Political Correspondence 1947–8, 1949–59, and 1947–53 respectively.

48 Interview with Nick Taylor, Dec. 1976; also taped interviews with J.G. Gardiner by Una Maclean Evans, 29 Dec. 1961–5, Jan. 1962, tape no. 6. These tapes are deposited in the Glenbow-Alberta Institute. In Mar. 1955, John Haar, a former officer in the Department of Citizenship, was appointed federal organizer in the province and from that time a series of conflicts occurred between Prowse and Stambaugh on the one hand and Prudham on the other. On the eve of 1957 election, Kidd reminded the Alberta people that 'nothing shakes public confidence in a political party more than evidence of internal dissension, bickering and bad feeling.' Vol. 651 (Alberta Liberal Association, GE 57), Kidd to Grodeland, 1 Apr. 1957. When Haar tried to secure a list of local officers over a five-year period from national headquarters, Kidd told him that such records were not kept: 'From one point of view it may be to your advantage *not to know* who has been in the organization in the last five years!' *Ibid.* (Alberta Liberal Association, 1954–5),

Kidd to Haar, 23 Mar. 1955 (italics in original). See, as well, J.W. Pickersgill, *My Years with Louis St Laurent: A Political Memoir* (Toronto 1975) 274–5.

49 Vol. 651, newsclipping, *Edmonton Journal* (7 Dec. 1957)

50 Vol. 764 (Alberta Liberal Association, 1961), John Decore to Pearson, 10 Nov. 1960

51 Vol. 728, Davey to Walter Gordon, 30 May 1963, and vol. 715 (Alberta Liberal Association 1963–5), Nick Taylor to Davey, 5 Dec. 1963

52 Vol. 715, 'Political Tape: J. Harper Prouse' [sic] (1963)

53 Vol. 1037, 'A Brief on the Federal Campaign Committee of Alberta,' presented by the Edmonton East Federal Liberal Association and the Norwood, Edmonton Northeast and Edmonton Centre Provincial Liberal Associations to the Liberal Convention of Alberta, Red Deer, 21 Nov. 1963

54 *Ibid.*, Davey to Pearson, 'Western Trip, November 22–November 28, 1963: Alberta'

55 Vol. 757, 'A Report on Preliminary Research Conducted in the Prairies for the Liberal Party of Canada' by International Surveys Ltd, Oct. 1963, 28 pp; based on interviews with leading Liberals in the three prairie provinces

56 Vol. 747, Thatcher to Pearson, 26 Feb. 1960

57 Davey to Jeanette Herback, honours student in political science, University of Saskatchewan, Nov. 1969. Before the Saskatchewan election, Davey wrote to Pearson that support for Thatcher 'would, once for all, doom any possibility of expanding our Party to the left.' Vol. 747, 3 Mar. 1967

58 Vol. 765, Thatcher to J.J. Connolly, nd (approximately 31 July 1961)

59 AM, Maybank Papers, File 85, Pearson to Maybank, 17 Dec. 1962

60 Vol. 1038, Lenore Andrews, President SWLA, to J.J. Connolly, 25 June 1963

61 Vol 765, Thatcher to Davey, 25 Oct. 1961

62 David E. Smith, *Prairie Liberalism: The Liberal Party in Saskatchewan, 1905–1971* (Toronto 1975) 294

63 Vol. 765, Davey to Pearson, 16 Nov. 1962 and vol. 1038, Davey to Pearson, memorandum on western trip and letter, 2 Dec. 1963

64 Vol. 1038, Thatcher to Pearson, 24 June 1963. The letter was signed 'with deep regret.' Thatcher described some members of the committee as 'eggheads.' This appellation, Davey later wrote, was 'the worst thing he can conceivably think to call anyone.' Vol. 728, Davey to Pearson, 10 June 1964

65 Vol. 1038, Davey to Pearson, memorandum and letter, 2 Dec. 1963

66 See Smith, *Prairie Liberalism* 303–4. The tenor of the dispute is suggested by Thatcher's rejection of one federal nominee whom he nonetheless described as 'a good Liberal–he is an able individual – he is a grand fellow.' Vol. 1038, Thatcher to John Nichol, 6 Aug. 1964

67 Vol. 728, Davey to Pearson, 10 June 1964

68 AM, Maybank Papers, File 91: Political Memoranda, diary entry, 19 Mar. 1948

69 M.S. Donnelly, *The Government of Manitoba* (Toronto 1963) 63; AM, Maybank Papers, File 85, Maybank to Pearson, 'Evisceration' [1962]; Vol. 881, 'Notes on Organization in Manitoba,' 6 pp ms [1960]

70 See 'How Manitoba Distributes Its Legislative Seats' in Paul Fox, ed., *Politics: Canada* (Toronto 1962) 264–6. See, too, David McCormick, 'The Dissolution of the Coalition: Roblin's Rise to Leadership,' *Transactions of the Historical and Scientific Society of Manitoba*, Series III, 28 (1971–2) 37–43.

71 AM, Maybank Papers, File 85, Maybank to Pearson, 'Evisceration' [1962]; File 99, Howard Winkler to Maybank, 21 Dec. 1957

72 News clipping, *Winnipeg Free Press* (28 June 1957). According to Gardiner, the 'Manitoba bunch [were always] a little different.' At the 1919 Convention 'we could hardly conduct our work in the room next to theirs because of the noise they made.' Glenbow-Alberta Institute, Gardiner Interviews, Reel No. 3

73 Vol. 757, 'A Report on Preliminary Research Conducted in the Prairies for the Liberal Party of Canada' by International Surveys Ltd, Oct. 1963, 28 pp

74 Vol. 1037, J.F. O'Sullivan to Nick Taylor, 9 Sept. 1963

75 *Winnipeg Free Press* (3 May 1969) 17

76 Winnipeg *Tribune* (4 Dec. 1976) 1, 3

77 Vol. 736 (Manitoba Liberal Association, 1963–5), 'Political Tape' transcript. Between 1951 and 1971 the combined populations of Calgary and Edmonton as a percentage of their province's population increased from 35 to 55 per cent; in Saskatchewan, for Regina and Saskatoon, the figures were 15 and 29, while for Winnipeg, the only metropolitan city in Manitoba, the figures were 46 and 55. In view of the fact that much of this growth is the result of rural depopulation, the problems of organizing political parties in both the metropolitan and rural areas have multiplied and also changed.

78 Vol. 1029, Prudham to Nichol, 19 Dec. 1966; interview with Mr Justice Walter Tucker, Aug. 1971

79 Vol. 728, Davey to Gordon, 30 May 1963

80 Vol. 765, Lang to Davey, 28 Sept. 1961

CHAPTER FIVE: PARTICIPATORY DEMOCRACY

1 Interview with A.R. O'Brien, National Director of the Liberal Party, 1966–9, Jan. 1977

2 Papers of Senator R.J. Stanbury, President of the Liberal Party of Canada (unless otherwise stated, all sources in this chapter are Stanbury Papers), vol. 6 (Liberal Federation Meeting, 25 Apr. 1969, Party and Political Review), 26 pp

3 Cited in Grattan O'Leary, *Recollections of People, Press and Politics* (Toronto 1977) 34

4 Vol. 9 (Speeches), Script for Communications Seminar, Video Taping (1971)

5 Vol. 3 (Correspondence, Jan.–June 1971), Stanbury to John Spink, 15 Mar. 1971

6 Vol. 12 (Exchange of views concerning leadership), Stanbury to John Godfrey, 25 June 1970

7 Vol. 6 (Liberal Federation Meeting, 25 Apr. 1969, Party and Political Review) 26

8 Vol. 7 (Ontario Advisory Committee, 28 Jan. 1969), Stanbury to Committee (draft), 23 July 1969

9 Vol. 1 (Correspondence, 1970), Stanbury to Paul S. Plant, 17 Feb. 1970

10 Vol. 1 (Correspondence, 1969), Barney Danson to Stanbury, 4 Sept. 1969

11 Vol. 2 (Correspondence, Sept.–Dec. 1969), Stanbury to Mark Inman, 29 Oct. 1969

12 Vol. 4 (Correspondence, July–Dec. 1971), Arthur Jordan to Harold Stafford, MP, forwarded to Stanbury, 12 Nov. 1971

13 Vol. 1 (Correspondence, 1969), Stanbury to Alan G. Martin, 28 Oct. 1969: 'But acting on a majority consensus is still not going to protect the rights of the minority, and the fact that they are now more knowledgeable about the problem and have expressed their opinion may well serve to alienate them from the government which sought their opinion but they rejected it in favour of the majority.' Ibid., Stanbury to Tom Bernes, Gloria Kunka and Fred MacDonald, 6 Feb. 1970

14 The convention format was approached with an open mind. One view of how to secure the most faithful representation of opinion was to involve the largest number of people. Regional conventions linked to a central convention by closed circuit television, computers, and electronic voting was one suggestion of how to demonstrate 'modern technology at the service of the people.' Costs and equipment, not will, stood in the way of its realization. Vol. 11 (National Liberal Convention: Memoranda and notes regarding organization ...). Memorandum from J.M. Davey to Stanbury [and others], 3 June 1969. Also vol. 3 (Correspondence, May–Sept. 1970), Stanbury to Trisha Jackson, 10 July 1970

15 Vol. 10 (National Liberal Convention, 1970 Correspondence and Memoranda regarding the Conference), Allen Linden, co-chairman of Policy Committee and Convention Organization Committee, 'Policy and Party Relevancy'

16 Vol. 3 (Correspondence, Jan.–Apr. 1970), Stanbury to David Anderson, MP, 4 Mar. 1970

17 An exception to this general statement would be the 'continentalist-nationalist' debate at the 1966 Policy convention. See Chap. 6.

18 These last figures were compiled from the list of participants (with addresses) found in the Stanbury Papers. Vol. 10 (Harrison Hot Springs Conference, Nov. 1969, correspondence and memoranda)

19 Compilation of press coverage; also Senator C.W. Carter to Stanbury, 20 Dec. 1969

20 Vol. 11 (Policy Formulation – Phase II, 1969–70, correspondence, memoranda, pamphlets), Stanbury to Sid Gershberg, 5 Feb. 1970

21 Stephen Clarkson, 'Democracy in the Liberal Party: The Experiment with Citizen

Participation under Pierre Trudeau,' in Hugh G. Thorburn, ed., *Party Politics in Canada*, 4th ed. (Scarborough, Ont. 1979) 157

22 Vol. 12 (Policy and research committee, correspondence and memoranda, 1968–71), James Davey to Stanbury, 10 Feb. 1971 and Davey to Torrence Wylie, National Director, 13 Oct. 1970

23 Vol. 10 (National Liberal Policy Convention, 1970, Correspondence and memoranda), Donald S. MacDonald, 12 Oct. and 1 Nov. 1971

24 Vol. 8 (Presidential Correspondence [miscell.] with MPs, Ministers and Assistants, 1970–2), Stanbury to James M. Davey, 4 Aug. 1971

25 Vol. 12 (Policy and Research Committee, correspondence and memoranda, 1968–71), Gordon Gibson (special assistant to the prime minister) to prime minister, 27 Sept. 1971

26 Clarkson, 'Democracy in the Liberal Party' 159

27 *Ibid.* (Post-election correspondence, 1972–3), Mel Hurtig to Stanbury, 15 Nov. 1972. See, too, Joseph A. Tannous to the prime minister, 11 Jan. 1973

28 Vol. 8 (Saskatchewan Liberal Association, 1968–72), Stanbury to Thatcher, 5 Feb. 1969

29 Vol. 1 (Correspondence 1968), A.R. O'Brien to File, 14 Oct. 1969

30 *Edmonton Journal* (26 Aug. 1971) 22

31 Vol. 1 (Correspondence, 1968), R. Fairclough, Director, Field Organization, to File, 13 Nov. 1968

32 At the time of the Saskatoon meeting of western Liberals in 1966, there was a rumour that some Liberals were thinking of breaking from the national party and running as 'Progressive Liberals.'

33 Vol. 5 (Alberta Liberal party, Correspondence and Notes, 1969–72) Stanbury to Alberto Romano, President of Calgary North Federal Liberal Association, 13 Mar, 1972

34 Vol. 6 (Manitoba Liberal party, 1968–72), Torrance Wylie to the prime minister, 11 July 1969

35 A decade before these events, a federal Liberal in Manitoba judged Bobby Bend, the provincial leader selected in 1969, 'as innocent of knowledge in regard to organizing as the most of them. He is, however, a thoroughly decent fellow and could be useful in any (party) council.' AM Maybank Papers, File 98, 'Persons' nd [1956]), 10 pp survey of Manitoba Liberals, presumably for national party headquarters. During the leadership campaign Bend acknowledged that 'it is not really politics I am concerned with as much as people.' *Winnipeg Free Press* (3 May 1969) 17

36 Vol. 1 (Correspondence, 1968), Otto Lang to Stanbury, 23 Sept. 1968

37 Vol. 10 (National Liberal Policy Convention, 1970, correspondence and memoranda), Stanbury to P.S. Elder, 26 May 1971

38 Vol. 11 (Resignation from Presidency, Correspondence of Senator Stanbury, 1973), Stanbury to Davey, 29 Sept. 1973

39 Richard J. Stanbury, 'Liberal Party of Canada: An Interpretation' (15 June 1969), 53 pp
   ms at 44–6 (in author's possession)

CHAPTER SIX: THE CONTRIBUTION OF POLICY

1 Interview with Harry Hays, minister of Agriculture, 1964–5, 1977. 'Socialistic' had
   many connotations. Arthur Laing, a member of both the Pearson and Trudeau governments between 1963 and 1972, had one explanation: 'I know what worries Western
   Canada. We are variously charged with "lack of competence to run a peanut stand," of
   burdening business big and small by demands for statistics, interfering with enterprise,
   the employment of kooks in the furtherance of protecting the ecology, of taxing to
   support dolts in other parts of Canada and centralizing here a stifling administrative ogre
   at once arrogant and incompetent.' Stanbury Papers, vol. 12, 'Post-election correspondence, 1972–73,' Laing to Stanbury, 18 Dec. 1972
2 NLF, Vol. 757, 'A Report of Preliminary Research Conducted in the Prairies for the
   Liberal Party of Canada,' International Surveys Ltd (Oct. 1963), 28 pp
3 Ibid., vol. 763, Jim Coutts to Pearson, nd (15 Dec. 1962) reports on meeting of Alberta
   Federal Committee with members of provincial agricultural organizations
4 Ibid.
5 Walter L. Gordon, A Political Memoir (Toronto 1977) 246
6 WP (18 Nov. 1971) 1–2 (E.K. Turner, president of SWP). The bond between government and pools is testified to by C.F. Wilson in his mammoth study of the grain trade, A
   Century of Canadian Grain: Government Policy to 1951 (Saskatoon 1978), as well as
   by Mitchell Sharp, then associate deputy minister in the department of Trade and
   Commerce and heading the Canadian delegation to talks on the International Wheat
   Agreement: 'At every step the official delegation [will] have the advice of its farm
   advisers consisting of representatives of the three Prairie Wheat Pools, the United Grain
   Growers and the Saskatchewan Farmers' Union.' WP (11 Dec. 1952) 5. According to
   Harold Winkler such close relations 'arouse[d] suspicion, and actually help[ed] in the
   rise of the MFU.' AM, Maybank Papers, File 100, Winkler to Maybank, 11 Feb. 1958
7 WP (18 Nov. 1971) 13 (A.M. Runciman, president of UGG)
8 Globe and Mail (5 Feb. 1975) 9; Edmonton Journal (30 Mar. 1976) 63; House of
   Commons Debates (13 Mar. 1975) 4055–6 and (27 June 1975) 7134
9 V.C. Fowke, 'Royal Commissions and Canadian Agricultural Policy,' CJEPS XIV
   (May 1948) 163–75
10 See Charles J. Hanser, Guide to Decision: The Royal Commission (Totowa, NJ 1965)
   Chap. 8, 'The Functions of the Royal Commission.' Hanser notes that 'the obstacles to
   handling problems really reduce to one – limited perspective – as found in a variety of
   forms (ignorance, indifference, misconception, vested interest, partisanship, fanati-
   cism) on the part of Government, blocs, the public, or individual citizens.' (p 157)

11 Wilson, *A Century of Canadian Grain*, notes that the first march on Ottawa was in 1910 when the prime minister and cabinet 'received the deputation on the floor of the house of commons, a courtesy not since repeated.' (p 42) In 1959 a petition in favour of deficiency payments and signed by over 300,000 farmers was presented to John Diefenbaker.

12 *WP* (24 Apr. 1969)

13 The fluidity of these periods is suggested in the following comment by Frank Eliason, secretary of the United Farmers of Canada (Saskatchewan Section), in a letter to F.W. Ferguson: 'When we organized the co-operatives a certain portion of the membership fell away. They came back into the movement when the organization went into politics in 1931, but others dropped out. We are, therefore, a peculiar type of organization.' AS, UFC (SS), General Correspondence, 4 Mar. 1935

14 For a recent example of this charge, see *House of Commons Debates* (28 Oct. 1976) 544.

15 Harry Hays, the only Liberal elected in either Alberta or Saskatchewan in 1963, was slow to make an impression on the electorate. International Surveys in October 1963 found out 'surprisingly little about what is thought of Mr Hayes [sic] even by the Party experts as far as his relation to the voter is concerned.' NLF, vol. 757. This was perhaps not altogether surprising since he was reported 'never [to have] had any ambition to enter federal politics [and] never [to have] voted Liberal in his life.' *WP* (23 May 1963)

16 In 1967–8 the Board reverted to the minister of Trade and Commerce, who at that time was John Turner. Among Mitchell Sharp's credentials was that he was Winnipeg-born but of this fact the *Western Producer* said: 'After graduating from the University of Manitoba and the London School of Economics, he became an easterner.' (23 Sept. 1963)

17 *WP* (24 Oct. 1963) 3. The feeling was reciprocated. According to Charles Wilson the farmers would not accept a French-speaking minister's being responsible for the Board. Interview, Jan. 1977

18 *WP* (17 Dec. 1964) 1. (The speaker was Harry Hays, minister of Agriculture.)

19 *Ibid.* (1 Oct. 1964) 1

20 *Ibid.* (19 Nov. and 3 Dec. 1964) 1, and (22 Sept. 1966) 1

21 *Ibid.* (11 Dec. 1964) 6 (edit.). Gordon's career touched Western politics a number of times, usually critically. In Oct. 1963, International Surveys reported that he was seen in the West as 'incompetent' and suggested that this unfavourable image might actually be taken advantage of by having him play the 'nasty minister' role as successor to C.D. Howe.

22 Wilson, *A Century of Canadian Grain* 650. In the debate on the first grain stabilization bill, in 1971, Lang made an impassioned defence of his and the farmers' cause: 'They are now saying ... that I should be in jail. Well, Mr Speaker, let me tell you that I am going to go on fighting for the Prairie farmer, trying to do the things I know will help

him. I am going to fight for his causes every way I know how. I am going to try to do things quickly, and sometimes take shortcuts ... instead of being held up in a legal morass ... Honorable members opposite cannot prevent me from doing everything that I know how to help the Prairie farmer by frightening me with threats of jail or defeat. Indeed ... I would gladly go to jail in the cause of the Prairie farmer.' *WP* (23 Oct. 1971) 2

23 *WP* (10 and 17 Jan. 1963) 2

24 It was at this time that the University of Saskatchewan agreed to accept grain in part payment for tuition fees.

25 *WP* (18 Dec. 1969) 6. One alternative to secession was unification and in the following year the most thorough investigation of this option took place. See David K. Elton, ed., *One Prairie Province?: A Question for Canada*, Conference Proceedings and Selected Papers (Lethbridge, Alberta, 1970)

26 *WP* (20 June 1957) 1

27 *House of Commons Debates* (25 Mar. 1976) 12140 and (13 Dec. 1971) 10389

28 *WP* (18 Nov. 1971) 1–2 (E.K. Turner)

29 *Ibid.* (3 and 17 Dec. 1970) 1

30 Interview, Jan. 1977

31 *House of Commons Debates* (23 Apr. 1970) 6194

32 *Ibid.* (16 Sept. 1971) 7928

33 *WP* (27 Jan. 1972) 1

34 *Minutes of Proceedings and Evidence of Standing Committee on Transport and Communications* (13 June 1978) 36: 29. (The Speaker was Mr Justice Emmett Hall.) To this statement, an unidentified honourable member replied: 'Right on!'

35 *WP* (1 Mar. 1973) 7

36 *Ibid.* (4 Oct. 1973) 3

37 *Ibid.* (23 Aug. 1973). When Trudeau 'for the first time ... made a speech dealing entirely with agriculture,' the *Western Producer* did not fail to note that 'it was made in Quebec province.' (17 Jan. 1972) 6 (edit.)

38 *WP* (16 and 23 May 1974) 10 and 8

39 For a description of the extensive consultation with farmers which preceded legislative approval of this new bill, see House of Commons Debates (26 Jan. 1976) 10320.

40 *WP* (19 Oct. 1972), speech by the prime minister at Swift Current, Saskatchewan

41 *Minutes ... Standing Committee on Transport and Communications* (13 June 1978) 36:13

42 See *Guide to Canadian Ministries since Confederation, July 1, 1867–April 1, 1973*, Public Archives of Canada (Ottawa 1974) v and 144

43 *WP* (12 July 1973) 2

44 Western Economic Opportunities Conference, 24–6 July 1973, *Verbatim Record and Documents* (Ottawa 1977) 22

45 *Vancouver Sun* (13 July 1973) 33

46 A sample of the article headings suggests the tone: 'The Growing Alienation of the Prairies,' *Globe and Mail* (7 May 1970) 7; 'Prairie Way of Life being Plowed Under,' *Star-Phoenix* (23 May 1970) 13; 'How the West is being Lost,' *Ibid.* (2 Feb. 1970) 13.

47 Stanbury Papers, vol. 12, 'Post-election correspondence, 1972–73,' Laing to Stanbury, 18 Dec. 1972

48 R.M. Burns, *Conflict and Resolution in the Administration of Mineral Resources in Canada* (Centre for Resource Studies, Queen's University, Kingston 1976) 39 and Wendy MacDonald, *Constitutional Change and the Mining Industry in Canada*, Working Paper No. 17, Centre for Resource Studies, Queen's University (Kingston 1980) 25–30

49 'Resource Taxation and Provincial Fiscal Capability' (13 and 14 Dec. 1976) 4

50 Stanbury Papers, vol. 12, 'Post-election correspondence, 1972–3,' Arthur Laing to Stanbury, 18 Dec. 1972

51 [1979] 1SCR 42 and [1978] 2SCR 545.

52 MacDonald, *Constitutional Change and the Mining Industry* 16–17

53 Blakeney, First Ministers' Meeting, 13 and 14 Dec. 1976, 'Statement by the Hon. Allan Blakeney' 6

54 This attitude, born out of the Minitoba, Saskatchewan, and Alberta acts and revived by use of the power of reservation and disallowance, now extends as a result of these recent decisions to the Court itself. For a discussion of the Court and the decisions, see P.W. Hogg, 'Is the Supreme Court of Canada Biased in Constitutional Cases?,' *Canadian Bar Review* LVII (Dec. 1979) 721–39.

55 Province of Saskatchewan, Opening Statement, Federal-Provincial Constitutional Conference (10 Feb. 1969) 3. See, as well, Strom's address entitled 'A Case for the West' to the same Conference.

56 *Winnipeg Free Press* (10 June 1968) 1

57 The best statement of this is Canada, *A National Understanding: Statement of the Government of Canada on the Official Language Policy* (Ottawa 1977). For more on multiculturalism, see Bernard Ostry, *The Cultural Connection: An Essay on Culture and Government Policy in Canada* (Toronto 1978) 117–18, 225; Jean Burnet 'Separate or Equal: A Dilemma of Multiculturalism,' in A.W. Rasporich, ed. *The Social Sciences and Public Policy in Canada* (Vol. 1, Calgary 1979) 176–83; and *infra*, 109–10 and 133–6.

58 See Stanbury Papers, vol. 6, for several files on 'Ethnic Affairs: press, advertising, ad hoc committee on etc.' As well, see vol. 12 for correspondence on related matters.

59 This would be one explanation for the tension researchers have found among descendants of the non-English: 'Children of Canadian-born parents … showed more anxiety about discrimination than did the children of immigrant parents. The feelings that their ethnic origin may be an obstacle to their future careers was strongest among the third

generation.' K.G. O'Bryan, J.G. Reitz, and I. Kuplowska, *Non-Official Languages: A Study in Canadian Multiculturalism* (Ottawa 1975) 372

60 Stanbury Papers, vol. 5, 'Alberta, Liberal Party in, Correspondence and notes 1969–72,' Robert D. Gillespie to Blair Williams, Executive Assistant to H.A. Olson, minister of Agriculture, 31 Jan. 1972

61 'Ethnic Language Retention and the Problem of Generations,' *Canadian Ethnic Studies* VIII, 2 (1976) 83. This article is one of several in a 'Roundtable' to discuss the Non-Official Languages report, *Non-Official Languages*.

62 Grants under the multiculturalism program for 1972–3 to the end of the second quarter of the fiscal year 1974–5 amounted to $4,288,881, of which Ontario received $2,179,000. Canada, *House of Commons Debates* (27 Jan. 1975) 2606. For the total budget for the federal multiculturalism program between Oct. 1971 and the fiscal year 1977–8, see *ibid.* (21 June 1978) 6624.

CHAPTER SEVEN: THE HOLD OF THE CENTRE

1 ([London] 1911) 149. He also suggests indoctrination of the young Albertans: 'The children in our schools would be taught to regard this Canada, this stepmother, as the incarnation of greed, tyranny and oppression.' A Liberal, Bramley-Moore sat in the Alberta Legislative Assembly from 1909 to 1913. He was killed in the First World War.

2 Brooke is quoted by Edward A. McCourt, *The Canadian West in Fiction* (Toronto 1949) 117–18. In his preface, McCourt describes the prairies' geographic unity 'hot in summer and cold in winter and the wind blows hard and often.' He also notes: 'They are young, aggressive and united in their hostility to Ontario.' There is one ghost such as Brooke speaks of: Louis Riel. The industry now growing around this figure and his translation from racial to regional significance belies the sentiment of another pre-First World War commentator: 'Canada had shown in prompt action [against the Métis] her united striking power, and the monuments of those who died for her at Fish Creek and Batoche linked Winnipeg closely to Ottawa and Toronto.' J.A.T. Lloyd, *The Real Canadian* (London 1913) 237

3 David H. Breen, 'The Turner Thesis and the Canadian West: A Closer Look at the Ranching Frontier,' in Lewis H. Thomas, ed., *Essays on Western History in Honour of Lewis Gwynne Thomas* (Edmonton 1976) 152 and Chester Martin, *'Dominion Lands' Policy*, ed. with introd., by Lewis H. Thomas (Toronto 1973) xiv

4 Foster Diary, 1 Aug. 1919 (quoting Julius Barnes, Wheat Director, US Grain Corp.), cited in C.F. Wilson, *A Century of Canadian Grain: Government Policy to 1951* (Saskatoon 1978) 232

5 Ronald Rogowski, *Rational Legitimacy: A Theory of Political Support* (Princeton 1974) 184ff

6 Reginald Whitaker, *The Government Party: Organizing and Financing the Liberal Party of Canada, 1930–58* (Toronto 1977) 208ff.
7 AS, Scott Papers, Scott to Thomas Jarrott, 8 Jan. 1904 (389[0]–MI–Scott General)
8 AS, Newspaper Clippings (Politics), *Edmonton Bulletin* (14 Dec. 1923)
9 Bruce W. Hodgins, 'Disagreement at the Commencement: Divergent Ontarian Views of Federalism, 1867–1871,' in Donald Swainson, ed., *Oliver Mowat's Ontario* (Toronto 1972) 67
10 For examples of the élites at work, see L.R. Pratt, 'The State and Province-Building: Alberta's Development Strategy, 1971–76,' in Leo Panitch, ed., *The Canadian State: Political Economy and Political Power* (Toronto 1977), and Manitoba, *Report of the Commission of Inquiry into The Pas Forestry and Industrial Complex* (1974).
11 Harold A. Innis, *Political Economy in the Modern State* (Toronto 1946) xi, 77–8, 'The University in The Modern Crisis.' In another paper with the same title as the took, Innis wrote that 'without a tradition of professionalism the social scientist has been the prey of governments and of private enterprise. The results have been scandalous.' (p 129) The 'seductions' in Canada were governments and in the United States private enterprise. How harsh a judgment this is may be debated. What is clear is that academics have played a major role in government. The Rowell-Sirois Commission and the B and B Commission, federally, and the establishment and promotion of the CCF in Saskatchewan, provincially, are prominent illustrations.
12 William Petersen, *Planned Migration: The Social Determinants of the Dutch-Canadian Movement*, vol. 2 (Berkeley: University of California Publications in Sociology and Social Institutions 1955) 130
13 David E. Smith, 'Instilling British Values in the Prairie Provinces,' *Prairie Forum* VI, I (forthcoming). Dr Riddell, the Canadian government representative to the League of Nations, advised the Oversea Settlement Committee, charged with administering the Act in England, to work through Canadian interest groups to bring pressure on the federal and provincial governments. He also advised patience; for 'with the change of Government in Canada which seems imminent the situation should improve.' PRO, CO 721/118, interview by Miss Potts of the Society for the Oversea Settlement of British Women with Dr Riddell, 9 Sept. 1925
14 Eli Mandel, 'Ethnic Voices in Canadian Writing,' in Wsevolod Isajiw, ed., *Identities: The Impact of Ethnicity on Canadian Society*, Canadian Ethnic Studies Association, V (Toronto 1977) 57–67. This would be true of 'the British' as well. The days had passed when Saskatchewan's political leaders would be described as 'a Gladstonian Liberal' (Dunning) or 'that detestable young Lloyd George of the prairies' (Martin). John Nelson, *The Canadian Provinces: Their Problems and Policies* (Toronto [1924]) 62–3 and AS, Martin Papers, clippings, *Medicine Hat Weekly News* (16 Nov. 1916)
15 'The manifest intention of the policy of multiculturalism has been to encourage and assist the preservation of cultural differences. Many members of various ethnic groups,

however, especially the white minority groups, see the policy as a way in which they can gain public recognition of their diverse subcultures, not as foreign, but as Canadian. On the psychological level this may serve to integrate ethnic identity with Canadian identity. Yet probably few members of the Anglo-Saxon groups would preceive the policy this way.' Raymond Breton, Jean Burnet, Norbert Hartmann, Wsevolod W. Isajiw, and Jos Lennards, 'The Impact of Ethnic Groups on Canadian Society: Research Issues,' in Isajiw, ed., *Identities*, 199–200

16 (London 1930); (Toronto 1933); (London 1914)

17 Peter Lougheed, 13 Oct. 1975, quoted in Pratt, 'The State and Province-Building' 1

18 Canada, *Report of the Royal Commission on the Natural Resources of Saskatchewan* (Ottawa 1935) 10, quoted in Saskatchewan, *A Submission by the Government of Saskatchewan to the Royal Commission on Dominion-Provincial Relations* (Canada 1937) 260–1. That the three prairie provinces were the creatures of the Parliament of Canada requires wider scholarly consideration than it has yet been given. For one thing it gave Canada a frontier, something which the Americans had but which Australia, the other great federal parliamentary democracy, did not have. There, each state had its own frontier. For an analysis by a Canadian of resource development in Australia, see Garth Stevenson, *Mineral Resources and Australian Federalism*, Research Monograph No. 17, Centre for Research on Federal Relations (Canberra 1976).

19 Canada, *Report of the Royal Commission on Dominion-Provincial Relations*, three books in one volume (Ottawa 1954) II, 246

20 H.V. Nelles, *The Politics of Development: Forests, Mines and Hydro-Electric Power in Ontario, 1849–1921* (Toronto 1974). See esp. Chap. 1, 'A Frontier of Monarchy.'

21 'The Place of Land in North American Federations,' *Canadian Historical Review* XXI (Mar. 1940) 64

22 Vernon C. Fowke, 'National Policy and Western Development,' *Journal of Economic History* XVI, 4 (1956) 461–79. See Martin, *'Dominion Lands' Policy* 120–2.

23 Edgar McInnis, 'Two North American Federations: A Comparison,' in R. Flenley, ed., *Essays in Canadian History* (Toronto 1939) 114

24 The momentum and direction of the United States's development is sharply distinguished from that of the Dominion, whose political system at the time it was formed 'was not charged with defining the goals of society nor ... its relationship to religious absolutes or absolutes of any kind.' John Conway, 'Politics, Culture and the Writing of Constitutions,' in Harvey L. Dyck and H. Peter Krosby, eds, *Empire and Nations: Essays in Honour of Frederic H. Soward* (Toronto 1969) 12

25 Martin, *'Dominion Lands' Policy* 29, 47

26 Canada, Report of the Select Standing Committee on Agriculture and Colonization, *Journals of the House of Commons* (1890), Appendix No. 5, pp 6–13. 'Agricultural Possibilities in Alberta: An 1890 View,' in Kevin H. Burley, ed., *The Development of Canada's Staples, 1867–1939: A Documentary Collection* (Toronto [1972]) 30–1

27 Report of Committee of Privy Council, 30 May 1884, *Sessional Papers of Canada*, 1885, No. 61. Quoted by Martin, *'Dominion Lands' Policy* 146. The failure of the French Canadians to participate according to their numbers is discussed in Chap. 1, *supra*.

28 Petersen 159

29 *Ibid.*

30 Daniel J. Elazar, 'Federal-State Collaboration in the Nineteenth Century United States,' in Aaron Wildavsky, ed., *American Federalism in Perspective* (Boston 1967) 210

31 For an interesting discussion of immigration as it relates to s-95 of the BNA Act, see W.H. McConnell, *Commentary on the British North America Act* (Toronto 1977) 304–7.

32 The reissue of Norman L. Nicholson's *The Boundaries of the Canadian Federation* (Toronto 1979) has helped remedy this oversight.

33 *Reminiscences* (Toronto 1912) 95, 178–9, 15

34 W.F.A. Turgeon, 'I'd Unite the Prairie Provinces,' *Maclean's* XLV (1 Feb. 1932) 17

35 Elazar, 'Federal-State Collaboration ...' 219

36 Bramley-Moore, *Canada and Her Colonies* 53

37 Canada, House of Commons, *Third Report of the Special Committee on Statutory Instruments*, Session 1968–9 (Ottawa 1969) 35

38 *WP* (13 Jan. 1972) 8. (Palliser Wheat Growers' Association delegate)

39 Bramley-Moore, *Canada and Her Colonies* 80

40 'Notes for Remarks by Premier Allan Blakeney,' Farm and Home Banquet, Saskatoon (11 Jan. 1978) 8

41 *Ibid.* 11

42 *Southern Politics* (New York 1949) 310–11

43 Anthony D. Scott, 'Government Policy and the Public Lands,' in Robert M. Clark, ed., *Canadian Issues: Essays in Honour of Henry F. Angus* (Toronto 1961) 159. The quotation is from a piece by Professor Angus: 'An Echo of the Past: The Rowell-Sirois Commission,' *Canadian Tax Journal* I (1953) 445–6.

44 Sir Richard Cartwright, *Reminiscences* (Toronto 1912) 352

45 NLF, vol. 601, 'Remarks of Premier Stuart Garson to the McGill Liberal Club,' 9 Oct. 1947

46 Sir Robert Herbert, ed., *Speeches on Canadian Affairs by Henry Howard Molyneux, Fourth Earl of Carnarvon* (London 1902) 125–6

47 *Transcript of the Prime Minister's Remarks at the Western Development Museum, Saskatoon, Saskatchewan* (19 Apr. 1977) 1

48 *Notes for Remarks by Premier Allan Blakeney, Saskatchewan Teachers' Federation* (31 Mar. 1978)

49 'Canadian Culture Today,' in Judith Webster, ed., *Voices of Canada: An Introduction to Canadian Culture*, Association for Canadian Studies in the United States (Burling-

ton, VT 1977) 3. See, as well, John Conway in Dyck and Krosby, *Empire and Nations* 3–17.
50 Marion I. Newbigin, *Canada: The Great River, the Lands and the Men* (London [1926]) 5
51 *My Discovery of the West: A Discussion of East and West in Canada* (London 1937) 251

CHAPTER EIGHT: THE LOST LIBERAL WEST

1 Ronald Rogowski, *Social Structure and Stable Rule: A General Theory*, Technical Report No. 3, Sept. 1969, Center of International Studies, Princeton University, III-43.
2 'Regions, Classes and Sections in American History,' *The Journal of Land and Public Utility Economics* XX (Feb. 1944) 39
3 H.A. Innis, 'The Rowell-Sirois Report,' *CJEPS* VI (Nov. 1940) 566
4 Leslie Fiedler, 'Canada and the Invention of the Western,' in Dick Harrison, ed., *Crossing Frontiers: Papers in American and Canadian Western Literature* (Edmonton 1979) 91
5 Rosemary Sullivan, 'Summing Up,' in Harrison, *Crossing Frontiers* 149
6 A.R.M. Lower, 'The Origins of Democracy in Canada,' in Welf H. Heick, ed., *History and Myth: Arthur Lower and the Making of Canadian Nationalism* (Vancouver, BC 1975) 27
7 The term is used by Howard R. Lamar, 'The Unsettling of the American West,' in Harrison, *Crossing Frontiers*. Lamar writes: 'Such incredible migration to the cities marks not only the defeat of pioneering, but of rural culture itself as part of the national character.' (p 47)
8 Leroy O. Stone, *Migration in Canada: Some Regional Aspects*, 1961 Census Monograph (Ottawa 1969) 40
9 See, too, Fredrik Barth, ed., *Ethnic Groups and Boundaries: The Social Organization of Culture Difference* (Boston 1969) introduction.
10 *Toronto Educational Governance/Multiculturalism Case Study: A Study of the Toronto School System in Terms of Governance and Multiculturalism and a Report of the IMTEC/US. Bicentennial Seminar on Managing Change in Urban Education* (Toronto 1977) 117
11 Material for the next few paragraphs is taken from annual reports of the Department of Tourism, Recreation, and Cultural Affairs (Manitoba), Department of Culture and Youth (Saskatchewan) and Department of Culture, Youth, and Recreation (Alberta) for the years 1970 to 1978.
12 Vol. II, *Detail of Budgetary Cash Outflow*, Culture and Youth, 'Culture and Multicultural Support' 69–77
13 William Christian, introd. and ed., *The Idea File of Harold Adams Innis* (Toronto 1980) 106. One is reminded of Richard Hofstadter's pungent opening sentence in Chap. 1 of

The Age of Reform: From Bryan to F.D.R. (New York 1955) 23: 'The United States was born in the country and has moved to the city.'

14 See Martha Fletcher and Frederick J. Fletcher, 'Communications and Confederation: Jurisdiction and Beyond,' in R.B. Byers and Robert W. Reford, eds, *Canada Challenged: The Viability of Confederation* (Toronto 1979) 171f

15 *Prairie Capitalism: Power and Influence in the New West* (Toronto 1979)

16 Between 1968 and 1979 six other Liberal cabinet ministers (excluding three ministers of state) came from the four western provinces. They were: Art Laing, Jack Davis, and Ron Basford of British Columbia; Jack Horner and H.A. Olson of Alberta; and James Richardson and Roger-Joseph Tiellet of Manitoba. Davis, Horner, Olson, and Richardson crossed party lines either on entering or exiting the Cabinet.

17 There was a ninth candidate: the Reverend Lloyd Henderson of Portage La Prairie, Manitoba, who received no support on the first ballot at the convention. The voting mechanics of the convention discourage caucusing. See, however, *Globe and Mail* (6 Dec. 1979) 8.

18 'The Relationship of the Origins of Immigrants to the Settlement of the Country,' *Papers and Proceedings of the Annual Meeting of the Canadian Political Science Association* II (May 1930) 49

19 *Winnipeg Free Press* (8 May 1969) 35. The subject of this comment aspired to lead the provincial Liberals.

20 *Ibid.* (9 June 1969) 8

21 NLF, Vol. 652, Geo. C. Marler to R.F.L. Hanna, 26 Feb. 1959

22 See Stanbury Papers, Vol. VI, 'Manitoba Liberal Party, 1968–72.'

23 *Edmonton Journal* (15 June 1955) 1, 24

24 On these issues nonconformity remains a novelty. See, for example, Kenneth H. Norrie, 'Some Comments on Prairie Economic Alienation,' *Canadian Public Policy* II (Spring 1976).

25 'The Role of Federalism,' in Daniel Elazar, ed., *Federalism and Political Integration*, Jerusalem Institute for Federal Studies (Ramat Gan, Israel 1979) 47

26 Letter to the editor, *WP* (28 Oct. 1971) 7

CONCLUSION

1 Klaus H. Burmeister, ed., *Western Canada 1909: Travel Letters by Wilhelm Cohnstaedt*, Canadian Plains Studies 7 (Regina 1976) 2

2 On the question of political perceptions, see Harold D. Clarke, 'The Ideological Self-Perceptions of Provincial Legislators,' *Canadian Journal of Political Science* XI (Sept. 1978) 617–33, esp. 624, and David J. Elkins, 'The Structure of Provincial Party Systems,' in David J. Elkins and Richard Simeon et al., *Small Worlds: Provinces and Parties in Canadian Political Life* (Toronto 1980).

3 *WP* (25 July 1974) 7 (Clarence Fairbairn, *WP* editor, 'Farmers themselves decide which crop to grow')

4 Quoted in G. Bruce Doern, 'The Development of Policy Organizations in the Executive Arena,' in G. Bruce Doern and Peter Aucoin, eds, *The Structures of Policy-Making in Canada* (Toronto 1971) 65

5 Submission to the House of Commons Standing Committee on Agriculture, in the matter of Bill C-196, An Act Respecting Grain. For more on C-196 and agrarian opposition, see *WP* (7 May 1970) 1, 2. A proposal of the federal task force on agriculture in 1970, which the Saskatchewan Wheat Pool among others found unattractive, was the creation of a national agricultural advisory council for the minister of Agriculture. According to the Pool, 'This kind of council might dilute farmer organizations' access to government.' *WP* (3 Dec. 1970) 1. See *ibid.* (28 May 1970) 1 as well.

6 The Lalonde paper is published in *Canadian Public Administration* XIV (Winter 1971) 509–37. The paragraph has been considerably altered. See 516 of the article and 15 of the original paper.

7 See Norman Ward, 'The Changing Role of the Privy Council Office and Prime Minister's Office: A Commentary,' *Canadian Public Administration* XV (Summer 1972) 375–7. I am grateful to Professor Ward for bringing this communication to my attention.

8 *Globe and Mail* (8, 9, 20 June 1970) 6, 7

9 *Report of the (Healy) Commission on Graduate Studies in the Humanities and Social Sciences: Summary* (Sept. 1978) 33

10 Saskatoon *Star-Phoenix* (16 June 1978) 1. In more recent years, provinces have actively sought changes in the operation of the Wheat Board or in the federal government's relationship to the Board. When Mr Thatcher sought to barter wheat for electric generators and by-pass the Board, the minister responsible had to step in. *WP* (14 June 1970) 8. In the seventies, Alberta has been a vigorous critic of the federal government's grain marketing practices, though not so unwise as to criticize the Board directly. See, for example, Saskatoon *Star-Phoenix* (17 June 1978) 1. Lang, however, construed the attack as such. *WP* (25 May 1978) 24

11 Notes for Remarks by Premier Allan Blakeney, Farm and Home Banquet, Saskatoon (11 Jan. 1978) 15

Index